Masters of Florence

WONDERS.
The Memphis International Cultural Series

Masters of Florence

CURATED BY
Annamaria Giusti
Director of the Museo dell'Opificio delle Pietre Dure, Florence

WITH
Cristina Acidini Luchinat
as scientific consultant
Soprintendente of the Opificio delle Pietre Dure, Florence

ESSAYS BY
Annamaria Giusti
Cristina Acidini Luchinat
Eugenio Martera and Patrizia Pietrogrande

CONTRIBUTIONS BY
Monica Bietti
Linda Carioni
Elena Carrara
Stefano Casciu
Alessandro Cecchi
Marco Chiarini
Maddalena De Luca
Annamaria Giusti
Magnolia Scudieri
Maria Sframeli
Maria Grazia Vaccari

EDITED BY
Contemporanea Progetti

PRESENTED BY

WONDERS
The Memphis International Cultural Series

TABLE OF CONTENTS

DEDICATION
Richard "Dick" Tillman

The heart of a community is often measured by the effort asserted to assist the less fortunate. The soul of a community is often best reflected by the vitality and excitement of its cultural, sporting, and entertainment institutions and events. Under the dynamic leadership of Richard "Dick" Tillman, Kroger has become the preeminent corporate supporter of all events, great and small, in Memphis and the Mid-South.

The Kroger-St. Jude Tennis Tournament, the Food Bank, Variety Club, and others too numerous to mention would not be possible without the support of Kroger and the personal involvement of Dick Tillman. Dick was instrumental in the development of WONDERS as a not-for-profit organization. Without his guidance and wise counsel as a long time member of the WONDERS Board of Directors, WONDERS would have certainly ceased long ago.

It is with deep affection, respect, and appreciation that this exhibition catalogue is dedicated to Richard "Dick" Tillman.

Lorenzo Ghiberti, *East Doors of the Baptistery (Gates of Paradise)*, 1425-1452
Florence, Baptistery

LETTER FROM THE MINISTRO PER I BENI E LE ATTIVITÀ CULTURALI, PROF. GIULIANO URBANI

Italia e Stati Uniti sono legati da profondi sentimenti di amicizia e solidi rapporti tra i due popoli e i due governi, che questa mostra ha il merito di consolidare ulteriormente.

Gli ultimi mesi hanno visto fiorire numerose iniziative: importanti imprenditori americani di origine italiana hanno creato una fondazione per lo scambio culturale tra i due Paesi, è stato rinnovato l'Istituto Italiano di Cultura di New York, sono stati realizzati progetti che hanno valorizzato il nostro cinema e hanno esaltato l'arte dei primi del Novecento italiano. In particolare, voglio ricordare le due mostre al Museo Guggenheim di New York, la prima dedicata a Federico Fellini nel decennale della sua scomparsa e la seconda incentrata su Boccioni e le avanguardie futuriste. Ora assistiamo alla grande rassegna di Memphis dedicata alla Firenze dei Medici.

Il sostegno della Fondazione WONDERS, che dalla fine degli anni Ottanta ha inaugurato un felice percorso di mostre annuali incentrate su grandi civiltà europee ed extraeuropee, permette di presentare al pubblico americano una sintesi della fervida storia artistica della capitale medicea tra il XIV e il XVIII secolo. La decisione della Fondazione Wonders di affidare all'Opificio delle Pietre Dure di Firenze, in origine antica manifattura d'arte nata e fiorita nei secoli grazie ai Medici, contribuisce inoltre a divulgare l'immagine di una cultura integrata al fare artistico, che per la città toscana rappresenta il senso del proprio passato, una chiave d'interpretazione del presente e un viatico per il futuro.

La generosità di molti musei ha reso possibile la mostra e ha inoltre permesso di costruire un percorso espositivo ricco e vario, per la presenza non solo di opere e oggetti che riescono a rendere in pieno il vivere quotidiano della civiltà fiorentina, ma anche di autentici capolavori. Basti ricordare la *Madonna Dolente* di Giotto dal Museo di Santa Croce, la *Madonna col Bambino* attribuita a Donatello dal Museo Bardini, la *Madonna della Loggia* di Sandro Botticelli della Galleria degli Uffizi, l'*Adorazione del Bambino* di Piero Cosimo dal Museo di Palazzo Martelli, i mirabili disegni di Michelangelo da Casa Buonarroti e di Raffaello dal Museo Horne.

Masters of Florence- Glory and Genius at the Court of the Medici, infine, offre la possibilità a molti cittadini statunitensi interessati alla civiltà del nostro Paese, ma lontani dalle classiche mete in cui vengono solitamente proposte simili iniziative, di poter conoscere a fondo l'arte e la storia italiane. Il nostro auspicio è che simili iniziative in futuro siano sempre più numerose, affinché la grande cultura del nostro Paese possa essere apprezzata ovunque negli USA.

Prof. Giuliano Urbani
Ministro per i Beni e le Attività Culturali
Repubblica Italiana

(Mr. Urbani, Italian Minister for the Cultural Patrimony and Activities, begins by noting the profound ties of friendship between the citizens and governments of the United States and Italy of which this exhibition is further demonstration.

He continues by citing other recent cultural initiatives such as the Italian Institute of Culture in New York and two exhibitions at the Guggenheim Museum, one dedicated to Federico Fellini and another focused on the Futurist avant-guarde. The Minister now endorses this important appointment in Memphis, dedicated to the Florence of the Medici.

He applauds the WONDERS organization for their long time support of cultural exhibitions that now permits this exhibition on the unique artistic history of Florence to be presented to the American public. The decision of the Wonders organization to entrust the curation to the illustrious Opificio of the Pietre Dure with historical ties to the Medici, only helps illuminate an image of Florence that represents a true sense of its past, a key to the present and the direction of the future.

He continues by noting that the participation of many museums has made possible this rich and varied exposition which includes such authentic masterpieces as the Virgin Mourning by Giotto from the Museum of Santa Croce, the Madonna with Child by Donatello from the Bardini Museum. the Madonna of the Loggia by Botticelli from the Uffizi Gallery, the Adoration of the Child by Piero di Cosimo from the Museum of Palazzo Matelli, and the admirable drawings of Michelangelo from Casa Buonarroti and Raphael from the Horne Museum.

He concludes by noting that the exhibition, Masters of Florence, offers many American citizens, interested in, but far away from exposure to the civilzation of Italy, the opportunity to deeply experience Italian art and history. He hopes that such initiatives become more numerous until the cultural patrimony of Italy can be appreciated everywhere in the United States.)

LETTER FROM AMBASSADOR OF ITALY TO THE UNITED STATES OF AMERICA, HIS EXCELLENCY SERGIO VENTO

I extend a warm welcome to all the visitors of this impressive exhibition, *Masters of Florence*, which WONDERS has so capably organized. To understand the Renaissance and the explosion of art for which it is known, one must also become acquainted with Florence and the powerful men and women who made of it a center of art, culture and wealth in Europe.

The present exhibition is not only a journey through priceless paintings, sculptures and drawings produced by the genius and talent of artists such as Michelangelo, Leonardo da Vinci, Botticelli, Raffaello; it is also a digression into a number of valuable elements that were part and parcel of this glorious period. These stopovers are a studied collection of the furniture, jewelry and other personal items of the denizens of power, offering a glimpse into the drama and intrigue of those who charted the course of a single period to an apex that is almost unparalleled in Western history.

This legacy, unique to Florence, has touched every corner of the world, and now it comes to Memphis in a flourish of art and artifacts that visit us from a world that is very different from ours perhaps in many ways, but so much like ours in many others. *Masters of Florence* then becomes more than an exhibition; it assumes the features of an intercultural exchange where the past informs the present, where the achievements and glories of an old age are brought to inspire and vitalize our own. The uncommon bond of fellowship and understanding uniting our two countries is deepened and expanded by these exchanges, reminding that culture is a form of communication to be shared and enjoyed and that a society that values culture is also a society of reciprocal understanding and a key to peace.

His Excellency Sergio Vento
Ambassador of Italy
to the United States of America

ACKNOWLEDGMENTS FROM CRISTINA ACIDINI LUCHINAT AND ANNAMARIA GIUSTI, OPIFICIO DELLE PIETRE DURE

The realization of an exhibition as ambitious as the one presented here was made possible in the first place, by the generous response given our initiative by those responsible for the many institutions involved, mostly Florentine, as well as the shared scientific and organizational support provided by Antonio Paolucci, Soprintendente Speciale per il Polo Museale Fiorentino and Domenico Valentino, Soprintendente per i Beni Architettonici e il Paesaggio e per il Patrimonio Storico, Artistico e Demoetnoantropologico di Firenze, Pistoia e Prato.

A special thank you is also extended to Direttore Generale Mario Serio, to Lucia Fornari Schianchi, Soprintendente per i Beni artistici e Storici di Parma e Piacenza, and to Francesco Buranelli, Director of the Musei Vaticani, who have all assured the participation of their prestigious institutions and to the private collectors who have made available significant works from their collections.

The occasion for this initiative was offered by the WONDERS organization of Memphis which we would like to thank for both their sustained willingness to fund the restoration of numerous works of art herein exhibited and their committment to the entire evolution of the project, competently curated in its organizational aspects by the staff of Contemporanea Progetti.

Before mentioning the individuals by name, we would like to reiterate our gratitude to the directors and staff of every museum and public institution, including our own Opificio, who have all with patience equal to their generosity, supported and contributed to the realization of our ambitious undertaking:

Carla Allegra, Maria Angeli, Elisabetta Archi, Franca Arduini, Umberto Baldini, Massimo Bartolozzi, Anna Bellinazzi, Fiora Bellini, Maria Grazia Benini, Licia Bertani, Massimo Bertolucci, Monica Bietti, Roberto Boddi, Angelo Bottini, Mirella Branca, Alberto Bruschi, Chiara Burgio, Mariagiulia Burresi, Loriana Campestrelli, Caterina Caneva, Ornella Casazza, Stefano Casciu, Alessandro Cecchi, Caterina Chiarelli, Marco Chiarini, Marco Ciatti, Curzio Cipriani, Susanna Conti, Giovanna Damiani, Cristina Danti, Maddalena De Luca, Marcello Del Colle, Daniela Dini, Corinne Diserens, Guy Faucher, Daniela Ferrari, Teresa Filieri, Antonia Ida Fontani, Carlo Francini, Stefano Francolini, Paolo Galluzzi, Giancarlo Gentilini, Cristina Gnoni, Andrea Gulizia, Sonia Iacomoni, Clarice Innocenti, Maria Rosa Lanfranchi, Isabella Lapi, Nadia Lastrucci, Mons. Angiolo Livi, Maria Pia Mannini, Rosalia Manno Tolu, Paola Mariotti, Massimo Medica, Silvia Meloni Trkulja, Lucia Meoni, Mara Miniati, Anna Mitrano, Rosanna Morozzi, Marilena Mosco, Miria Nardi, Elisabetta Nardinocchi, Antonio Natali, Fausta Navarro, Antonella Nesi, Patrizio Osticresi, Serena Padovani, Claudio Paolini, Beatrice Paolozzi Strozzi, Mauro Parri, Roberta Passalacqua, Annamaria Petrioli Tofani, Serena Pini, Paola Pirolo, Rosanna Proto Pisani, Maria Prunai Falciani, Giancarlo Raddi delle Ruote, Pina Ragionieri, Alessandra Ramat, Mario Scalini, Magnolia Scudieri, Maria Sframeli, Chiara Silla, Carlo Sisi, Laura Speranza, Giorgio Strano, Salvatore Sutera, Brunella Teodori, Rita Toma, Maria Grazia Vaccari, Mons. Timothy Verdon.

Cristina Acidini Luchinat
Soprintendente dell'Opificio delle Pietre Dure

Annamaria Giusti
Direttore del Museo dell'Opificio delle Pietre Dure

ACKNOWLEDGMENTS FROM PATRIZIA PIETROGRANDE, CONTEMPORANEA PROGETTI

Just as it takes many individuals to make a village, it takes the collaboration of many individuals to make an exhibition, particularly one with the scope and magnitude of *Masters of Florence*, involving 222 works of art and historical documentation coming from 62 lending institutions. This initiative began with a chance, but opportune meeting four years ago between ourselves, Contemporanea Progetti and WONDERS, the Memphis International Cultural Series so we would like to begin by thanking Glen Campbell and Steve Masler for their vision, their dedication to the vision and at times, their patience with their Italian "shipmates" in the realization of this exhibiiton and its catalogue.

On the other hand, none of this would have been possible without the committment of Annamaria Giusti as curator and Cristina Acidini Luchinat as scientific consultant so I would like to thank them both for their committment and particularly, Annamaria Giusti for her continual dedication to many details, both small and great, that has rendered this exhibition so rich in the comprehensive experience it offers its visitors as an exhibition and its readers as a catalogue.

We must also thank the many other individuals who collaborated on the project from the many museums, libraries, churches and private collections of Florence and Tuscany; not only the responsible professionals from the various Soprintendenze and the museum directors, but their colleagues as well, and the many assistants and secretaries who so generously collaborated with our staff at Contemporanea in the organization of countless details.

We would also like to thank the many professional individuals who helped make both the exhibition and catalogue possible. They include diversified restoration experts who have restored more than 33 works of art for this exhibition, made possible by the funding of WONDERS. Eleven other museum professionals and art historians have made important contributions to the catalogue as well as two professional translators. We have various photographers to thank but we would like to particularly thank Niccolo Orsi Battaglini for his tireless contribution to the photography of the catalogue.

And finally, I would like to personally thank my colleagues and staff at Contemporanea Progetti. I thank all my partners for their support but I would like to specially thank Eugenio Martera and Linda Carioni for their dedication to the project. I would also like to thank the various individuals and professionals from our staff who have worked on the project over the course of the last four years but in particular, all who have seen it through its home stretch – Piernicola Assetta, Cecilia Barbieri, Raffaella Conti, Emanuela Corradino, Leda Cosentino, Mimma Delle Grottaglie, Natalie Fischer, Silvia Gatta, Mirjam Kink and Benedetta Marchi.

In closing, I would again like to reiterate that it takes many individuals to realize an exhibition, many more than those mentioned here, and I would like to thank all personally and collectively for their contribution to the realization of this very important exhibition that hopes to heighten awareness and stimulate interest in the unique cultural and artistic patrimony of Florence, Italy.

Patrizia Pietrogrande
President
Contemporanea Progetti

LIST OF LENDERS

Archivio di Stato, Florence

Archivio di Stato, Mantua

Biblioteca Laurenziana, Florence

Biblioteca Marucelliana, Florence

Biblioteca Nazionale Centrale, Florence

Biblioteca Riccardiana, Florence

Alberto Bruschi Collection, Grassina

Carlotta Bruschi Collection, Florence

Casa Buonarroti, Florence

Cenacolo di Andrea del Sarto, Florence

Chiesa di Ognissanti, Florence

Chiesa di Santo Stefano dei Cavalieri, Pisa

Comune di Firenze, Florence

Convento di San Domenico, Fiesole

Eredità Bardini, Florence

Fioratti Collection, New York

Galleria dell'Accademia -
Museo degli Strumenti Musicali, Florence

Galleria d'Arte Moderna, Florence

Galleria degli Uffizi, Florence

Galleria del Costume, Florence

Galleria Nazionale, Parma

Galleria Palatina, Florence

Gualtieri Collection, Florence

Istituto e Museo di Storia della Scienza, Florence

Musée des Beaux Arts, Nantes

Musei Vaticani, Vatican City

Museo Archelogico Nazionale, Florence

Museo Bardini, Florence

Museo Civico, Bologna

Museo Civico, Prato

Museo degli Argenti, Florence

Museo delle Cappelle Medicee, Florence

Museo della Città e del Territorio, Monsummano Terme

Museo dell'Opera di Santa Croce, Florence

Museo dell'Opera di Santa Maria del Fiore, Florence

Museo dell'Opificio delle Pietre Dure, Florence

Museo di Palazzo Davanzati, Florence

Museo di Palazzo Martelli, Florence

Museo Diocesano, Pistoia

Museo di San Marco, Florence

Museo di Storia Naturale, Sezione Mineralogia, Florence

Museo Horne, Florence

Museo Nazionale del Bargello, Florence

Museo Nazionale di Castel Sant'Angelo, Rome

Museo Nazionale di Palazzo Mansi, Lucca

Museo Nazionale di Palazzo Reale, Pisa

Museo Nazionale di San Matteo, Pisa

Museo Nazionale di Scienza e Tecnologia
"Leonardo da Vinci", Milan

Museo Nazionale di Villa Guinigi, Lucca

Museo Storico della Caccia e del Territorio, Cerreto Guidi

Ospedale di Santa Maria Nuova, Florence

Palazzo Vecchio, Florence

Private Collection, Montecarlo

Private Collection, Naples

Private Collection, Florence

Provincia di Firenze, Florence

Salvadori Carnevali Collection, Florence

Torrini Collection, Florence

Villa La Quiete, Florence

Villa of Poggio a Caiano, Florence

EXHIBITION

Curated by: **Annamaria Giusti, Director of the Museo dell'Opificio delle Pietre Dure, Florence**
   with Cristina Acidini Luchinat, Soprintendente of the Opificio delle Pietre Dure as scientific consultant

Exhibition Concept and General Organization: **Contemporanea Progetti, Florence**
Project Management: **Patrizia Pietrogrande, Eugenio Martera, Linda Carioni**
Project Coordination: **Emanuela Corradino, Leda Cosentino**
Project Research: **Cecilia Barbieri**
Graphic Design: **Piernicola Assetta, Benedetta Marchi, Mirjam Kink**
Exhibition Video: **Contemporanea Progetti**
Transportation: **Arteria Srl, Florence**

CATALOGUE

Curated by: **Annamaria Giusti, Director of the Museo dell'Opificio delle Pietre Dure**
Essays by: **Cristina Acidini Luchinat, Annamaria Giusti, Eugenio Martera, Patrizia Pietrogrande**
Entries by: **Monica Bietti (M.B.), Elena Carrara (E.C.), Stefano Casciu (S.C.), Alessandro Cecchi (A.C.), Marco Chiarini (M.C.),**
   Annamaria Giusti (A.G.), Magnolia Scudieri (M.S.), Maria Sframeli (M.Sf.), Maria Grazia Vaccari (M.G.V.)
Translation by: **Linda Carioni, Diane Kunzelman, Eve Leckey**

Edited by: **Contemporanea Progetti, Florence**
Catalogue Organization: **Eugenio Martera, Patrizia Pietrogrande, Linda Carioni**
Catalogue Research: **Cecilia Barbieri, Benedetta Marchi, Raffaella Conti, Leda Cosentino**
Catalogue Design: **Mirjam Kink, Benedetta Marchi**
Cover Design: **Mirjam Kink**
Coordination of Photography: **Emanuela Corradino**

EXECUTIVE STAFF CONTEMPORANEA PROGETTI

President: **Patrizia Pietrogrande**
Managing Director: **Eugenio Martera**
International Relations: **Linda Carioni**
Advisory Board: **Patrizia Pietrogrande, Eugenio Martera, Stefania Ippoliti, Linda Carioni, Silvia Gatta, Massimo Marchi, Eva Parigi**
Executive Assistant: **Natalie Fischer**

WONDERS
The Memphis International Cultural Series

BOARD OF DIRECTORS

Diane Rudner, Chair

Doug Browne

Leslie Dale

Judge Bernice Donald

Greg Duckett

Kate Duignan

Erwin Geiger

Rusty Hensley

Larry Jensen

Tom Pittman

Agnes Pokrandt

Honey Scheidt

Pat Tigrett

Dick Tillman

Kevin Wright

EXECUTIVE STAFF

Richard C. Hackett, President & Chief Executive Officer

Glen A. Campbell, Vice-President & Chief Operating Officer

Ted Ferris, Chief Financial Officer

Sandy Lammey, Executive Assistant

Steve Masler, Chief Curator

Meredith Cain, Curatorial Assistant

Twyla Dixon, Director of Marketing & Public Relations

Joyce Ann Parker-Fegette, Director of Sales

Carolyn Daugherty, Volunteer Manager

Lee Person, Gift Shop Manager

Major Jim Kelly, Director of Security

John T. Duncan, Manager of Security

Travis Graves, Manager of Security

WONDERS STAFF

ART HANDLING, TRANSPORTATION, AND INSTALLATION

Alexander International
Neely Mallory III, President
W.L. Wadsworth, Executive Vice-President
LeRoy Pettyjohn, Vice-President, Fine Art Handling
Jennifer Scism, Fine Art Supervisor
Bill Ramia, Director of Import Services
John Hearn, Import Services

Arteria
Antonio Addari, General Manager
Marcello Contrucci, Operations Manager

Fine Art Installation Team
Larry Anderson
Edna Bomar
Tammy Braitwaite
Judd Childress
C.B. Jolly
Jewel Rosenberg
Brian Sharp
David White

DESIGN AND CONSTRUCTION

Architectural Design/Team Management
Askew Nixon Ferguson Architects, Inc.
Lee Askew III, FAIA, Principal-in-Charge
Leslie Smith, AIA, Project Architect
Kenneth Parks, Documentation

Exhibition Design
Design 500
Scott Blake, Exhibit Designer

Graphic Design
K. Design
Kathy Kelley

Solution Graphix
Jamie Tillman

Exhibit Lighting
Moonshine Lighting, Inc.
Randy Ridley, Project Manager
Robert Dicken, Project Design

Graphic Production
Bennett Creative Services
John Bennett

Mountmaking
Multiform Studios
James Leacock

Exhibit Construction and Specialty Manufacturing
Advance Manufacturing
David Craig, President
Greg Robison, Estimator
Mike Frye, Job Superintendent

Exhibition Maintenance
Nash Service Group
Will Nash

Exhibition Insurance
Summitt Global Partners
Chip Moreland

CURATORIAL AND EDUCATION

Teachers Guide
Heather Baugus, Layout Design
Darla Linerode-Henson, Lesson Plans

Curatorial Assistance
Kaywin Feldman, Director, Memphis Brooks Museum of Art
Walter R. Brown, Associate Professor and Assistant Chair of the Department of History, University of Memphis
Victor Coonin, Associate Professor and Chair, Department of Art, Rhodes College Memphis Brooks Museum of Art

Introductory Video
Contemporanea Progetti
Eugenio Martera, Producer

Audio Tour
Antenna Audio, Inc.
Alicia Simi
Margo Wallace
Allison Dufty

Catalogue Production

Design and Editing
Contemporanea Progetti
Eugenio Martera
Patrizia Pietrogrande
Linda Carioni

Printing and Production
Creative Graphics, LLC

SALES, MARKETING, AND PUBLIC RELATIONS

Advertising and Marketing
Sossaman & Associates
Donna Gordy, President
Chris Taylor, Account Manager
Walter Rose, Creative Director
Kenny Patrick, Art Director

Randall Hartzog, Production Services
Wil Hugh, Media Services
Mike Villanueva, Interactive Services

Speakers Bureau
Marjorie Gerald, Coordinator

Packaging and Group Travel
Sweet Magnolia Tours
Jay Kirkpatrick, Director of International Sales
Kathleen Green, Sales Manager

Concessions and Special Event Catering
Chef's Choice Catering

Promotional Assistance
Memphis Brooks Museum of Art
Memphis Convention & Visitors Bureau
Memphis Marriott Downtown
Memphis Zoo and Aquarium
Pat O'Brien's Memphis
The Peabody Hotel
Peabody Place

Direct Mail
Memphis Presort, Inc.

The Pyramid/SMG
Alan Freeman, General Manager
Chuck Jabbour, Assistant General Manager
Terri Knight, Executive Assistant

Gala Event
Girls Inc.
Sandra Burke, President and Executive Director
Tammie Ritchey, Development Director
Nicole Perino, Special Events/Promotions Manager
University of Memphis Athletic Department
R.C. Johnson, Athletic Director
Melissa Moore, Assistant Athletic Director

Ticketing Equipment and Services
Ticketmaster Vista

Sponsors

PRESENTING SPONSORS

THE PLOUGH FONDATION THE BUCKMAN FAMILY

PRINCIPAL SPONSORS

AUTOZONE

MAJOR SPONSORS

ASSISI FOUNDATION   MEMPHIS CONVENTION & VISITORS BUREAU

FEDERAL EXPRESS   THE PEABODY HOTEL

INTERNATIONAL PAPER   PEABODY PLACE

THE SCHEIDT FAMILY FOUNDATION

CITY OF MEMPHIS
DR WILLIE W. HERENTON, MAYOR

MEMPHIS CITY COUNCIL
Chairman, Joe Brown
Councilwoman, Carol Chumney
Councilman, Ed Ford
Councilwoman, Janet Hooks
Councilman, E.C. Jones
Councilman, Myron Lowery
Councilman, Tom Marshall
Councilman, Scott McCormick
Councilman, Ricky Peete
Councilman, Jack Sammons
Councilwoman, TaJuan Stout-Mitchell
Councilwoman, Barbara Swearengen-Holt
Councilman, Brent Taylor

SPONSORS

MAJOR SUPPORTERS

B. Lee Mallory

Bell South Advertising

Memphis Sight and Sound

City of Memphis, Division of Police Services
James H. Bolden, Director

Coors Brewing Co.

Clear Channel Communications

Lipscomb & Pitts Insurance, LLC

Memphis Arts Council

Memphis Marriott Downtown

Memphis Sight & Sound

Mednikow Jewelers

The Pyramid/SMG

Shelby County Government,
AC Wharton, Mayor

Time Warner Communications

UNICO

Quantum Showroom

SUPPORTERS

Backyard Burgers

The Bogatin Law Firm, LLC

Catholic Diocese of Memphis Schools

Chef's Choice Catering

The Downtowner Magazine

Memphis Area Transit Authority

Memphis Brooks Museum

Memphis City Schools

Metro Memphis Hotel Lodging Association

Metro Memphis Attractions Association

University of Memphis

Shelby County Schools

WKNO-TV, Channel 10

WREG-TV, Channel 3

Barbara Williams

The Embassy of Italy
Sergio Vento, Ambassador
Pasquale Ferrara, Chief Consul

The Embassy of The United States of America
Mel Sembler, Ambassador
William W. McIlhenny, Consul General, Florence

Masters of Florence

Annamaria Giusti

Still another exhibition on art during the time of the Medici? The question is not all that farfetched, considering how many important exhibitions over the last thirty years have followed the traces of this ruling dynasty, and have encountered along the way many less-explored facets of Florentine art. The first of these exhibitions dedicated to *The Last of the Medici* was held in Florence and Detroit in 1974. This show was an international event, with a two-fold appeal: on the one hand, for its focus on the Florentine Baroque, an era often obscured by the light cast by the shining stars of the Medieval and Renaissance periods, and on the other hand, for its acknowledgement of the excellence and international prestige of the decorative arts, which was an expression of Florentine culture that was anything but "minor", especially during the 17th and early 18th centuries.

The numerous initiatives centering on the Medici during 1980 were all concentrated on the *Cinquecento* (1500's). Although this period was already well investigated by art-historical studies, the vision was broadened on these occasions to include multiple aspects that helped to create the Florentine hot-house environment of culture in many forms that was so closely bound to the fortunes of the Medici family, already a ruling dynasty. This broadened, interdisciplinary perspective in the analysis of a historical period provided the criteria for subsequent "Medici initiatives", such as the centennial celebration of Lorenzo the Magnificent in 1992, which finally offered a comprehensive reconstruction of such a complex personality.

On a parallel track, these initiatives that broadened the body of knowledge also helped to deepen and refine research, both about certain aspects of the Medici patronage of the arts, (among the many possible examples, I would like to recall another exhibition curated in 1988 by the Opificio, *Splendori di pietre dure*) and about chronological issues that could be considered through the multiplicity of their artistic components. This was the case in the 1997 exhibition, *Magnificenza alla corte dei Medici*, which concentrated on the period of Francesco I and Ferdinando I, or the more recent *Ombra del Genio*, in which an important selection of Florentine art dating from the century between Cosimo I and Cosimo II de' Medici, was presented in Florence and the United States in 2002-2003.

The events to which we have briefly referred have played an important role beyond that of the temporary occasion of the exhibition or the more lasting one represented by the catalogue. They have formed a reserve of knowledge, which has become integral to the increasing attention dedicated to Medici themes. This is true whether speaking of a specialized sphere of study and research, or of exhibitions whose scientific and communicative goals are oriented towards introducing a non-Italian public to Medici artistic themes. Two distinct exhibitions, recently organized by the Florentine Soprintendenza may be seen in this light; each united a meaningful selection of works deriving from the patronage of the Medici Grand Dukes. One was presented in China, in Beijing and Shanghai (1997-98), and the other in Europe, in Munich, Vienna, and Blois (1998-99).

In light of this, one may quite easily understand the interest of the Opificio in evaluating and then accepting the idea of an exhibition that unites the themes of Florence and the Medici. The proposal came from WONDERS, the Memphis International Cultural Series, which has been promoting exhibitions in the city of Memphis for more than a decade now. Aimed at presenting a representative selection of various artistic cultures ranging from antiquity to European and non-European art, these

MASTERS OF FLORENCE

initiatives have regularly been rewarded with very high public attendance. This will be an occasion for us to introduce a relatively new public to Florentine history and culture. It is not by chance that the term history precedes that reference to art. Beginning with the initial planning of the exhibition, we decided to avoid a parade of masterpieces and "treasures", giving precedence to providing the historical context in which "major" and "minor" expressions of Florentine culture and art might find their place, following a chronological pathway traced through almost five centuries.

"Too much to choose from!", one might almost say, considering the overwhelming abundance of art that Florence has to offer. There is in fact no pretense to synthesize all of this in just one exhibition. Instead the intent is to highlight moments in time, "flashes", capable of communicating their message in a clear yet suggestive way; moments which find their unity in the timeline of the Medici family from the 1300's up to the fatal year of 1743 that witnessed their extinction.

Nor is it a pretext that the *trait d'union*, (the connection) of the Medici family, first as it emerged and later as it ruled Florence, is intrinsic to the history of Florence. The exhibition is planned to unfold accordingly: the first section offers a glance at the Florence of the 1300's inhabited by, but not dominated by the Medici, while the subsequent sections are constructed through references either direct or contingent to the Medici presence.

For the loans essential to the realization of our project, we have applied to a series of Florentine and Tuscan museums, as prestigious as numerous. All have replied very generously to our requests, thus assuring both the quality and variety of works, and permitting us to put together a total of about 220 works. These are representative of the Florentine artistic culture in all the many forms that its extraordinary creativity has produced: the rise of sculpture in the *Quattrocento* (1400's), represented in the exhibition by milestones in the work of Ghiberti, Donatello and Verrocchio; the leading role of painting, first in Medieval times through the work of Giotto and subsequently, as the acme of Renaissance expression, with Beato Angelico, Ghirlandaio, Botticelli, Piero di Cosimo, Raphael.

Florence, however, is not only about the Renaissance, nor the so-called "major arts": in the exhibition, the artistic creations and personalities of the 1600's and early 1700's, have found a place corresponding to their very valued importance in grand ducal Florence. Among these are such internationally renowned artists as Pietro da Cortona and Rubens, but to an even greater degree, a broad range of artworks and objects belonging to the applied arts. Within the long arc of time embraced by the exhibition, many of the artworks were selected as an expression of the artistic excellence achieved in the field of decorative arts. Other objects document customs and life-styles, sometimes-daily routines of "normal" life, as is natural when dealing with a family, even a royal family. In any case, the selection of the objects has been based on what can best illustrate the web onto which a "grand" history has been woven, and also serve as a means of bettering our understanding of it. In this light can be found the explanation for the co-presence of masterpieces of art, which certainly could not be lacking in an exhibition which strives at least to suggest the idea of the heights reached by the Florentine Renaissance, with certain almost "commonplace" objects; items that create a more immediate contact with the past, through human sentiments or common habits from everyday life. This is demonstrated in the little drawing of a newborn baby that Maria de' Medici, about to become the Queen of France, sketched on a letter to her sister who had become a mother. It is also demonstrated in the household slippers we can imagine being worn by Michelangelo, as he composed his Neo-Platonic verses, or worked on one of the drawings that can be seen in the exhibition.

The city of Florence, prestigious for art and culture yet still approachable in its human dimensions, also speaks to the visitor throughout the varied but well-articulated exhibition, formulating almost the ideal premise for the features of a future museum - "Florence as it once was".

I do not wish to further "explain" the exhibition that we have structured to be eloquent in itself. I would only like to add that in the catalogue, we have followed the same criteria. The objects are presented, grouped into the five sections which form the exhibition itinerary and in a sequence determined by the relationships between the various objects according to a coherent historical context, as outlined in my brief prefaces for each section. Most of the entries are also in the form of brief outlines, in order to favor easy consultation on the part of the visitor, and also enable the catalogue to be a clear "guide" to the exhibition, even for those who have not seen it. Both the short entries and the lengthier ones dedicated to significant works of art, or to those works that provide a "key" to better understanding of the exhibition "story", have been prepared by specialists who have accepted the task of synthesizing their certainly more in-depth knowledge. I am particularly grateful to all of them for this, knowing all too well that brevity and modesty are rather rare merchandise among us art historians.

And if any other art historians are curious enough to leaf through this certainly not too "weighty" catalogue, then they may perhaps find some pleasant insights, and maybe even a few bits of news.

The Birth of the Legend of Florence

Cristina Acidini Luchinat

The city of Florence, its immediate surroundings and the entire region of Tuscany (which still covers more or less the same area as the old Grand Duchy that only in 1860 became part of the Italian State under the Savoy dynasty) are internationally famous for the quality of architecture, art, craftsmanship and the natural setting which man has so wisely cultivated over the centuries.

Indeed, if we consider the city of Florence alone, we realize that within the relatively limited area of the historic center there is a concentration of monuments and masterpieces that is extraordinary not only for their number, and therefore density, but also for the standard of excellence. Many are famed in their own right, such as the Ponte Vecchio, the Cathedral, Botticelli's *Primavera* and Michelangelo's *David*, to name just some of the most renowned. Florence is remarkable for this concentration even in comparison with other Italian cities of art such as Venice, Rome or Naples, and at the beginning of the Renaissance her politicians, writers, and historians quickly became aware that an exceptional cultural and artistic patrimony was being created and accumulated in the city. The civic pride of writers such as Leonardo Bruni, Cristoforo Landino and many others has left us with the image of a beautiful, vibrant and wealthy city, enclosed by a circle of undulating hills where villas, gardens and estates nestled.[1]

Clearly there was no single reason for such a burgeoning of the arts, but rather a fortunate sequence of causes, including primarily the city's economic success that began in the 13th century and saw Florence's products, merchants and bankers in demand, traveling throughout the Italian peninsula and to many European countries. But there was also the solidity of the civil and religious institutions and the participation of numerous lay associations (corporations, guilds, confraternities) in the running of the community, and indeed the sophistication of the language (vernacular Tuscan) which over the centuries would come to be considered and adopted as the purest form of Italian, thanks to poets and writers like Dante and the *Stilnovisti*, Petrarca and Boccaccio.

Other reasons may lie, on the one hand, in faith and devotion which gave rise to religious works and the sacred arts, mostly supported by private donations; and on the other, in the study of ancient pre-Christian writings and artifacts (which were available locally and especially in Rome) and the early emergence of a humanistic literary culture imbued with inherently natural values.

And lastly, although not scientifically measurable, but fascinating all the same, some writers of the day claimed that insubstantial factors also had a role, such as the "subtle influence in the very air" and the amount of "talented men that were being born in Tuscany".

These two quotations are taken from Giorgio Vasari's fundamental text which was published in two volumes in the second half of the 16th century.[2] This monumental work of art literature is packed with biographical details and information on the works of artists from the Middle Ages to Michelangelo, encompassing almost three centuries.

According to Vasari's progressive vision of art, it was the Tuscan — and especially Florentine — artists who revived the arts that had

Michelangelo, *David,* 1501-1504
Florence, Galleria dell'Accademia

THE BIRTH OF THE LEGEND OF FLORENCE

declined after the fall of the Roman Empire in the west, giving way to the affected and hieratic forms that developed in Byzantium, the capital of the Eastern Empire. By liberating art from the domination of the "Greek Masters" - those Byzantine artists who lived and worked in the Italian peninsula - Cimabue, Arnolfo di Cambio, Niccolò Pisano and later his son, Giovanni, helped give birth in Tuscany to an early artistic re-awakening (at the end of the 13th and beginning of the 14th century) inspired by the study of antiquity and also enriched by a renewed attention to nature. According to Vasari, the uninterrupted rise of the arts in Tuscany culminated in his own lifetime with the titanic figure of Michelangelo Buonarroti, insuperable in all the arts (and, it should be added, quite a fine poet), "everyone might admire and follow him as their perfect exemplar... and he would be acclaimed as divine."[3] During the prosperous period as a free *comune*, both inside and outside the small area enclosed by the second ring of defensive walls, Florence was almost entirely a building site of monumental works. The new cathedral was under construction, dedicated to Santa Maria del Fiore abandoning the previous devotion to Saint Reparata (legendary girl martyr from Pannonia, now Hungary) and introducing the veneration of Christ the Redeemer incarnated in the virginal image of the Madonna, flower and fruit of the biblical Tree of Jesse. This religious veneration had a civic counterpart in the Florentine new year which fell on 25 March, date of the Annunciation by the angel to Mary and the conception of Jesus, so that for many centuries, the Florentine year began *ab incarnatione* (since conception). But work was also taking place on the church of Orsanmichele, the Palazzo dei Signori (today's Palazzo Vecchio), the great churches such as the Dominican Santa Maria Novella and the Franciscan Santa Croce, the bridges, city walls, palaces, loggias, public monuments such as the San Zanobi column, raised in 1384 in memory of the transfer of the miraculous remains of the saintly Bishop from San Lorenzo to the Cathedral, and even on the first sculpted stone lion, known as the *Marzocco* and a symbol of the city, at the entrance to the palace of the government.

The artistic "idol" of the day was Giotto, whose irresistible rise was observed and recorded by an illustrious witness of the times – Dante Alighieri, Florentine politician and scholar in exile, whose religious poem, the *Divine Comedy* was for a long time considered to be a theological work, later becoming a cornerstone in the development of vernacular Italian. In *Purgatory* in the second canticle are the famous lines,[4]

"Once Cimabue thought to hold the field
as painter; now Giotto is all the rage,
dimming the lustre of the other's fame."

The lines express in synthesis, but probably quite precisely, the rapid transition of Italian painting. The vast and widely-spread output of Giotto and his helpers and followers developed into an innovative artistic espression, completely free from the Byzantine legacy. Flexible and narrative, this new artistic expression introduced the feeling of weight, space, and the physical substance of people and things.

In Florence, Giotto's name is still primarily associated by all with the *campanile* of the cathedral, the tall, square-built tower that houses the cathedral bells, which he designed and began work on in 1334, overseeing the construction as far as the completion of the lower decorative order. However, his work as a painter is to be found in the churches of the city, the monumental crosses (the recently restored cross in Santa Maria Novella is splendid), several paintings of the Madonna enthroned (Uffizi Gallery, Diocesan Museum), and many other panel paintings in churches and museums, as well as memorable fresco cycles in the Bardi and Peruzzi chapels in Santa Croce.

On the last of his numerous journeys throughout Italy, he travelled to Milan, sent by the Council of Florence to work in the service

THE BIRTH OF THE LEGEND OF FLORENCE

of Azzone Visconti. This is an important indication of the awareness that had rapidly developed at the highest levels of Florentine political power of the "value" of artists and of works of art as ambassadors for the city at an international level. Almost a century and a half later, Lorenzo the Magnificent would send the best Florentine artists, including Botticelli, to paint the walls of the Sistine Chapel in Rome as confirmation of the peace recently signed with Pope Sixtus IV.

Artists after Giotto established the lasting tradition of panel and fresco painting, of marble and bronze sculpture, and of highly aesthetic applied arts created with superb technical skill. The devastating Black Death of 1348 slowed down this artistic ferment but did not bring it to an end.

That entirely Florentine phenomenon known as the Renaissance or "Early" Renaissance took place in this cultural and urban context at the beginning of the 15th century, evolving during the 16th century into the "High" or "Late" Renaissance. During the first thirty years of the 15th century many skilled *maestri* continued to produce Gothic-style art, but with exquisite variations derived from intelligently grafted classical elements (as in the works of the goldsmith and scupltor Lorenzo Ghiberti) and unusual techniques (the paintings of Lorenzo Monaco and Gentile da Fabriano). But the small group of innovators who all knew each other and were constantly in contact, succeeded in developing a new and different vision of the world in which the moral and physical figure of Man dominated the center of the universe, now definable and measurable through perspective.[5]

While the philosophical and literary activity of the great Tuscan humanists was enthusiastically directed towards rediscovering and reinterpreting ancient Greek and Roman texts, the artists were intent on studying the antiquities of Rome and the reinvention of that lost classicism. The opening pages of any text or manual on the Florentine and Italian Renaissance are dedicated to Filippo Brunelleschi, architect, sculptor and goldsmith, to Donatello, versatile sculptor, and to Masaccio, a panel and fresco painter. Brunelleschi's research into optics and geometry was known to other artists, and lead to the invention or discovery of "artificial perspective", which Donatello soon applied in sculpture and Masaccio shortly after in painting. The architect Leon Battista Alberti then codified the rules of perspective in his writings thereby spreading its use and knowledge.

From then on, western European art is strongly distinguished by perspective as a way of seeing and representing the world, differentiating it from the visual and figurative conventions of other continents.

The rational appropriation of reality, which was spreading from Florence throughout Italy and

Giotto, *Bell Tower*, 1334
Florence, Santa Maria del Fiore

THE BIRTH OF THE LEGEND OF FLORENCE

beyond, also brought about immense progress in geography and cartography, inspiring the great navigators at the close of the century. In planning his voyage towards the Indies, Christopher Colombus was helped and assisted by Paolo Dal Pozzo Toscanelli, an elderly Florentine mathematician who had known and frequented Brunelleschi in his youth.

From the early decades of the century this triumvirate of supreme masters was surrounded by other outstanding talents; the architect Michelozzo di Bartolomeo, who, among many other achievements, designed Palazzo Medici on Via Larga; the sculptors Nanni di Banco and Luca della Robbia; the painters Masolino, Beato Angelico, Paolo Uccello, Domenico Veneziano, Filippo Lippi, Andrea del Castagno, and numerous other important artists and great masterpieces that would fill pages and pages.

With the Renaissance of the age of humanism, and the construction of Santa Maria del Fiore, which quickly became the supreme symbol of this golden moment for the arts, Florence made a unique, but not only architectural, achievement. The building of the dome was, above all, a daring challenge on every technical level. The original plan by Arnolfo was modified and extended during the 14th century, until in about 1370 the measurements of the three naves and their chapels were established, as well as the dome which was to be built at the crossing of the naves and the trilobate apse. But when the moment came to vault the dome, at the

Filippo Brunelleschi, *Dome*, 1436
Florence, Santa Maria del Fiore

beginning of the 15th century, it became obvious that it was impossibile to build such a massive structure with the traditional method of scaffolding from the ground. After public competitions and meetings of experts, the project was assigned to Filippo Brunelleschi, who made the revolutionary proposal to *voltarla senza armatura* (to build it without support). With this method, no scaffolding would be used and a double structure (consisting of an internal and external shell with an accessible passageway between) would be raised, resting directly on the drum, the mighty octagonal prism that supports it, and gradually adjusting the curve with moveable centering until it closed at the top, 90 meters above the ground. His achievement (for which he obtained the complete support of the authorities of Santa Maria del Fiore, despite the audacity of this pioneering technique) marked an astounding advance in the "science of building", both theoretically and practically, but also and above all, it demonstrated the power of human inventiveness. The dome was completed in 1436 and was crowned after the death of Brunelleschi (1446) by the small marble temple forming the lantern, based on his design. The image of the dome with its lofty curve, which eight white marble ribs divide into eight segments covered with red tiles, has since then dominated the urban skyline of Florence from both near and afar and it is also accepted as a visual limit for the entire territorial organization of the area.

THE BIRTH OF THE LEGEND OF FLORENCE

The pride felt for the dome was intense and was perfectly expressed by Leon Battista Alberti who defined it as, "such a large structure, rising above the skies, ample to cover with its shadow all the Tuscan people (...)" ("*structura sì grande, erta sopra e cieli, ampla da choprire chon sua ombra tucti e' popoli toscani*").[6]

With building sites in strategic locations around the city (though all were interrupted and often altered by his successors), Brunelleschi introduced distinctive features to Florentine civil and religious architecture which, by tradition and revival, were part of the local architectural scene until the beginning of the 20th century. The architectural style inspired by classical models is evident in the beautiful churches of Santo Spirito and San Lorenzo, with *pietra serena* or stucco moldings and broad harmonious surfaces of whitened plaster. *Pietra serena* and plaster, the hefty sandstone walls, the decorations in glazed terracotta, named after their inventor, Luca della Robbia, bronze and marble sculptures, all these elements formed the rational measure of the visual outline and the somber harmony so typical of Florence and other Tuscan towns.

With the advent of the Medici there was a boom in the increasingly complex and sophisticated artistic commissions and collecting undertaken by other important families as well as the church.

In the 15h century, the family of Giovanni di Bicci, a branch of the Medici, were influential bankers; in the 16th century their descendents were popes in Rome, and dukes and grand dukes in Florence. Two Medici women, Catherine and Maria, married kings of France. As Annamaria Giusti fully describes in this catalogue, in the three centuries of the Medici's dynastic rule, the cultural achievements of Florence encompassed a concentration of monuments and collections of international acclaim, the very density of which is quite exceptional.

Both in town and country the "early" Medici, descended from the *Pater Patriae*, Cosimo the Elder, Piero the Gouty and Lorenzo the Magnificent, who all invested vast sums of money in buildings either directly commissioned by them such as palaces and villas, or in churches and chapels that were under their protection. Quite splendid examples of Medici patronage are to be found around the area of San Giovanni, starting at the Baptistery and Cathedral and proceeding to the the Dominican monastery of San Marco. Panel and fresco paintings by Beato Angelico are in the monastery, and the library that housed rare and valuable codices was designed by Michelozzo. On the other side of the road, where the Medici Casino stood, were the gardens of San Marco, where some of the family's classical antiquities were kept and which Lorenzo The Magnificent made available to young artists so that they could study and draw them; among the most talented of the youthful apprentices between 1490 and 1492 was the young Michelangelo. Standing on both sides of today's Via Cavour were houses of the various branches of the family, including the impressive Palazzo Medici, strategically placed on a corner. The building was originally an impressive "cube" of stone faced with rustic *bugnato*, but it was enlarged by the later proprietors, the Riccardi in the 17th century, and today the façade is much longer than originally. Just around the corner to the west, the complex of San Lorenzo represents a complete synthesis of Medicean history: the Old Sacristy (begun by Giovanni di Bicci, who is buried there with his wife); the church itself, designed by Brunelleschi and housing masterpieces by Donatello; the Treasury enriched by Medici popes with rare furnishings and semi-precious stone vases belonging to the family and used as reliquaries; Michelangelo's New Sacristy where Dukes Lorenzo and Giuliano who both died at an early age are buried; the Biblioteca Laurenziana, also designed by Michelangelo to house the Medici codices and right from the start open to scholars for consultation. In the 17th century, the octagonal Chapel of the Princes, entirely decorated inside with precious marble, was built as a mausoleum for the Medici family; and finally in the 18th century Anna Maria Luisa, the Electress Palatine and last of the dynasty, completed the Medici's three centuries of construction at San Lorenzo by building the slender bell tower.

THE BIRTH OF THE LEGEND OF FLORENCE

The astounding artistic initiative of both patrons and collectors at the time of the high Renaissance was due greatly, but not only, to the Medici. The most important artistic workshops of the later 15th century were at the service of the old aristocracy, the mercantile bourgeoisie, the religious orders and long-standing institutions. While Pollaiolo's workshop grew famous, in Andrea del Verrocchio's versatile studio the young Leonardo da Vinci and Sandro Botticelli studied and worked, both destined to have brilliant, though very different, careers. Leonardo was highly gifted in the arts and sciences, an intelligent researcher and observer of nature, tireless inventor, an experimenter of techniques and technologies. Restless and always ready to travel, he worked for different patrons until his death in France at the court of Francis I. Sandro Botticelli, instead, remained in Florence throughout his long life (except for brief trips and sojourns in nearby villas). He studied and illustrated Dante's *Divine Comedy*, the literary monument of Florentine culture, and was profoundly and essentially a painter, creating an artistic style that was particularly understood and appreciated at the time of the pre-Raphaelites in the 19th century.

In 1504, the Republic of Florence, which had dismissed the Medici some ten years previously, experienced a unique moment in the history of art. Michelangelo was completing the immense marble statue of the *David*, but he was also preparing the cartoon for the *Battle of Cascina* for a fresco in the Palazzo Vecchio in the same council chamber (now of the *Cinquecento* – Chamber of the 500) where Leonardo would paint the *Battle of Anghiari*. The young Raphael too was in Florence and would remain until 1508 refining the skills he had acquired in Umbria by capturing the softness of Leonardo and the grandeur of Fra' Bartolomeo. His masterpieces, the Doni portraits and the *Madonna with Goldfinch* were painted during this period. During the following years, power passed from the Medici to the Republic until they once more took control as dukes, followed by the siege of the city by the Emperor in 1529. Yet these tumultuous political events coincided with an artistic subtlety that developed at the same rate as intellectual unease. Painters who were young at the time of Michelangelo's *Stories of the Old Testament* (1508-12) in the Sistine Chapel were quite overpowered by the work and drew inspiration from it for a "new style" of art which, some three centuries later, would be called "Mannerism". In the unfolding of the scenes and figures, which have a complex spatial relationship with the illusionistic architectural features, an inexhaustibly diverse and continually superb design is combined with a background of pure color shot through with gleams of light, which 20th century restoration has carefully brought brilliantly to light. Without the ceiling of the Sistine Chapel, the vivid and visionary paintings of Pontormo, Rosso Fiorentino and the Sienese Beccafumi would have been impossible. And it was still Michelangelo - also the author of sublime sculptures and the magnificent fresco of the *Universal Judgement* on the vast wall behind the Sistine Chapel altar - who provided inspiration for the next generation of artists who had trained in Florence and Rome, and in the mid 16th century sought work at the first "court" of Florence, in the service of Duke Cosimo I. These included Francesco Salviati, Giorgio Vasari and Bartolommeo Ammannati.

The prodigious legacy to architecture and sculpture left by Michelangelo in the New Sacristy in San Lorenzo – the tombs of Duke Lorenzo of Urbino and Duke Giuliano of Nemours – must have been decisive for the future development of Florentine art. The interior of the Sacristy and the tombs form a powerful unity of architecture and sculpture, integrated into a single coherent concept, the essential elements of which could be taken up by other artists, such as Niccolò Tribolo and Giorgio Vasari when Michelangelo departed from Florence in 1534 leaving the work incomplete. Michelangelo sculpted seven statues: Giuliano with *Night and Day*, Lorenzo with *Dawn and Dusk* and the *Madonna and Child*. Also attibuted to him is the *Adolescent*, destined for the Sacristy and now in the Hermitage in St Petersburg. The architecture, but especially the statues, or parts of them, were copied by numerous artists in the following decades, and the best sculptors of the mid-16th century - Baccio Bandinelli, Benvenuto Cellini,

THE BIRTH OF THE LEGEND OF FLORENCE

Vincenzo Danti and Giambologna - were able to study these unique pieces, developing their own style.

Although Michelangelo never returned to Florence in the thirty years between his departure for Rome and his death, he remained a point of reference for the city's art and politics. His visitors questioned, listened and flattered him and he thus continued to exercise his authority from afar, and was even appointed head of the Academy of Arts and Design (the first artistic academy in Europe) when it was founded in 1563, the year before his death. And it was his death that finally brought about Michelangelo's triumphal return to his native city, following the Duke's quite exceptional decision that he should receive a solemn funeral in San Lorenzo, the Medici family's own church and the site of his greatest architectural and sculptural creations. An oration by the great historian Benedetto Varchi and an impressive display celebrated Michelangelo as supreme in the arts of architecture, painting, sculpture and poetry. This was the first and only time that an artist was to receive an honor that, after him, was reserved only for grand dukes and sovereigns beginning with Cosimo de' Medici in 1574. Michelangelo's funeral in 1564 signalled a change in the

Michelangelo, *Night and Day*, 1520-1534
Florence, New Sacristy, Medici Tombs, Church of San Lorenzo

propaganda of the Medici grand dukes, now increasingly focused on art, and intended to export an image of the small Tuscan state as being the source of international taste and the cradle of aesthetics. In Florence, and gradually in other towns and cities of Tuscany, new buildings and monuments began to modernize the earlier urban context of mainly medieval architecture with 15th century additions. To mention just a few examples, Cosimo I made profound changes to the center of Florence, building the loggias of the New Market, the magistrates' building (now the Uffizi), the corridor that connects Palazzo Vecchio to the new palace on the other side of the river, the Palazzo Pitti and the Boboli Gardens. His sons and successors continued and developed this building policy working with the court architects Vasari and Ammannati and the talented and versatile Bernardo Buontalenti. Statues such as Cellini's *Perseus*, fountains like Ammannati's *Neptune*, equestrian figures of the grand dukes by Giambologna, all contributed to the spectacular artistic impact of public squares. These bronze and marble figures had an allegorical meaning and importance drawn from Greek and Roman mythology or from dynastic celebration confirming concepts of a political nature, such as the supremacy of Good over Evil with the government of the grand dukes, resolute but pacificatory.

The interest that the Medici, and other important Tuscan families, had in the land gave rise to the development of rural villas that not only worked the land for agricultural purposes, but equally importantly respected the beauty of the landscape and villages. Florence is encircled by Medici and aristocratic villas and, from the 16th century on, entranced travellers have left enthusiastic

THE BIRTH OF THE LEGEND OF FLORENCE

Giorgio Vasari, *Corridor*, connecting Palazzo Vecchio and the Pitti Palace, 1564

descriptions of them.

In fact, Florence exported more that just an artistic image. The court was noted too for the fine and rare objects that were sometimes presented to rulers or influential personages who had visited the city or sometimes sent to other European courts as diplomatic gifts and the exquisite items that were part of the dowry of the Medici princesses. Even today the sumptuous objects belonging to Florentine collections and museums that are lent to temporary exhibitions throughout the world are, in a certain sense, ambassadors of the Tuscan heritage of art and history.

As is evident from studies and exhibitions of the last 20 years, the decorative arts in Florence were highly considered and merited the most precious materials, the most skilled craftsmen and immense financial resources. Cosimo I brought weavers from Flanders and established a tapestry factory that operated for two centuries producing numerous splendid tapestries woven with wool, silk, gold and silver. His oldest son, Francesco I, an enthusiast of natural history and keen on experimentation, brought hard stone cutters from Milan and glass makers from Venice. And it was Francesco who was the first person in Europe to discover the secret of imitating the beautiful, fine Chinese porcelain in the Medici Casino at San Marco. The skill of working inlaid marble enabled the grand dukes to emulate the magnificence of the ancient emperors and their ambition reached its peak in the 17th century with the building of the Chapel of the Princes, a sumptuous and somber burial chamber encrusted with colored marble and semiprecious stones.

Research into the natural world, its creations and treasures, so beautifully represented in Francesco's *Studiolo* (study) in Palazzo Vecchio (1572) developed into further scientific study. The alliance that was established in Florence in the late 16th century between art and science put the technical resources of drawing, painting and superb craftsmanship at the service of rapidly evolving disciplines such as zoology, botany, mechanics, cosmography and astronomy. Some of the most fascinating items of 16th-17th century craftsmanship are, in fact, the scientific instruments used at the Medici court, many of which are now exhibited in the History of Science museum.

THE BIRTH OF THE LEGEND OF FLORENCE

Within the first thirty years of the 17th century in Florence, the artistic philosophy inherited from Michelangelo and the Mannerist artists was reduced to simplified and austere forms of art and architecture, inspired also by the precepts of the Catholic counter-reformation that restored sacred art to the communicative simplicity of its origins. The frescoes in the room decorated by Giovanni di San Giovanni in Palazzo Pitti synthesized an erudite, lively and communicative artistic culture. But genuine artistic renewal came from outside – from Rome, the undisputed leader of art in the Italian peninsula, where the newly developing style was Baroque, a style destined to extend well beyond the Alps and become both a European and south American artistic expression during the 18th century.

Pietro da Cortona was in fact a Tuscan painter and architect who had trained in Rome and arrived in Florence in 1637 to paint the ceiling frescoes of the "Planets" in the reception rooms in the Pitti Palace (now the Palatine Gallery). His work demonstrated to local artists a new and different style of painting, with a fresh and natural method of composition where a knowledge of perspective was used to create an illusion of spatial expansion. The range of radiant colors that recent restorative cleaning has emphasized, transposed onto the fluidity of Tuscan drawing, the richness of the Venetian palette.

The second important manifestation of Baroque painting in Florence occurred in 1682 with the arrival of the Neapolitan Luca Giordano. This masterly, brisk fresco painter left two masterpieces in Florence that would provide examples of dynamic and airy compositions for local painters: the ceiling of the Corsini chapel in the Church of Santa Maria del Carmine and especially the *Apotheosis of the Riccardi Family* in the long gallery of Palazzo Medici Riccardi.

However, the artistic circles of the grand duchy greeted the rapid spread of this popular new Baroque style with caution and remained faithful to the teaching of drawing which was still the foundation of Florentine artistic training. Just as architecture maintained its measured and severe equilibrium, with the minimum of ornamental detail, so sculpture limited the dynamism of figures and groups to an evenly balanced movement often preferring the more poetic and restrained form of the small bronze to monumental statuary. Meanwhile, painting was developing into increasingly numerous genres with not only sacred, historical and mythological subjects but also portraits, still-life, battle scenes, views, miniatures, not to mention *bambocciate* (low-life and trivialities), *stregonerie* (sorceries) and caprices. The expansion of collectionism to Italian centers of art, as well as to other European countries brought foreign and especially Flemish and Dutch paintings and drawings to Florence. The variety of subjects in painting was therefore matched by a wide range of stylistic techniques.

The penetration of the Baroque even within the decorative arts, provoked thoughtful and creative results. For example, the Florentine technique of inlaid marble and semiprecious stone that had developed in the 16th century as entirely two-dimensional, evolved a more sculptural quality and portrayed three-dimensional elements such as fruit, flowers and birds in high relief, made by highly skilled craftsmen. Renowned masters such as Giovanni Battista Foggini and Massimiliano Soldani Benzi were the masters of decorative arts for the later Medici and over the last several decades, specialized studies have shown that their skills represented the height of Florentine artistic production at that time.

It was however, a period of general decline for the Grand Duchy; with European politics now dominated by large nation states, the region was relegated to the background and the extinction of the ruling dynasty was by now inevitable as the last grand duke had failed to produce an heir. Yet this dismal situation was illuminated by the farsighted wisdom of the last of the Medici, Anna Maria Luisa. For many years happily married, though without children, to the Elector Palatine Johann Wilhelm von der Pfalz-Neuburg, after his death she returned to Florence from the German city of Düsseldorf and managed the tricky passage of the

THE BIRTH OF THE LEGEND OF FLORENCE

throne from the Medici to the Hapsburg family, and in 1737, she and her successors subscribed to a fundamental document known as the "Family Pact".

If, in a drastically simplified history, one were forced to identify the key moments that changed the destiny of Florence, I would have no hesitation in naming three. The first, at the beginning of the 14th century was the period of Dante and Giotto, when the city formulated the literary and artistic means of expression that would become established throughout the Italian peninsula.

The second was in the mid-16th century, when Michelangelo was honored with a state funeral, recognizing his "divine quality" as an artist, the supreme ambassador of the Medici duchy in the world.

The third was indeed 1737, the year of the "Family Pact", by which the last of the Medici established, with full legal force, that the immense collections of the family would become the property of the succeeding dynasty but that they would not be removed from the city of Florence. It is thanks to this enlightened Grand Duchess (who died in 1743) that the city was not emptied of its treasures, but is still endowed with them today, continuing to provide knowledge, stimulate research and kindle interest both inside and outside Florence's splendid museums and magnificent libraries.

Moreover, the legacy of the Electress went far beyond the, albeit important, material aspect. In the agreement stipulated with her successors, a fundamentallly important clause establishes that the estate will remain permanently in Florence and be openly available not only as categories of books and objects, but also for its originally intended purpose. So precise and so charming is the text of Article III of the Family Pact that it deserves to be fully quoted, "that [the heritage of paintings, statues, libraries, jewels, relics etc.] being for the ornamentation of the State, for the benefit of the people and as an inducement for the curiosity of foreigners nothing will be removed or taken out of the Capital and State of the Grand Duchy".

All histories of museums and cultural institutions, not only in Florence, should start with this quotation, for in effect, the Electress identified for the first time and with exemplary lucidity, the purpose of collections of art and books. In referring to three aspects, the intrinsic beauty of the environment, the moral advantage for citizens and the increase of "cultural tourism", Anna Maria Luisa stated in striking synthesis, the aesthetic, educational and promotional purposes that are often discussed verbosely and repetitively in writings on museums today.

The history of Florence does not end in 1743, but with the Medici ended an incomparably creative period that had brought an enormous contribution to western civilization.

The exhibition is dedicated to this long history and artistic heritage and, with Annamaria Giusti, we have planned it to be wide-ranging and plentiful with exhibits that are not only of artistic value, but also provide historic information, scientific facts, details of the customs and habits of the period.

Thanks to Wonders which has shared our vision from the beginning and was so determined to host the exhibition at the Pyramid Center, and thanks to Contemporanea Progetti who managed the organization so expertly, this important show brings to Memphis for the first time a many-faceted image of Florentine culture, with the hope that it represents not only an enjoyable experience now, but that it may also provide the stimulus to visit Florence, for full immersion in the place where, six centuries ago, the Renaissance was invented.

THE BIRTH OF THE LEGEND OF FLORENCE

Giorgio Vasari and Federico Zuccari, *Universal Judgment*, 1572 - 1579,
Florence, Dome of the Cathedral of Santa Maria del Fiore

1) On the origins of the urban view of Firenze in drawing, painting and cartography, see M. Chiarini and A. Marabottini (edited by) *Firenze e la sua immagine. Cinque secoli di vedutismo* (Florence), Venice 1994.

2) G. Vasari, *Le vite de' più eccellenti architetti, pittori et scultori italiani, da Cimabue insino a' tempi nostri*, Lorenzo Torrentino, Florence, 1550 2 voll; ed. curated by L. Bellosi and A. Rossi, Giulio Einaudi Editor, Turin, 1986; and G. Vasari, *Le vite de' più eccellenti pittori, scultori e architettori...di nuovo ampliate*, Giunti, Florence 1568 3 voll.; ed. in *Le opere di Giorgio Vasari*, curated by G. Milanesi, Le Monnier, Florence 1878-1885, 9 voll. I-VII 1878-1881. G. Vasari, *Lives of the Artists*, Volls. 1 and 2 ed. by George Bull, Penguin Books 1965; the volumes first appeared in Florence in 1550 with the title *Lives of the most Excellent Italian Architects, Painters and Sculptors, from Cimabue to our Times* (*Le vite de' più eccellenti architetti, pittori et scultori italiani, da Cimabue insino a' tempi nostri*). The quotations are from the Preface of the above in English, ed. p. 45.

3) G. Vasari, *Le Vite* edited by G. Milanesi, Le Monnier. Firenze 1878-1885, 9 voll. I-VII, 1878-1881. From the Proemio, di tutta l'opera, vol. I 1878, p. 104. Vasari, *Lives of the Artists*, from the Preface; see op.cit. pp.
Vasari's teleological vision of Italian art, and specifically Florentine, art as a development that reached the apex of perfection with the modern age, then declining imperceptibly towards excessive artistic expressions, such as later on the Baroque, or cerebral expressions, such as Neoclassicism, or sentimental art such as Romanticism had a very strong influence on some schools of history and criticism in Italy, surviving, indeed, right into the 20th century and up to the eve of the Second World War.

4) *Purgatorio*, canto XI, vv. 94-96; *Purgatory*, canto XI, vv. 94-96, Penguin Books, 1985, trans. by Mark Musa.

5) For a recent reconstruction of the early phases of Renaissance art, see the catalogue *Masaccio e le origini del Rinascimento* (San Giovanni Valdarno, AR), Milan, 2002.

6) L.B. Alberti, *On Painting*, Prologue, (1435-36); trans. with introduction and notes by John R. Spencer, New Haven, 1970.

The Architecture of the City

Eugenio Martera, Patrizia Pietrogrande

The architectural and artistic patrimony of every city is an essential part of its cultural identity. The history of Florence, even during periods of democracy, remains in large part the history of its leading families, first among them the Medici family, a dynasty of bankers and great patrons of artistic monuments and masterpieces.

Tuscany was under their dominion for more than three centuries during which Florence was the cultural and intellectual center of all of Europe. The accumulation of wealth permitted an unprecendented artistic growth in the city. For their role in this, the Medici name is indivisibly linked to the history of Florence, the city which symbolized the most splendid historical period of the entire Italian peninsula. The economic power of Florence was manifested and could be measured through the beauty and omnipotence of its architecture, in particular the Baptistery, religious heart of the city and the Palazzo Vecchio, proud emblem of civic power. During the 1300's, the city was enriched by extraordinary architectural accomplishments such as the Cathedral and the Bell Tower of Giotto while other city churches were adorned by cycles of frescoes such as the Domenican Church of Santa Maria Novella and the Franciscan Church of Santa Croce.

Also significant in this sense was the arrangement along the main streets of the city of the seats of commerce and banking; their architecture viewed as a prestigious cultural statement and symbol of the power of the corporate order or the family, such as the Medici, that had commissioned them. Just how influential was the cultural politics of the Florentine economy can be understood through the importance of the works undertaken by the Medici dynasty. From the very first Medici onwards, their talent lay in coupling an affirmation of the family with a cultural and artistic patronage of forceful impact; their ambition was to enrich the city with emblems of the family's power manifested in imposing monuments and architecture. This family prerogative was formulated in the splendid artistic period that occurred in Florence in the early decades of the 1400's when the first of the Medici, Giovanni

di Bicci would establish the financial and cultural basis of the family empire. He began by hiring Filippo Brunelleschi to rebuild the family church, San Lorenzo as well as the Spedale degli Innocenti (Hospital of the Innocents)

Thus the years between 1420 and 1446 and the work of Filippo Brunelleschi, inserted into a medieval context with boundaries already defined, became the decisive moment in the architectural and urban form of Florence. Although medieval in substance, the form of all of Brunelleschi's work demonstrates such strength of invention and such a new vision of the city as to forever transform the city's visual aspect; from the 1400's onwards, and still it can be said today, Florence is a Renaissance city.

His work undoubtedly exceeded any expectations of the public for Brunelleschi was never asked to give the city this new order; his objective was to control a space logically with proportion, rationally perfect in its every part. More importantly, his conception of the city with a new vision and with a new rational order in which the past took on new meaning, had other lasting implications

Anonymous, *La Catena,* Florence in 1490, copy of 1890, (detail)
Florence, Museo Firenze com'era, Archive

for architecture.

The work of Brunelleschi should be seen as an effort in critical interpretation and as the creation of a new order perceived by an elite, and can be considered as the first artistic avant-guarde in the modern sense. Moreover, it should be pointed out that in the span of these few years, a decisive step was taken in architectural history; the manual activity of building walls became a mental act. In the figure of Brunelleschi, practical application and intellectual abstraction are so integrated as to create the "being" of an "architect" according to the modern conception.

Another leading figure in Renaissance architecture was Leon Battista Alberti who was the first to propose in a modern sense, the theoretical problems of the artistic experience. The different dimensions of the architectural experience of Brunelleschi and Alberti is evident in the relationship established with classical antiquity. Brunelleschi resolved every reference in the actual process of building as he went along, while Alberti proceeded by scholarly understanding and the theorization of imitation according to studied criteria. The Florentine works of Alberti demonstrate an intellectual perfection of the type of solutions already confronted by Brunelleschi: the great dome, the city piazza (SS Annunziata), the facade of the palace (Palazzo Rucellai) the chapel within a religious organism (San Pancrazio), and an open air loggia in the urban environment (Loggia Rucellai). This jump in quality of structure and form in 15th century Florentine architecture is also reflected in both contemporary figurative and literary expressions of the urban image.

Throughout the 15th century, the Medici family chose to develop the western zone of the city to their advantage, and in particular Via Larga. At the intersection with the street that led to the Basilica of San Lorenzo, according to the design of Michelozzo, the grand Palazzo Medici was constructed, becoming the prototype for the new Renaissance palace.

Thus the zone of San Lorenzo became the central node for Medici strategy. The church was completely rebuilt by Brunelleschi while the convent was restructured and enlarged by Michelozzo. At the end of Via Larga was the Convent of San Marco which was a center of activity, not only religious, but aboveall, cultural and of great relevance to the Medici. Cosimo the Elder, a universal man, founded first in the family palace and then in San Marco, the first modern libraries of the western world. Another library was built around 1450 in the complex of SS Annunziata, designed by again, Michelozzo.

It is under Lorenzo the Magnificent, however, that Florence is affirmed as the capital of art and culture. In was in the so-called "Medici orchards" near San Marco that Lorenzo in fact opened a school of sculpture where among others was Michelangelo Buonarroti who would then live for four years in the residence on Via Larga, treated as a son. During the same years, Leonardo da Vinci could be found working in Florence. To the numerous Medici villas located in the Florentine countryside, Lorenzo would add in 1485, the villa at Poggio a Caiano, designed by Giuliano Sangallo, and the villa at Careggi.

In the 1500's, the focal point of Medici architectural initiatives would again be the Church of San Lorenzo. Pope Leo X promoted a competition for the facade and then Pope Clement VII would build the New Sacristy, intended as a family mausoleum, as well as the Biblioteca Laurenziana. For this project, Michelangelo departed from the traditional Florentine architecture of Brunelleschi and Giuliano da Sangallo, and offered a very personal vision that instead of eliminating the contradictions of his time that rendered impossible any solution, resolved the contradiction itself, the contrast internal, in one value.

Cosimo I knew no limits in rendering his dominion absolute through architectural and urbanistic structures that were clearly derived from a policy towards culture that used artistic objects and the qualification of the environment as a means of prestige

THE ARCHITECTURE OF THE CITY

for the affirmation of the State. In Giorgio Vasari, he found an indispensible supporter; one who would constantly underline the rapport between his artistic ideas and the desires of the Duke.

In this environment, the relationship between new architecture and pre-existing structures profoundly changed. Arnolfo di Cambio, architect of the 1300's, configured a city in respect of its preceeding edification. Brunelleschi assumed the past into a new rational order in which everything, including the past itself, assumed new meaning. The initiatives of Cosimo I, realized by his artists and architects, respected the past only where it served political motives. The organization of the absolute State coincided with the organization of the city.

The wedding of Francesco I with Joanna of Austria in 1565 constituted a fundamental moment in the reign of Cosimo I and signaled, on the plane of elaboration of the urban form, the moment of greatest force, both for a series of lasting modifications to the central part of the city and for a concentrated operation that aimed to transform the urban environment into some sort of proposal for an ideal city. The politics to potentialize the center part of the city concluded with the transfer of the court to Palazzo Pitti and the construction in only five months of the corridor by Vasari that connected Palazzo Pitti with Palazzo Vecchio.

With this extraordinary feat, the architectural and urban aspect of Florence that still today characterizes the city, was completed. Oversight of the urban fabric today reveals all the fundamental passages taken throughout this remarkable history. What is most extraordinary is the figurative power of every single architectural intervention and at the same time, its urban significance. Still today the city of Florence can be considered an unsurpassed model of equilibrium and order between its architectural singularity and its urban fabric: work such as the Dome of Brunelleschi and Vasari's Corridor remain insuperable as a synthesis of this concept and it is in this that their contemporaneity can be found, not withstanding they were built so long ago.

Giorgio Vasari and Giovanni Stradano, *View of Florence during the siege of 1529 - 30* (detail)
Florence, Palazzo Vecchio, Quarters of Leo X, Hall of Clement VII

GIOVANNI DI BICCI DE' MEDICI (1360 - 1429)

Founder of the Medici dynasty; his sons would sire the two historical branches of the family.

The prosperity of medieval Florence in the late 1300's induced Giovanni (di Bicci) de' Medici to abandon agriculture and engage in commercial activities, namely banking in Florence. Little interested in politics, he was first of all a businessman and soon proprietor of a bank with branches throughout Europe, credited with the first truly international banking system.

Later in life he proved himself both a philanthropist and patron of the arts. In 1419 he financed the construction of the charitable hospital, Spedale degli Innocenti, designed by Brunelleschi who was also employed for the renovation of the ancient Basilica of San Lorenzo. Despite the banker's preference for the architecture of Brunelleschi, it would be a young Ghiberti who in 1401 won the competition for the doors of the Baptistery.

1350 ■ 1347-50 Black Plague devastates Europe

■ 1387- Geoffrey Chaucer writes *The Canterbury Tales*

FILIPPO BRUNELLESCHI
1377-1446
Leading architect of the early Renaissance. Best known for the design and construction of the dome of the Cathedral, (1434).

LORENZO GHIBERTI
1378-1455
Trained as a goldsmith, one of the most important sculptors of the early Renaissance. Best known for the third set of bronze doors he designed for the Baptistery, the *Gates of Paradise* (1452).

DONATO DE' BARDI
CALLED **DONATELLO**
1386-1466
Leading sculptor of the early Renaissance. His rediscovery of the technique for the fusion of bronze allowed the large, life-size statues of antiquity to be reproduced.
Best known for the bronze statue of *David* commissioned by Cosimo the Elder (1430).

The Medici Dynasty
Linda Carioni

COSIMO (THE ELDER) DE' MEDICI (1389 - 1464)

Son of Giovanni de' Medici; proclaimed *Pater Patriae* (Father of the Fatherland) upon his death.

Cosimo the Elder embraced politics to extend the family's power and influence. Financial shrewdness and political astuteness established him as the supreme arbitrator of Florentine affairs however he would first endure imprisonment and exile. Summoned back to Florence in 1434, he wisely consolidated power. As his banking empire expanded so did the coffers of the family fortune.

Under his guidance, Florence experienced the beginning of the Renaissance. All the great painters, architects, and artisans of the day were busy at work. The Della Robbia family perfected techniques for glazed terracotta. For Cosimo the Elder, the first Renaissance palace was built; its interior courtyard was decorated with bronze statues by Donatello. Fra' Angelico frescoed the walls of the Convent of San Marco where in 1444, Cosimo the Elder established a library to house the Medici collection of antique manuscripts, maps and charts.

■ 1431- Joan of Arc is
burned at the stake

1450

FRA' GIOVANNI DA FIESOLE
CALLED **FRA' ANGELICO**
1395 CA.-1455
Born Guido di Pietro, early Renaissance painter who combined life as Dominican friar and painter. Best known for the frescoes painted in the Convent of San Marco (1436 ca.).

PAOLO DI DONO
CALLED **PAOLO UCCELLO**
1397-1475
Renaissance painter best known for three versions of *The Battle of San Romano* (1456).

TOMMASO DI SER GIOVANNI DI MONE CALLED **MASACCIO**
1401-1428
First great painter of the Renaissance known for use of scientific perspective. Best known for frescoes painted for the Brancacci Chapel, in particular, *The Tribute Money* and *The Expulsion from Paradise* (1424-1427 ca).

LUCA DELLA ROBBIA
1400 CA.-1482
Founder of family's terracotta workshop; originator of glazed terracotta bas-reliefs.

THE MEDICI DYNASTY

LORENZO (THE MAGNIFICENT) DE' MEDICI (1449 - 1492)

Grandson of Cosimo the Elder, son of Piero de' Medici.

Under his leadership, Florence was the epicenter of the Renaissance, thanks to the intellectuals and artists of his court - Verrocchio, Ghirlandaio, Botticelli, Michelangelo, Leonardo da Vinci - as well as philosphers, writers and poets.

His intellectual gifts and complex personality allowed him to function in a myriad of roles - scholar, statesman, collector of antiquities, patron of the arts and protector of artists. He founded a school for sculpture in the Medici Orchards where the young Michelangelo was discovered. Dedicated to the diffusion of Platonism, he expanded the family collection of ancient manuscripts which became the core of the Biblioteca Laurenziana. He spent lavishly on the construction and embellishment of the Medici villas situated in the Florentine hillsides.

Although he never held public office within the republic, he was an extremely astute political leader. Unfortunately, his death signaled turbulent times for Florence; his heir was incapable of governing and the family was exiled.

Much admired by Niccolò Machiavelli as the perfect example of a benevolent dictator, he was the model for Machiavelli's *The Prince*.

1450 ■ 1450- The Gutenberg Bible is printed

■ 1492- Lorenzo the Magnificent dies
■ 1492- Columbus discovers America

ANDREA DI FRANCESCO DI CIONE CALLED
ANDREA DEL VERROCCHIO
1435-1488
A leading sculptor and painter of the early Renaissance known for the artist workshop he led in Florence. Pupils included Botticelli and da Vinci.

ALESSANDRO DI MARIANO FILIPEPI
CALLED **SANDRO BOTTICELLI**
1445-1510
One of the greatest of Renaissance painters; often commissioned by the Medici. Best known for his elegant masterpieces, *Allegory of Spring* and *The Birth of Venus* (both 1482 ca.).

DOMENICO BIGORDI
CALLED **GHIRLANDAIO**
1449-1494
One of the great masters of the Fiorentine school of painting who depicted the refined style of Florentine life with detailed clarity. Best known for the frescoes painted for the Church of Santa Trinità and the Church of Santa Maria Novella.

LEONARDO DA VINCI
1452-1519
Legendary master of the Renaissance; celebrated painter, draftsman, architect, engineer and scientist. Began his career in Florence for the Medici.
Most famous masterpiece, the *Mona Lisa (La Gioconda)*, known for the enigmatic smile of the subject (1503-1506).

THE MEDICI DYNASTY

CLEMENT VII (GIULIO DE' MEDICI) (1478 - 1534)

Cousin of Leo X. Elected Pope in 1523, his immediate concern was the raging conflict between European powers. His equivocal policies led to the Sack of Rome in 1527. Patron of sculptor and goldsmith, Benvenuto Cellini and Michelangelo who he commissioned to paint *The Last Judgement* for the Sistine Chapel in 1536.

LEO X (GIOVANNI DE' MEDICI) (1475 - 1521)

Son of Lorenzo the Magnificent.
In 1513, Giovanni de' Medici became Pope Leo X, restoring Medici influence in Florence and Europe. His controversial policy of "selling indulgences" led to the excommunication of Martin Luther and the Protestant Reformation.
As patron of the arts, his preferred artist was Raphael who was already working on a series of frescoes for the Vatican Palace.

CATERINA DE' MEDICI (1519 - 1589)

Great granddaughter of Lorenzo the Magnificent. Her uncle Pope Clement VII arranged for her marriage to Henry of Orleans, heir to the French throne, but she was distrusted as a foreigner, especially by her husband who was enamored with his mistress. Finding the French aristocracy uncouth, she imported the use of many Florentine refinements to her court. Of her ten children, three would be kings. Upon her husband's sudden death, she became regent for her sons.

■ 1504- Michelangelo completes the statue of *David*

■ 1517- Martin Luther nails the 95 Thesis to the doors of Castle Church in Wittenberg.

■ 1519- Conquist of Mexico by Cortez

■ 1532- Henry the VIII establishes the Church of England

1550

PIERO DI LORENZO
CALLED **PIERO DI COSIMO**
1461/62-1521
Florentine Renaissance painter known for his religious works and imaginative mythological scenes.

MICHELANGELO BUONARROTI
1475-1564
Arguably the greatest figure in art history. Architect, painter and sculptor. Began his career in Florence for the Medici; worked extensively in Rome for various Popes. Among his masterpieces are the frescoed ceiling of the Sistine Chapel and the statue of *David*, symbol of the Florentine republic, one of the world's most famous works of art (1501-1504).

RAFFAELLO SANZIO
CALLED **RAPHAEL**
1483-1520
Master Renaissance painter born in Urbino, well known for the numerous Madonna paintings of his Florentine period. In 1508 he was called to Rome to paint a series of frescoes for the Vatican. Best known work is one of those frescoes, *The School of Athens* (1508-1511).

BENVENUTO CELLINI
1500-1571
Florentine sculptor, engraver and goldsmith with powerful patrons, both Pope Clement VII and Cosimo I de' Medici. Although known for his defense of Rome during the sack of 1527 and an autobiographical account of his turbulent life, his best known artistic work is the bronze statue of *Perseus* (1545-1554).

THE MEDICI DYNASTY

COSIMO I DE' MEDICI (1519 - 1574)

The first Grand Duke; son of the secondary branch of the Medici family. Called to Florence to impose order after the assassination of his cousin, he quickly consolidated power and through military prowess defeated rival city-states. In 1569, he was proclaimed Grand Duke with rights of hereditary succession, forever ending the Florentine republic. His building plans were equally ambitious. Palazzo Vecchio, the seat of city government, was renovated into a family residence by his favorite architect, Giorgio Vasari. His wife, Eleonora of Toledo purchased the Pitti Palace on the other side of the Arno River, entrusting its massive renovation into a royal palace to Bartolomeo Ammanati while Niccolò Pericoli known as Tribolo created the surrounding Boboli Gardens. Vasari was also commissioned to construct the *Uffizi*, (offices) to administer the duchy and the Vasari Corridor that spans the river over the boutiques of the Ponte Vecchio and connects the two palaces. With a pragmatic eye towards the arts, he commissioned the best artists of the day – Bronzino, Santi di Tito, Cellini, Giambologna – to produce portraits and masterpieces that glorified his accomplishments and the Medici family.

1550   ■ 1558- Elizabeth I becomes
Queen of England

JACOPO CARRUCCI
CALLED **PONTORMO**
1494-1556
Early Mannerist painter known for the frescoes of the villa of Poggio a Caiano and the recently restored *Deposition from the Cross* in the Church of Santa Maria Felicita (1526).

AGNOLO DI COSIMO
CALLED **BRONZINO**
1503-1572
Outstanding Mannerist painter of the Medici court known for the elegant poses of his portraits. Best known work, *Portrait of a Young Man* (1550-55 ca.).

GIORGIO VASARI
1511-1574
Writer, painter and architect known for the construction of the Palazzo of the Uffizi, but perhaps better known as author of *The Lives of the Artists*, a definitive source about the lives of Italian Renaissance painters (1550, revised 1568).

THE MEDICI DYNASTY

FRANCESCO I (1541 - 1587)

First born son of Cosimo I.
He succeeded his father as Grand Duke in 1574.
More scholar than sovereign, his interests were in the natural sciences, chemistry and alchemy.
He hired architect Bernardo Buontalenti to enclose the loggia of the upper floors of the Uffizi to create a gallery to house the family art collections, in effect creating the museum that today is known as the Uffizi Gallery.

FERDINANDO I (1549 - 1609)

Second son of Cosimo I.
Upon his brother's death in 1587, Ferdinando I would give up his life as a cardinal in Rome to assume his role as Grand Duke in Florence bringing with him his collection of Greek statues.
To ensure the future of the dynasty, he married Cristina of Lorraine; their wedding celebrations would be the finest ever seen in Florence. For twenty two years he would prove to be an accomplished statesman.
Despite his passion for antiquities, he also followed new artistic developments and founded the Opificio delle Pietre Dure (still operating today) specializing in the cutting and inlay of hard stones.

MARIA DE' MEDICI (1573 - 1642)

Her marriage to Henry IV of France was arranged by her uncle, Ferdinando I for political reasons.
Unhappy at court, betrayed by love, ill-advised as regent for her son, her life would end in exile.
She commissioned from Pieter Paul Rubens the famed allegorial canvases that illustrate events in her life for her Luxembourg Palace.

■ 1588- The Spanish Armada is defeated by the English

1600

BARTOLOMEO AMMANNATI
1511-1592
Sculptor and architect known for the renovation of Palazzo Pitti.
Also known for the *Neptune Fountain* (1576) and the *Santa Trinità Bridge* (1567-70).

JEAN DE BOULOGNE
CALLED **GIAMBOLOGNA**
1529-1608
Born in Flanders, the most successful Mannerist sculptor, known for the airy elegance of his bronze statues of Mercury. Best known for marble statue *Rape of the Sabine* in the Loggia dei Lanzi (1583).

PIETER PAUL RUBENS
1577-1640
One of the most important painters of the 17th century, defining the exurberance of the Baroque.
Known for the allegorical canvases of the Luxembourg Palace that depict the life of Maria de Medici (1625).

THE MEDICI DYNASTY

COSIMO II (1590 - 1621)

First born son of Ferdinando I.
Only seventeen when he ascended the throne, the family coffers were empty and he closed the Medici bank, yet once again the Pitti Palace was renovated through tax revenue.
His most significant cultural act was the protection and patronage extended to Galileo Galilei whose controversial observations were making enemies among the inquisitional followers of Church doctrine. He nominated Galileo as "Head Mathematician of the Grand Duke".

FERDINANDO II (1610-1670)

First born son of Cosimo II.
Like his father, he would protect Galileo after his condemnation and sentencing to house arrest by gifting the Villa at Acetri to the old scientist.
Married to Vittoria della Rovere, a dark forbidding religious fanaticism descended upon the family yet the family art collection was particularly enriched by the works of art brought in 1631 by Vittoria delle Rovere from the Court in Urbino as her dowry, including works by the Venetian master Renaissance painter, Titian, in particular *The Venus of Urbino*.

1600
- 1600- The East India Company is founded
- 1604- Cervantes writes *Don Quixote*
- 1604- Shakespeare writes *Hamlet*
- 1620- The Pilgrims land in New England

GALILEO GALILEI
1564-1642
Considered the father of modern physics; known for his astronomical observations and the invention of a telescope powerful to see the moon. Although protected by the Medici, forced to retract his controversial theories by a tribunal of the Inquisition (1633).

PIETRO BERRETTINI CALLED
PIETRO DA CORTONA
1596-1669
Leading painter of high Baroque. Best known for the frescoed ceiling, *Allegory of Divine Providence and Barberini Power* (1639) of the Barberini Palace, Rome. Painted similar frescoes for rooms of the Pitti Palace in Florence.

JUSTUS SUTTERMANS
1597-1681
Noted portrait painter of the Medici court; in keeping with his Flemish roots, his official portraits were modeled on works by other Flemish masters, Rubens and Van Dyck. Best known work is his portrait of Galileo (1636).

GIOVANNA GARZONI
1600-1670
One of the most important female painters of Italian art history. Known for her delicate watercolors of still life painting, in particular *Chinese Plate with Cherries and Bean Pods* (ca. 1620).

THE MEDICI DYNASTY

COSIMO III (1639 - 1723)

Son of Ferdinando II.
Due to irreconcilable differences, his wife would return to her native France. He would live for eighty-one years, but his three children, the last generation of the Medici, were subject to the fanaticism of their grandmother. Although all three would marry, all would remain childless.

GIAN GASTONE (1671 - 1737)

The last Grand Duke. Upon the death of his older rebellious brother, the second son of Cosimo III, the melancholy Gian Gastone would become the last Grand Duke until his death in 1737.

ANNA MARIA LUISA DE' MEDICI (1667 - 1743)

Daughter of Cosimo III and the last of the Medici. Upon her brothers' death, the Grand Duchy passed to Francis of Lorraine (Austria) as territorial possession but the family possessions passed to the seventy year old sister of the last Grand Duke, widow of the Elector Palatine. She would live out her life in relative seclusion in the Pitti Palace, ever the Medici, working to complete the Chapel of the Princes and collecting still life. Upon her death in 1743, her last testament expressly prohibited in perpetuity the dispersion of the vast patrimony of the Medici from Florence.

1696- Peter I the Great becomes Czar of Russia ■ 1724- Farenheit invents the thermometer ■ 1725- Jonathan Swift publishes *Gulliver's Travels* ■ 1752- Benjamin Franklin invents the lightening rod ■ 1756- Wolfgang Amedeus Mozart is born **1760**

BARTOLOMEO BIMBI
1648-1729
Specialized in large naturalistic paintings of the fruits and vegetables of the gardens of the Medici villas; known for the authenticity of his portrayal of nature, even in its aberrations.

ANTON DOMENICO GABBIANI
1652-1726
A favorite painter of Ferdinando de' Medici and student of Suttermans. Best known for his portraits of court musicians, in particular *Portrait of Ferdinando de' Medici with his Musicians* (1685 ca.).

NICCOLÒ CASSANA
1659-1713
Noted Medici portrait painter.

Genealogy of the Medici

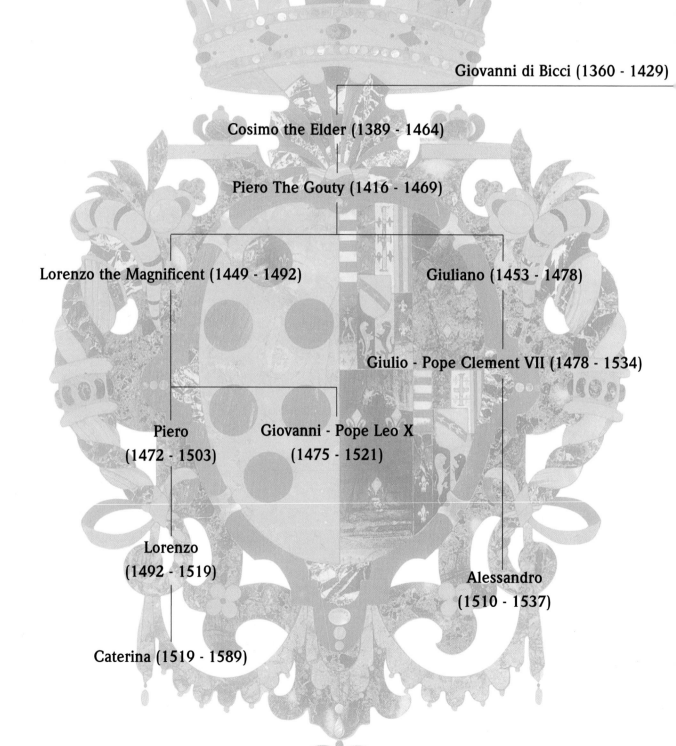

Giovanni di Bicci (1360 - 1429)

Cosimo the Elder (1389 - 1464)

Piero The Gouty (1416 - 1469)

Lorenzo the Magnificent (1449 - 1492)

Giuliano (1453 - 1478)

Giulio - Pope Clement VII (1478 - 1534)

Piero
(1472 - 1503)

Giovanni - Pope Leo X
(1475 - 1521)

Lorenzo
(1492 - 1519)

Alessandro
(1510 - 1537)

Caterina (1519 - 1589)

Giovanni di Bicci (1360 - 1429)

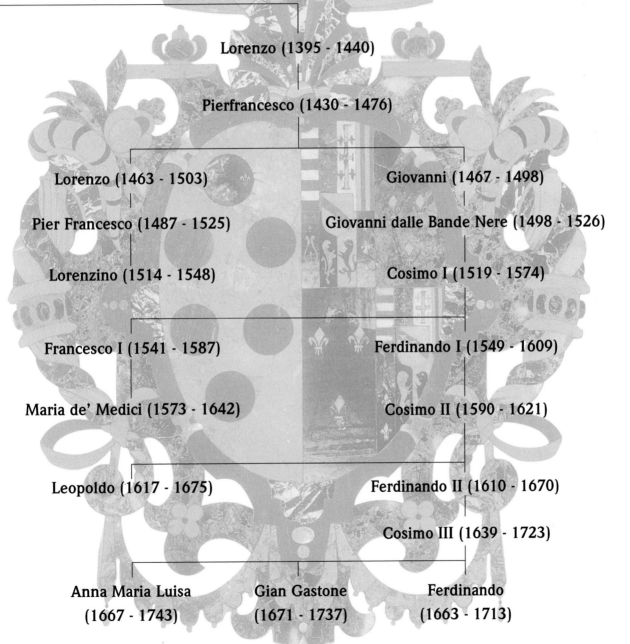

Lorenzo (1395 - 1440)

Pierfrancesco (1430 - 1476)

Lorenzo (1463 - 1503)

Giovanni (1467 - 1498)

Pier Francesco (1487 - 1525)

Giovanni dalle Bande Nere (1498 - 1526)

Lorenzino (1514 - 1548)

Cosimo I (1519 - 1574)

Francesco I (1541 - 1587)

Ferdinando I (1549 - 1609)

Maria de' Medici (1573 - 1642)

Cosimo II (1590 - 1621)

Leopoldo (1617 - 1675)

Ferdinando II (1610 - 1670)

Cosimo III (1639 - 1723)

Anna Maria Luisa
(1667 - 1743)

Gian Gastone
(1671 - 1737)

Ferdinando
(1663 - 1713)

Florence before the Medici

Annamaria Giusti

The Medici family was part of the mercantile middle-class that began to establish itself in the 1200's, becoming the most important social class of the free commune of Florence. It was a time in which the city's development continued unabated by either the conflict between political factions, the Guelphs and Ghibellines, that convulsed the Italian peninsula in the 1200's, or the subsequent division in Florence among the Guelphs that led to the permanent exile of Dante Alighieri.

The growing political and economic power of Florence was manifested in its imposing architecture as exemplified by the Baptistery, religious heart of the city, encrusted with precious marbles in imitation of Imperial Roman temples, and the Palazzo of the Signoria (Palazzo Vecchio), proud emblem of civic power with its fortified turrets.

In city affairs, the *Corporazioni delle Arti* (artisan guilds), representing all within the city who exercised a profession or craft, were of widespread political and social importance. Of particular importance were the *Arte della Lana* (Woolmakers' Guild) and the *Mercanzia* (Merchants' Guild) which represented the interests of Florentine merchants who imported and exported goods throughout Italy and Europe. The merchants undertook banking activities as well, servicing even the major ruling houses of Europe. The gold florin coin, hammered in Florence, became in the 1300's the predominant currency of the continent.

At the same time, culture and the figurative arts in Florence experienced an extraordinary enrichment that was destined to continue through the coming centuries; the genius of Giotto opened new directions in painting, establishing the leading position of Florence that was to last until the 1500's. During the 1300's, the city was enhanced by monuments and masterpieces of art: the Duomo cloaked in marble, witnessed the rise of the Bell-Tower designed by Giotto; the Baptistery, embellished by the first of its extraordinary gilded bronze doors by Andrea Pisano; many city churches, notably Santa Maria Novella and Santa Croce, adorned in frescoes and paintings on gold backgrounds.

The artistic splendor of the city and the refined style of life of its prosperous population continued virtually unaffected by certain dramatic events of the 1300's such as the pestilence of 1348, the brief rule of a French tyrant, the Duke of Athens, or the conflict of the lower classes with the merchant class which by the end of the century had established its dominance. Within a short time, from within its ranks, would emerge the family destined to govern Florence for three centuries.

Andrea di Cione called **Orcagna**
(Florence 1320 ca. - 1368)

THE EXPULSION OF THE DUKE OF ATHENS
After 26 July 1343
Detached fresco, originally circular in form, 290 x 260 cm
Florence, Palazzo Vecchio

Originally in a tabernacle in the courtyard of the *Stinche* prison, built between 1299 and 1301 and demolished in 1833 to make way for the present Verdi Theater, this detached fresco portrays Saint Anne, on whose feast day, July 26, 1343, the Florentines rebelled against the tyrant Gualtieri di Brienne, Duke of Athens and beseiged Palazzo dei Priori (Palace Vecchio).

Saint Anne, the mother of the Virgin, sits on a throne that is guarded by two angels and decorated with the arms of the city council and of the people of Florence. With the right hand she consigns to the knights of Florence the three emblems of the city, the red lily of the town, the red cross on a white field of the people and white on red. With the left hand she protects the Palazzo dei Priori (now Palazzo Vecchio) seen with the outer gates of the main entrance and Customs House doorway, installed as part of the fortifications undertaken by the Duke of Athens and carried out by Giovanni Pisano.

On the right, in front of an empty throne alluding to the loss of the city's ruler, is an archangel, probably Michael, bearing a column, the symbol of Strength, and banishing the tyrant. In his arms he carries a monstrous personification of Fraud whose unjust government had trampled and broken the laws and liberties of Florence, symbolized by the sword, the scales, book and ensign lying broken on the ground.

The scene must have been frescoed at the time of the rebuilding of the prison, burnt down by the Florentines after the prisoners had been liberated during the uprising that lead to the Duke's expulsion.

Many different names have been proposed for the identity of the artist of this fresco, from a generic allusion to the School of Giotto, then to Giottino, or to an artist close to Maso di Banco and to Nardo di Cione, or to Maso di Banco himself, or Taddeo Gaddi, Orcagna, or his brother, Jacopo di Cione, or Cennino Cennini who wrote a treatise on painting while in fact imprisoned in the *Stinche* prison. Recently, the attribution to a young Andrea Orcagna proposed by Boskovits, has been generally accepted. (A.C.)

Bibliography: P. Fraticelli, *Delle antiche carceri di Firenze denominate Le Stinche*, Florence 1834; G. Krejtemberg, *Orcagna- Andrea di Cione*, Mainz 2000, no. 3, pp. 34-38, and in particular note 54 at p. 37.

The "Biadaiolo" Master
(active Florence 1325 - 1335)

THE MIRROR OF HUMANITY BY DOMENICO LENZI
1328 - 30
Parchment manuscript, 38,5 x 27 cm
Florence, Biblioteca Laurenziana, Ms. Tempi 3

This is the so-called "*Biadaiolo* " codex, composed by Domenico Lenzi, a grain merchant as the name of the work suggests, who annotated on it the prices of cereals for the Florentine marketplace located at Orsanmichele between 1321 and 1335, together with bits of news, verses, and reflections of various sorts. The precious miniatures which decorate the codex are attributed to an anonymous artist, known as the "*Biadaiolo*" Master. Views of the city of Florence itself may be identified on sheets 57v-58r (Giotto's bell tower still under construction, the Cathedral of Santa Reparata, not yet destroyed, the tower of the Bargello, the bell tower of the Badia), in scenes which represent the welcoming of the poor people evicted from Siena during the food shortage of 1328-30. The manuscript was donated to the Biblioteca Laurenziana by the Florentine family of the Tempi in 1839. (E.C.)

Bibliography: M. Tesi, *Biblioteca Medicea Laurenziana*, Florence 1986, p. 126.

Florentine

UPPERMOST PART OF THE COLUMN OF SAN ZANOBI
Mid - 14th century ca.
Marble, diorite and iron, 273 x 73 cm
Florence, Comune di Firenze (once in Piazza del Duomo)

The column dedicated to St. Zanobi was located just north of the Baptistery in Florence; it was erected on the site where it was said that new foliage had sprung from a dead elm tree, at the passage of the urn containing the relics of the patron saint of the city, during its solemn transfer from San Lorenzo to Santa Reparata. Documents attest to the column being newly erected, shortly after having collapsed during the flood of 1333. This piece, consisting of a large marble cross sustained by a cone-shaped element made of diorite - a green stone with golden inclusions which in its original state must have appeared very bright - was probably added to the top of the column on this occasion. (E.C.)

Bibliography: G. Morolli, *L'architettura del Battistero e "l'ordine buono antico"* in *Il Battistero di Firenze*, Modena 1994, p. 54.

Florentine

STONE SLAB WITH GEOMETRIC DECORATIONS
First quarter of the 13th century

White marble inlay with green marble of Prato,
54 x 131 x 6 cm
Florence, Museo dell'Opera di Santa Maria del Fiore,
inv. no. S.B.A.S. 09/00188439

The marble slab was originally part of the group which formed the baptismal font and choir enclosure of the Florentine Baptistery, demolished by Bernardo Buontalenti in 1576, to make place for the scenery designed by him for the solemn baptismal ceremony of Prince Filippo, son of Grand Duke Francesco I de' Medici.

The ancient font was in the form of a basin, following the Ambrosian rite by which the catechized were baptized while standing.

The Florentine Baptistery, which is thought to have been erected on the site of a temple dedicated to Mars, was already in the 13th century the religious and municipal symbol of the city. The city of Florence entrusted the custody of its *Carroccio* and military trophies to this ancient place. St. John the Baptist was made the patron saint of Florence and the symbol of its wealth (his image is reproduced on the florin, the ancient coin of Florence, several

examples of which are displayed in the exhibition).

The recovery of fragments of the ancient baptismal font, including the one presented here, took place by chance in 1909. This produced such in-depth studies as Poggi's (1910), who first connected the work to the choir in San Miniato al Monte and to the pulpit once in San Pier Scheraggio, assigning the fragments to the Romanesque style of the 13th century. (M.B.)

Bibliography: L. Becherucci, B. Sani in L. Becherucci, G. Brunetti, *Il Museo dell'Opera del Duomo a Firenze*, Milan 1969-70, Vol. I, pp. 214-215.

Tino di Camaino
(Siena 1285 ca. - Naples 1337)

HEAD OF ST. JOHN THE BAPTIST
1320 - 21 ca.

White marble, 55 x 41 x 25 cm
Florence, Museo dell'Opera di Santa Maria del Fiore,
inv. no. S.B.A.S. 09/00153347

Around the year 1320, the Sienese sculptor Tino di Camaino carved three groups to be placed above the doors of the Baptistery in Florence. Three centuries later, these sculptures were substituted with other groups representing the same subjects, carved by Andrea Sansovino (*Baptism of Christ*, east door), Vincenzo Danti (*Beheading of St. John the Baptist*, south door), and Giovan Francesco Rustici (*Preaching of the Baptist*, north door).

The fragment exhibited here is the only surviving piece from the group originally above the north door, substituted by another *St. John the Baptist preaching to a Pharisee and a Levite*, commissioned by Rustici in 1506.

Arriving in Florence from Siena, Tino da Camaino, always very closely tied to local artistic traditions, came under the influence of Arnolfo di Cambio, who had been assigned with planning the *Opera del Duomo* and with the decoration of the Cathedral façade. (M. B.)

Bibliography: G. Brunetti in L. Becherucci, G. Brunetti, *Il Museo dell'Opera del Duomo a Firenze*, Milan 1969-70, Vol. I, pp. 228-229; C. Montrésor in *Il Museo dell'Opera del Duomo a Firenze*, Florence 2000, pp. 16-17, 20.

Anonymous
(Florentine)

PORTRAIT OF DANTE ALIGHIERI
after 1436

Paper manuscript, written in antique-style bastard gothic; leather binding with dry and black stamps, gold inscriptions on the spine; 29,5 x 20 cm

Florence, Biblioteca Riccardiana, Ms. Ricc.1040

This manuscript, which collects the *Rime* (Rhymes) by Dante Alighieri, the *Canzoni* (Songs) by Bindo Bonichi and *Sonetti* (Sonnets) by Mariotto Davanzati, was transcribed after 1436, according to what is written on c. 55v; this is also confirmed by the presence on several folios of a Florentine watermark, which may be ascribed to the years 1439-1448, and by the structure of several of the initials. The fame of the codex is mainly due to the portrait of Dante to be found before the beginning of the textual part. The painter, whose identity has been variously hypothesized, seems to have followed quite closely the description of the poet given to us by Boccaccio. A taste for realism (in the dark flesh tones, for example) is evidenced by the strongly characterized facial traits, leading us to identify the painter as an artist already aware of the new style introduced by Masaccio, Brunelleschi and Donatello. Furthermore, the visibly pulsing vein on the temple and the severely frowning profile might also bring to mind Alberti's indications regarding portraiture. Giovanni del Ponte and Domenico Veneziano are among the names suggested, but whoever the artist was, he was undoubtedly working during the first half of the 14th century. (E.C.)

Bibliography: G. Lazzi in *Danti Riccardiani. Parole e figure*, Florence 1996, pp. 69-72; G. Lazzi, *Biblioteca Riccardiana e Moreniana in Palazzo Medici Riccardi*, Florence 1998, p. 76.

Giovanni Mochi

(Florence 1829 - Santiago del Cile after 1892)

DANTE PRESENTING GIOTTO TO GUIDO NOVELLO FROM POLENTA

1855 or 1862

Oil on canvas, 84,5 x 108 cm

Florence, Galleria d'Arte Moderna, inv. Acc. no. 349

This work, done in the prevailing style of historical painting at mid-19th century, was presented in 1855 to the Florentine *Società Promotrice di Belle Arti* and then to the *Accademia*, winning for its author the prize of 666 *francesconi* offered by the Grand Duke in exchange for the work itself. In a Gothic style interior, we see the poet presenting Giotto to Guido

Novello, seated at a desk. Dante, who had been exiled from Florence in 1301, arrived in Ravenna in 1318, where he was hosted by Guido Novello from Polenta. Guido, taking up at this time an intention already manifested by his father, was seeking an affirmed artist for the restoration of the basilica in Ravenna dedicated to St. John the Evangelist. Dante suggested Giotto, then working in Ferrara for the Estensi; as a consequence, the frescoes in the churches of San Francesco and San Giovanni in Ravenna are attributed to the artist. The innovative spirit of Giotto's art was immediately recognized by his contemporaries, Dante first among all; the poet in fact celebrates his friend in the immortal verses of the *Divine Comedy* (*Purgatory* XI, 94-96). (E.C.)

Bibliography: S. Pinto in *Cultura neoclassica e romantica nella Toscana Granducale*, Florence 1972, p. 72; A. P. Torresi, *Neo-Medicei*, Ferrara 1996, p. 163; C. Mariani in *Giotto e Dante*, Milan 2001, pp. 61-66.

Giotto
(Colle di Vespignano 1267 ca. - Florence 1337)

MADONNA DOLENTE
1311 - 1315 ca.
Detached fresco, 64 x 45 cm
Florence, Opera di Santa Croce

The fresco, representing a female figure most plausibly identifiable as the *Virgin Mourning*, is a fragment of an originally much larger composition, perhaps a *Crucifixion* as is suggested by the darkened sky in the background. It was removed with the section of wall from an unknown building during the demolition of the old center of Florence that took place at the end of the 19th century. Although restored and transferred to a different support during the 20th century, it shows all the signs of the vicissitudes it has managed to survive.

The surface color is extremely worn and the pigments of the cloak and dress – probably the traditional blue and pink – have disappeared entirely as they were clearly applied *a secco* (to a dry surface). An appreciation of the work is therefore extremely difficult as it is no longer possible to see the original chromatic relationships. On the other hand, however, the loss of the pigment on the clothing permits the interpretation, otherwise impossible, of an intermediate phase in the creation of the work – the drawing in chiaroscuro outlined *a fresco* on smooth plaster with the red color used for sinopie. This stage of painting is most important to an understanding of the style and technique of the artist. Thus a very free and rapid drawing is revealed that succeeds in defining the outline of the figure and the process of modeling, accentuating some elements and softening others, simply by flexible use of the brush. On the technical level, the use of red here is interesting; traditionally associated with the sketch (known

as a sinopia) made on the first layer of rendered plaster, here it is used instead of the greenish pigment more usual for the detailed drawing made on the final smooth layer of plaster.

A close study of the drawing confirms the high quality of the the work also evident in the remaining painted sections and contributes towards its attribution to Giotto, as recently confirmed by Miklos Boskovits. The skillfully achieved impression of grandeur emanating from the figure together with the softness of the brushwork and intensely expressive details is the gift of a great master and excludes the possibility of a later interpretation of the artist's style as has been maintained by some scholars. Indeed, the attention to realistic detail and the softening of the form with a particularly delicate chiaroscuro are characteristic features of Giotto's more lyrical and naturalistic phase, which began with the frescoes in the Magdalene Chapel in Assisi towards 1310. This fragment shows many similarities to these as can be seen on comparing it to the head of the Saint in the fresco *Mary Magdalene receives robes from the hermit Zosimo*, which would date the Florentine fresco to the period immediately following Giotto's return to Florence from Assisi in 1311. (M.S.)

Bibliography: M. Boskovits in *Giotto*, Florence 2000, pp. 88, 141-143; A. Tartuferi in *Una mostra e alcune spigolature giottesche* in *Giotto*, Florence 2000, p. 27

Florentine

TEXTILE FRAGMENT
15th century
Red cut velvet with gold foil, 165 x 82 cm
Florence, Museo Nazionale del Bargello, inv. stoffe, no. 10 M.

This fragment of a precious Florentine velvet and gold foil textile attests to the variety of silk, wool, and in general of fine textile production carried on in Florence since the Middle Ages, for which the city was famous throughout the entire world then known.

In particular, this portion of red cut velvet over gold cloth is decorated with the so-called "pomegranate" design, one of the fundamental textile patterns used in Florence during the 15th century; the fragment itself is formed of three pieces sewn together and bordered to form an altar frontal. The decorative pattern is composed of a serpentine trunk rising vertically, broken by large plant motifs, and intertwined with another smaller and less evidently marked branch going in the opposite direction, which culminates in stylized thistle flowers. The velvet part of the trunk and lobed leaf are *allucciolati*, that is, they are woven with gold *bouclé* loops. The pomegranate motif continued to develop from the late 15th to the early 16th centuries, for use in woven compositions. This textile piece is similar to the ones found in the Badia Fiorentina, used until recently to line the entire interior walls during religious celebrations.

The pattern present on this textile may be seen in many Italian and Flemish paintings of the 15th century (Van Eyck, Petrus Christus, Antonello da Messina, Mantegna, Piero della Francesca), proof of how extended the market for Florentine textiles actually was, merit also of the constant dedication of the Medici to banking and mercantile activities. (M.B.)

Bibliography: Tessuti serici italiani 1450-1530, Milan 1983, p. 84 (for similar examples).

Follower of Bernardo Daddi

MADONNA ENTHRONED WITH THE CHILD AND THE STS. FRANCIS, JOHN THE BAPTIST, HELEN AND JACOB

1343 ca.

Tempera on panel, 57 x 27 cm
Florence, Museo Horne, inv. no. 43

This little panel is the pendant of another representing the *Crucifixion*, conserved in the same museum (no. 42); together they formed the wings of a diptych, typical example of a small portable altar commissioned for private devotional purposes. The art of painting in Florence was of very high quality during the course of the 1300's, and enjoyed wide diffusion. It was expressed not only through works destined to the churches, but also in small yet exquisitely made painted panels, suitable for the private residences of the wealthy Florentine society, and for following the city's merchants as they traveled.

Bernardo Daddi, a Florentine artist who received his primary formation in the school of Giotto, is the painter who has long been held responsible for this little panel. It is in reality the work of a close follower of Daddi, done in his workshop during the fourth decade of the century. This is confirmed by the similarity with the *Crucifixion* in the gallery of the Accademia in Florence (inv. 1890, no. 8570), dated 1343.(M.B.)

Bibliography: R. Offner, K. Steinweg, *A Critical and Historical Corpus of Florentine Painting,* Sec. III, Vol. IV, Florence 1991, pp. 50-54.

Bernardo Daddi (?)
(active Florence, 1320 - 1348)

SAINT CATHERINE OF ALEXANDRIA WITH DONOR AND CHRIST BLESSING
1340 ca.
Tempera on panel, 207 x 85 cm
Florence, Museo dell'Opera di Santa Maria del Fiore,
inv. 1890, no. 3457.

The painting is an iconical representation of a saint who has always enjoyed much popularity. Saint Catherine of Alexandria, virgin and martyr of regal origin, as can be seen from her precious crown and elegant clothing, was a courageous supporter of Christianity who, condemned to death by the Emperor Maxentius, with the help of angels overcame even torture and death by spiked wheels, her usual attribute together with a book and a martyr's palm leaf. The statuesque figure, portrayed standing against a gold background enhanced with a minute engraved decoration around the edge and on the halo, holds out the folds of her cloak to protect the donor of the panel, kneeling in everday clothes at her feet, according to traditional 14th century custom. A trilobate arch surmounts the image of the saint and above is another panel, also trilobate, with a bust of *Christ Blessing*. At the base of the panel are two Medici coats of arms which seem to have been added at a later date. The form, type and dimensions of the painting, without lateral scenes or *predella*, indicate that it was made in the 14th century to adorn columns in churches, a decorative element common in Florentine art of the period. Historical sources mention its presence, from the mid 17th century to the mid 19th century, on a column in the Cathedral of Florence, near the Trinity altar on the left side of the church.

The flowing and elegant outline, the tenuous coloring and the soft forms in a solid structural arrangement, giottesque in style, are characteristics that indicate without any doubt, the work of Bernardo Daddi. One of Giotto's most important followers, he adopted the great master's suppleness of form and developed it into a gentler and more decorative style influenced by Sienese art and by Maso di Banco. As was normal at that time, many apprentices, overseen by Daddi himself as required, contributed to the vast production of his workshop, often producing works that were barely distinguishable from those of the master. Such is the case of this panel which Richard Offner believes to be the work of the "Assistant of Daddi", while others maintain it is by Daddi himself. (M.S.)

Bibliography: R. Offner, K. Steinweg in *A critical and Historical Corpus of Florentine painting*, Vol. V, Florence 2001, pp. 222-26.

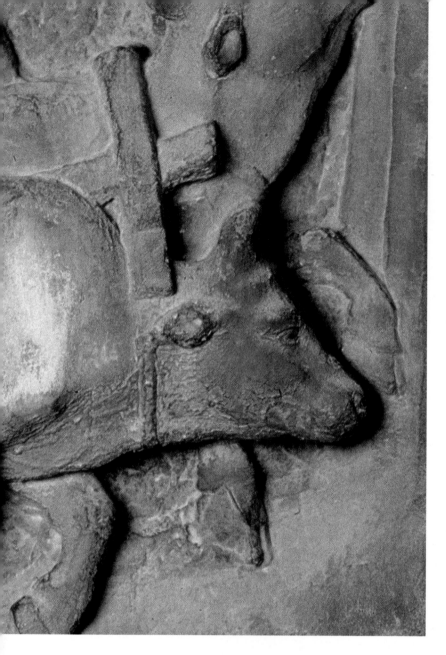

Andrea Pisano
(Pontedera 1290 ca. - post 1348)

AGRICULTURE
1337 - 1341
Marble relief, 83 x 69 cm
Florence, Museo dell'Opera di Santa Maria del Fiore,
inv. no. S.B.A.S. 09/00153298

The relief is one of a series of 26 hexagonal panels that decorated the first level of the Cathedral bell tower in Florence, now substituted by copies while the originals are in the museum of the *Opera di Santa Maria del Fiore*. The sculptural decoration of the bell tower includes a second level with diamond-shaped panels and a third with statues in niches and follows a prescise iconographical arrangement illustrating the history of man from his creation to his progressive civilization through various activities and arts to his eventual salvation. The cycle begins on the main façade, to the west, with panels dedicated to Genesis with the descendents of the forefathers and their inventions and continues on the south and east sides with panels portraying man's work and the arts, each separated by symbolic representations of those who have contributed to the civilization of man. In the diamond-shaped panels on the second level are the Planets, the Virtues, the Liberal Arts - necessary to elevate man above material needs - and the Sacraments, the means of salvation. In niches above are statues of those who had announced man's salvation: Kings, Sybils, Prophets and Patriarchs. The program, reflecting a concept developed by medieval Scholastic philosophy and common in the decoration of Gothic cathedrals in northern Europe was, at the time, entirely new on a bell tower which also had considerable importance as a civic symbol. The desire to represent the evolution of man's skills was also therefore a matter of civic pride at a time of intense economic and cultural success in Florence.

The sculptural decoration was carried out in several successive phases by Andrea Pisano with the help of various assistants. Pisano began work under Giotto and, assuming the role of master builder on his death in 1337, continued until 1341. Of the panels generally believed to be by him, *Agriculture*, penultimate in the group of the *Artes Mechanicae* (Mechanical Arts), indicates a shift by Pisano from the Gothic style of the first group to the more classical style evident in the second. The composition itself, clearly organized according to principles of symmetry, and conceived with a strong horizontal arrangement, suggest the "continuous frieze" of classical origin. The reference to classical models which must certainly have inspired the sculptor is even more evident in the sculpted faces and the natural treatment of the oxen, clearly revealing a precocious interest in a return to classicism, a practice that would be more actively followed only in the 15th century. (M.S.)

Bibliography: G. Kreytenberg in *The Dictionary of Art*, 1996, no. 24, pp. 874-876; C. Montrésor, *Il Museo dell'Opera del Duomo a Firenze*, Florence 2000, pp. 77-87; A. Fiderer Moskowitz, *The sculpture of Andrea and Nino Pisano*, Cambridge 1986, pp. 137-140.

1a)

1b)

2a)

2b)

1) TWO GOLD FLORINS, FLORENTINE MINT
1252 -1303, (III series)
Diameter 2,03 cm
Florence, Museo Nazionale del Bargello, inv. nos. 117, 119

2) SILVER FLORIN OF THE FLORENTINE REPUBLIC
1182 - 1252
Diameter 1,8 cm
Grassina, Alberto Bruschi Collection

Florence did not have its own mint until the beginning of the 13th century, having until then adopted money coined by the more prosperous and powerful cities of Lucca and Pisa. Starting in November, 1252, Florence began to mint the gold florin, which was destined to be universally honored (as was the gold *genovino* minted in Genoa), thus becoming a stimulus for commerce all over Europe. The Florentine mint was independent from the *Signoria* (Lords), and was linked to the activity of dispatching gold and silver practiced by merchants and bankers. Two of the major guilds, *Mercanzia* (Merchants' Guild) and the *Cambio* (Bankers' Guild), administrated the mint, electing the officials charged with its government; the administrators were changed every six months in order to avoid the forming of privileges. In 1284, the *Comune*, or city government, instituted the so-called office of the *Saggio* (Wise man), required to check the weight of florins of anyone wishing to avoid the risk of imitations and forgeries. The Merchandise Council nominated actual monetary officials, aided by two members from each of the major guilds in keeping the monetary system under control. Starting in 1375, the "gentlemen of the Mint" began impressing their own personal arms on the money coined by them. The technique of coinage consisted in fixing the

underlying minting die (*pila*) to an anvil, then hammering on the die placed on top (*torsello*), thus obtaining the stamping of the metal slip set in between.

The florin has maintained its original appearance, weight (3.54 grams) and purity (24 karat gold), over the centuries: the floral symbol of Florence is stamped on the front, with the inscription FLORENTIA; on the rear is St. John the Baptist, with the inscription S. IO[H]ANNES B. The gold florin preserved the iconography of the old silver florin (the fleur-de-lis and St. John), although with several variations. In 1252, one gold florin corresponded to 20 silver florins (equal to one *lira* or pound), while in 1533, this proportion had become 1 to 150. In 1289, the Venetian gold *ducato* was coined with weight and value equal to the florin, thus rendering them interchangeable. In 1533, Alessandro de' Medici stopped coinage of the florin, substituting it with the gold *scudo* in imitation of the money circulating in France. (E.C.)

Bibliography: B. Paolozzi Strozzi, *Monete fiorentine dalla Repubblica ai Medici*, Florence 1984, pp. 9-13; L. Camerini, *Il fiorino in 1492: un anno fra due ere*, Florence 1992, pp. 198-199.

3a)

3b)

4a)

4b)

3) GOLD FLORIN COINED IN AVIGNON
14th century
Diameter 1,8 cm
Grassina, Alberto Bruschi Collection

4) GOLD FLORIN COINED IN CAMBRAY
Bishop Guido IV of Ventadour (1342 - 1349)
Diameter 1,9 cm
Grassina, Alberto Bruschi Collection

Soon almost all the mints of the Western world were coining gold florins, often with the result of producing poor imitations of the Florentine original. The town of Florence, Guelph and republican, developed during the course of the *Trecento* (1300's) into the most florid city in Tuscany, at the expense of Pisa, defeated both militarily and commercially by Genoa.

Florentine commerce had always greatly flourished in France. Tuscan merchants were already solidly established in Paris, in fact, since the first decades of the 13th century. It was natural, therefore, that they should expand their activity towards Avignon, when this city became papal seat in the 14th century and consequently developed into the Provençal commercial capital.

The Medici also established a limited partnership in Avignon in 1446, transforming it into an actual affiliate in 1448.

Florins were also minted in Cambray, city at the far limits of the Empire and of French rule, often convulsed by struggles between the city's Bishop and the populace which alternated with moments of perfect accord. (E.C.)

Bibliography: M. Bernocchi, *Zecche di imitazioni e ibridi di monete fiorentine* in *Le monete della Repubblica fiorentina*, Florence1978, p. 76; C. Bec *Firenze mercantile e i Medici* in *Idee, istituzioni ed arti nella Firenze dei Medici*, Florence 1982, pp. 1-28.

Tuscan

MONEY COFFER
16th century
Iron, wood, 43,5 x 87 x 40 cm (closed), 87 x 87 x 43 cm (open)
Lucca, Museo Nazionale di Villa Guinigi, inv. no. 314

Wills describing the contents of strong boxes and caskets, used for the safe keeping of money or other precious objects, testify to their common presence among domestic furnishings during the Middle Ages and the Renaissance. During the 14th and 15th centuries, they could be found in a variety of forms, sometimes very refined, often quite massive in appearance. The strong box presented here is very similar to an actual safe. Its iron structure has a solid lock hidden beneath the lid, and hardly any ornamental features, excepts for such practical elements as hooks, handles, and locks, which have been fashioned in a somewhat decorative way. (E.C.)

Bibliography: I. Belli Barsali, *I forzieri e gli scrigni dei mercanti* in *I palazzi dei mercanti nella libera Lucca del '500,* Lucca 1980, pp. 516, 518.

Florentine

PANEL WITH THE EMBLEM OF THE ARTE DEL CAMBIO
1430 ca.
Pietra serena relief, 68 x 50 cm
Florence, Museo di San Marco, inv. 1904, no. 29

The panel shows the emblem of the *Arte del Cambio* (Bankers' Guild), consisting of an oval shield covered with coins (in painting, golden bezants on a red background) hung on a band from the neck of a lion and surrounded by branches with rich, fleshy leaves and a flower at the tip. The Bankers' was one of the seven major guilds that governed the city and had its headquarters in that part of the old center of Florence, demolished between 1881 and 1895, where many of the oldest houses of the city were as well as other important guilds or professional corporations active in the city.
The panel came from a house in Via Porta Rossa and probably dates from 1430, the year in which the Bostichi family donated the building to the Bankers' Guild, although the type of emblem and relief are still 14th century in style, especially the lion which recalls the heads sculpted by Andrea Pisano on the south door of the Baptistry. (M.S.)

Bibliography: P. Pruneti in M. Sframeli, *Il centro di Firenze restituito,* Florence 1989, p. 266.

Florentine

FLORENTINE FLEUR-DE-LIS AMONG EMBLEMS OF THE AGNUS DEI

Second half of the 15th century

White marble relief with red marble inlay, 113 x 59 cm
Florence, Museo dell'Opera di Santa Maria del Fiore,
inv. no. S.B.A.S. FI 09/00228840

This bas-relief, whose original location remains unknown, represents the insignia of the *Arte della Lana*, or Woolmakers' Guild, among which we may discern the Florentine fleur-de-lis, present in the form of a red marble inlay, while another emblem on the far right has either been chipped away or left unfinished.

The guilds were freely organized professional corporations or associations of artisans, in which the craft and merchant classes held a pre-eminent place. Originating during the 13th and 14th centuries in various cities throughout Italy, including Florence, the guilds each possessed a coat of arms and a patron saint. The Florentine guilds were divided into seven major ones (such as the Woolmakers' Guild itself) and fourteen minor ones. The Woolmakers' Guild, one of the richest together with the Merchants' Guild, was made responsible in 1331 for work on the Cathedral. The first stone of the new Cathedral of Santa Maria del Fiore had been laid on September 8, 1296, and while the newly-founded *Opera del Duomo* was charged with taking decisions about the work to be done, the financial burden was left to the Republic. When serious economic difficulties emerged in 1331 and patronage was assigned exclusively to the Woolmakers' Guild, the *Opera* assumed the Guild's emblem (*Agnus Dei*) as its own. Only in 1770, when the Guild was abolished by the Hapsburg-Lorraine, was this bond broken forever. (E.C.)

Bibliography: L. Becherucci, G. Brunetti, *Il Museo dell'Opera del Duomo a Firenze*, Milan 1969-70, Vol. I, p. 292; C. Montrésor, *Il Museo dell'Opera del Duomo a Firenze*, Florence 2000.

From Merchants to Power

Annamaria Giusti

By the end of the 14th century, Giovanni di Bicci de' Medici had formulated the basis of the financial fortune of the family, a fortune that would continue to grow until the end of the 15th century due to his acumen as businessman and banker. To him is credited the development of the Medici Bank with numerous branches in various Italian and European cities.

From the beginning of the 15th century, his political weight in city affairs increased, as did his personal prestige. He welcomed the anti-Pope Giovanni XXIII after he had reconciled with the Pope and obtained for him the rare privilege of burial in the Baptistery; the tomb commissioned by the Medici from artists of the caliber of Donatello and Michelozzo. In the splendid artistic season enjoyed by Florence in the first decades of the 1400's, another favorite of Giovanni de' Medici was the great architect, Brunelleschi to whom was entrusted the reconstruction of the Church of San Lorenzo, near the Medici residence on Via Larga and already known as the "family" church. Also noted among the civic projects under his patronage was the construction of the Ospedale degli Innocenti, (Hospital of the Innocent) another outstanding chapter in the activities of Brunelleschi, and whose ultimate humanitarian purpose was to provide shelter to abandoned infants.

Upon his death in 1428, the head of the family became his forty year-old son, Cosimo (the Elder). Although wise and prudent in exercising the growing Medici power, he could not avoid the opposition of other important Florentine families that in 1432 forced him into two years of exile. Upon his return, due to support from both the common and upper middle classes, Cosimo assumed the role of undisputed arbitrator in city affairs, contributing to the emergence of Florence in the panorama of 15th century Italy.

With Cosimo, the Medici ability to merge affirmation of their power with artistic and cultural patronage of great impact was fully evident, an ability that would remain the prerogative of the family in future centuries. On Via Larga, the family home was transformed into a supremely grandiose residence, prototype for the new Renaissance palace that in Florence found immediate expression in the noble residences of the Rucellai and the Strozzi. On many an occasion, however, Cosimo preferred to leave the palace to his son Piero who was adding rich decoration and artistic treasures, to retreat into meditation in the two cells, frescoed by Fra' Angelico, reserved for him at the Convent of San Marco, place of spirituality and also art created by his patronage.

The precious manuscripts of classic antiquity and more recent Italian authors, often splendidly illustrated, that the Medici were collecting in their palace on Via Larga would not remain the guarded patrimony of one family; Cosimo founded the first public library by offering their accessibility to qualified scholars first in the palace itself and then, building to the side of the Church of San Lorenzo, a proper library that would be enlarged by his descendants. When in 1464, Cosimo died, he would become forever known by public decree as *Padre della Patria* (Father of the Fatherland).

Of the two legitimate sons of Cosimo, Giovanni would die before his father. The other, Piero the Gouty, appears next to his father and half-brother, Carlo, born of a Circassian slave, in the sumptuous frescoes of the *Procession of the Magi* which shortly before

the death of Cosimo, would come to adorn the walls of the chapel of Palazzo Medici, in an exquisite testimony also to the refined artistic taste of Piero. Less fortunate in public office, the five years of his "government" (1464-69) witnessed a new conspiracy from within the city aristocracy and war with Venice.

Upon his death, the reins of Florence would be taken by the oldest of two sons, the twenty year-old Lorenzo, born of Lucrezia Tornabuoni, a profoundly cultured and literary woman. Under the leadership of Lorenzo the Magnificent (1469-1492) Florence was the undisputed capital of art and culture with its political actions pivoting on the interests of the Magnificent. Little interested in the traditional financial activities of the family, in Lorenzo, the evolution from exponent of the wealthy bourgeousie to intellectual "prince" was completed. The family fortune began its decline although his international prestige was so great that he procured the hostility of the Pope aligned with the never ending opposition of a part of the Florentine nobility. In 1478, a conspiracy led by the Pazzi family attempted to assassinate both Lorenzo and his beloved brother Giuliano. Confronted with swords and daggers at the Easter mass in the Cathedral, Guiliano was slain while Lorenzo was saved by refuge in the sacristy. The city, however, was solidly pro-Medici and the conspirators were swiftly apprehended and executed.

A busy public life combined with the role of mediator in the agitated political situation of the time, did not prevent Lorenzo from an unflagging promotion of art and culture. Himself cultured and literate, he invited philosophers and poets to select reunions at his palazzo on Via Larga. He financed the rebirth of the ancient University of Pisa and founded the University of Florence, making it the only in Europe where Greek could be studied. In the Medicean Orchards near San Marco, he opened a school of sculpture attended by Michelangelo. In 1488 adding to the villas that the Medici had built in the surrounding Florentine countryside, he constructed Poggio a Caiano which would become his favorite. In the Medici villa of Careggi, Lorenzo would die in 1492, at forty-three years of age, calling to his bedside the Domenican priest Girolamo Savonarola who for three years had been promulgating a purifying and austere response to the worldly corruption of Florence and the Medici court.

Two years later, the son of Lorenzo, Piero known as the Unfortunate, would suffer humiliation in Florence due to the presence of the French army led by Naples. Consequently, the disfavor of its citizens who would order the exile of the family. In the ensuing years, Florence, deprived of political leadership, returned to internal strife with the Savonarola gathering in the lead. His implacable moralizing although finding favor with part of the citizenry and the artistic world, would earn the intolerance of the Pope who would convince the Florentine *Signoria* (Lords) to hand him over to the papal legates. They would condemn him as a heretic to burn at the stake in 1498.

Giovanni di Ser Giovanni called **Lo Scheggia**
(San Giovanni Valdarno 1406 - Florence 1486)

THE STREET GAME CALLED "GIOCO DEL CIVETTINO"
1450 ca.

Tempera on panel, diameter 59 cm
Florence, Museo di Palazzo Davanzati, inv. no. 328

The wealthy families of Florence dedicated growing care to the interior decoration of their houses and palaces in the course of the 15th century. Giovanni di Ser Giovanni called Lo Scheggia, brother of Masaccio, was one of the favorite artists for the painting of scenes on marriage chests, strongboxes, or birth plates, and in general for the ornamentation of furniture and household fittings, such as the decorative wall paneling of nuptial chambers, hat racks, beds.

The *desco da parto* was used in the *Quattrocento* (1400's) to celebrate the birth of children to noble or wealthy families. Either round or octagonal in shape, painted on one side or sometimes on both with sacred and profane subjects, it was used to carry food and drink to the new mothers. Such objects were not only offered as gifts for the birth of a child, but also to augur fertility on the occasion of a matrimony.

The panel's recent restoration has shown that, although it has suffered from past interference, its circular shape is original. The subject matter is in line with the playful tone characteristic of birth trays and wall paneling, showing the gaiety of a street game called "*della civetta*" or "*civettino*", still known today. The scene is set outdoors, in an open area in front of a door in the city walls; on one side is a Renaissance palace with ashlar-work and semi-circular arched windows on the façade; on the right there are two palaces of an older type, with jutting corbels and curtained windows, similar to those in the background of the scene on the Adimari marriage chest, in turn taken from the cityscape frescoed by Masaccio in the Church of the Carmine. We thus have an evocative although idealized vision of 15th century Florence, with its architecture, customs, clothing, and scenery represented in a very effective way. (M.B.)

Bibliography: Il Museo di Palazzo Davanzati a Firenze, Milan 1971, p. 216, no. 242; M. Sframeli in *L'età di Masaccio*, 1990, p. 240; S. Francolini, M. Vervat, *Il gioco del civettino dello Scheggia. Il ritrovamento di un ulteriore dipinto e la tipologia dell'oggetto*, in "Kermes", no. 42, 2001, pp. 51-63.

Filippo Brunelleschi (attributed to)
(Florence 1337 - 1446)

WOOD MODEL FOR THE DOME BY BRUNELLESCHI
Before 1465
Walnut (?); central part 100 x 90, lateral parts 56 x 63 x 37 cm
Florence, Museo dell'Opera di Santa Maria del Fiore,
inv. no. S.B.A.S. FI 09/00161656

Filippo Brunelleschi was charged with building the dome of the Cathedral of Florence, dedicated to Santa Maria del Fiore, beginning in 1417. At this time, he began to study the method of construction, together and in competition with other master woodworkers and mathematicians. His project – presented with Donatello and Nanni di Banco – was chosen in the contest promoted by the *Opera del Duomo*, preferred over the one by Ghiberti. Brunelleschi vaulted the dome "without arming it", (that is, without supplying a support to hold it up while it was being constructed, as instead was traditional). Work began in 1426, with the construction of a double wall structure, whose two portions were capable of holding each other up as they were being erected. In 1432 work was quite far along, and in 1436 the two walls, at that point finished, were blessed by the Bishop of Florence, Matteo Federighi. The novelty of this dome, which makes a superb banner visible far beyond the limits of the city, "so that it covered with its shadow all the people of Tuscany", as Leon Battista Alberti commented, was not so much in its form or design, which followed the preceding architectural traditions, but rather in the logic behind its construction, so innovative as to be still astonishing today. Precise documentation of this great undertaking is conserved in the archives of the *Opera del Duomo*, part of which was published by Cesare Guasti in 1857.

The dome is covered with terracotta from Impruneta; its vaults are divided into segments by eight marble ribs which are the ideal continuation of the eight angled corners of the drum (constructed between 1413 and 1417). The cupola is composed of a double shell of two walls of different thicknesses, an inner and an outer one, bound together by a total of 24 buttresses; the corner buttresses form the main ribs covered with marble. Horizontal arches connect the buttresses to the two walls, and are connected one to another with portions of wall structures, which also provide walkways designed both for static solidity and access for inspection. The vaults, constructed in the form of trapezoidal segments, curve as they rise upwards, until they meet and are united by the so-called *serraglio*, or key, on top of which the temple-shaped lantern is placed. Brunelleschi, who died in 1446, did not succeed in terminating the lantern as he had planned it from the start; it was finished only after 1445, when work was taken on first by Michelozzo, then by Ciaccheri and Rossellino. The top piece is a gilded sphere; the one made by Andrea del Verrocchio in 1468-69 was knocked down by a thunderbolt in 1601, and was reconstructed in 1604.

The model for Brunelleschi's dome presented here was probably made before 1465, that is before the drum was covered with marble, although some are convinced that it was the work of Brunelleschi himself, at a moment close to the beginning of the dome's construction (1418). (M.B.)

Bibliography: M. Scolari in *Rinascimento da Brunelleschi a Michelangelo*, Venice 1994, p. 586, no. 261

TURNBUCKLE
16th/17th century
Iron, 174 x 80 cm
Florence, Museo dell'Opera di Santa Maria del Fiore,
inv. no. S.B.A.S. FI 09/00228878

TURNBUCKLE
16th/17th century
Iron, 108 x 14 cm
Florence, Museo dell'Opera di Santa Maria del Fiore,
inv. no. S.B.A.S. FI09/00228877

PINCERS
16th/17th century
Iron, 145 x 64 cm
Florence, Museo dell'Opera di Santa Maria del Fiore,
inv. no. S.B.A.S. FI 09/00228871

An imaginary reconstruction of Brunelleschi's work site has been re-created inside the museum of the *Opera di Santa Maria del Fiore* in Florence, with old tools recovered in the fake tribunes of the Cathedral dome (these are the four semi-circular structures around the drum of the dome, only two of which were finished at the time of Brunelleschi's death). Brunelleschi, in fact, quite aware of the difficulty of the undertaking, prepared a series of machines directly on site, designed to help out with work. Having proceeded in a basically empirical way, there are no surviving drawings of his for this equipment, although we know of numerous sketches made by other engineers of the period, such as Francesco di Giorgio, Leonardo da Vinci, Bonaccorso Ghiberti, Taccola and Giuliano da Sangallo.

Although probably not original, these old instruments are likely similar to those used by Brunelleschi himself, because the efficiency of such utensils made their use in construction work last unvaried for a very long time. The turnbuckle was employed for the precise placement of structural elements, even those of noticeable size and weight. The central piece, when inserted between the two outer keys previously fixed into the load to lift, forces them to expand, thus producing a very tight grip; removal of the middle key instead releases the load. Brunelleschi possessed the technical skills of the goldsmith and metal caster, having worked as such, and therefore knew how to take advantage of the differing degrees of friction which are produced by the contact between various metals. Taking into account the fact that friction will be reduced when a metal is placed in contact with another formed of a different alloy, he in fact equipped the turnbuckles and hooks with an iron screw made to turn in a bronze nut. These scissors-like pincers could be adjusted to various widths, in order to adapt to the different objects to be grasped and moved. (E.C.)

Bibliography: M. Preti, *Il Museo dell'Opera del Duomo di Firenze*, Milan 1989, p. 34; *Rinascimento da Brunelleschi a Michelangelo*, Milan 1994, p. 486; P. Galluzzi, *Gli ingegneri del Rinascimento da Brunelleschi a Leonardo da Vinci*, Florence 1996, p. 96; C. Montrésor *Il Museo dell'Opera del Duomo di Firenze*, Florence 2000, p. 151.

GRAND DUCAL SEDAN CHAIR
18th century
Wood and leather, 140 x 60 cm
Florence, Opera di Santa Maria del Fiore

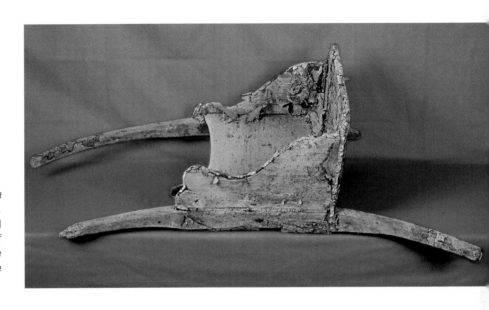

The sedan chair has been recovered in the deposits of the *Opera di Santa Maria del Fiore*, and is presented here for the first time. It was expressly made for the purpose of transporting the Grand Duke, probably the elderly Cosimo III, up the steep stairway of the Cathedral dome, as may be deduced from the shape of the handles, intentionally curved to permit the sedan chair's passage up the narrow spiral staircase. (E.C.)

WOODEN MOLDS
15th century
Wood, 40 x 25 cm
Florence, Museo dell'Opera di Santa Maria del Fiore,
inv. no. S.B.A.S. FI 09/00228884

These wooden molds served to make the *conci* or bricks for the construction of the dome of the Cathedral of Florence. There are 8 of such molds conserved in the Florentine museum of the *Opera*, divided into four groups: type "A", 2 molds for forming rectangular bricks of 19.5 x 37.5 x 5.5 cm. (weighing 6.435 kg); type "B", 2 molds for making rectangular bricks of 28.9 x 49.1 x 5.8 cm. (weighing 13.168 kg); type "C", 3 molds with an angle of 135° for bricks weighing 8.161 kg; type "D", 1 mold with an angle of 135° for bricks weighing 10.339 kg. A note dated 1425, which revises the 1420-21 project, indicates the need to make "large" bricks, weighing between 25 and 30 pounds, for construction of the wall in a herring-bone pattern; this corresponds to 13.950 kg, therefore to type "B". (E.C.)

Bibliography: G. Petrini, *Gli stampi dei mattoni grandi per la cupola di Santa Maria del Fiore a Firenze*, in "Parametro", no. 239, 2002, pp. 88-89.

Pseudo Pier Francesco Fiorentino

ADORATION OF THE CHILD WITH THE YOUNG ST. JOHN
1480 - 1490 ca.
Tempera on panel, 110 x 68 cm
Florence, Museo Bardini, inv. no. 854

Fifteenth century inventories often mention the so-called *colmi da camera*, which were small curved-top tabernacles for personal devotion, frequently produced in series and destined to a broad range of patrons. Such works, often by artists linked to Neri di Bicci, Lippi and Pesellino, done quite rapidly with few variations or even on the basis of the same cartoons, testify to the prolific activity of Florentine workshops in the second half of the *Quattrocento* (1400's). The painting exhibited here, still in its original frame, is a typical example of this type of object: work by an unidentified Florentine artist, formerly identified as similar in style to Pier Francesco Fiorentino (1474-1497), an artist close to Benozzo Gozzoli, but is now held to be from the workshop of Pesellino or Lippi. The subject derives from the panel commissioned by Cosimo the Elder from Filippo Lippi, which later became the property of the Riccardi family. It was in the Medici palace on Via Larga until its sale in 1814, subsequently passing from the Solly Collection to the Berlin Museums. This work offered a very successful model – a copy by Lippi's workshop is still on the altar in the chapel of Palazzo Medici Riccardi - almost to the point of its "mass reproduction", testified to by numerous versions of the Virgin in adoration of the Child, seen lying nude on a cushion in the foreground and watched over by the young St. John, generated from the Lippi, Botticini, Ghirlandaio, Jacopo del Sellaio and Pesellino workshops, as well as those of other lesser known Florentine painters of the second half of the 15th century. This panel differs from most of the other versions of the subject, in that the background is a delightful rose garden, rather than the usual gilding. (M.B.)

Bibliography: A. M. Bernacchioni in *Maestri e botteghe*, Florence 1992, pp. 160-161, no. 5.3; B. Paolozzi Strozzi in *I restauri nel Palazzo Medici Riccardi*, Florence 1992, pp. 32-49 (for the original model); M. Tamassia in *Pulchritudo Amor Voluptas*, Florence 2001, p. 130, no. 29.

Alessandro Pieroni (copy)
(Florence 1550 - Livorno 1607)

PORTRAIT OF COSIMO THE ELDER DE' MEDICI
1600 ca.
Oil on canvas, 53 x 44 cm
Florence, Eredità Bardini, inv. no. 5515

Cosimo the Elder (1389-1464), called *Pater Patrie*, was a progenitor of the Medici dynasty which governed Florence for more than three hundred years. The great merchant family was originally from the Mugello area, which lies north of the city at the foot of the Tuscan-Emilian Apennines. Cosimo, who had received a humanistic education, played many important political roles, beginning in 1414; he was also a great patron of the arts, and as such was a stimulus to the development of the Renaissance. It was thanks to Cosimo the Elder that the Church of San Lorenzo and the Old Sacristy were rebuilt, according to Brunelleschi's design; he also commissioned the construction of the palace on Via Larga, the villa at Cafaggiolo, and the Church and Convent of San Marco, assigned to Michelozzo. He was also patron to the most famous sculptors and painters of the time (Donatello, Filippo Lippi, Fra' Angelico, etc.), commissioning many works of art from them. Cosimo was exiled from Florence between October, 1433, and the same month of the following year, as the result of an accusation of having subverted the State in the war against Lucca. In 1434, after returning to Florence, he again became head of the city's internal political affairs, gaining great prestige for having succeeded in transferring from Ferrara to Florence (1439), the council summoned by Eugenio IV to further the unification of the Western Latin and Eastern Greek churches. Also very important from a political point of view was an alliance with the Sforza: the loyalty of a lasting ally was assured by having aided them in the inheritance of the Milanese duchy. Another important political act was the peace treaty of Lodi (1454), following Turkish conquest of Constantinople; this ratified Cosimo's tactics of constantly striving for an equilibrium that maintained political tranquility. Thanks to Cosimo the Elder, the Medici expanded their banking activity, developing an enormous system of markets in Italy and abroad, which made them the protagonists of the entire economy of the world then known. To his wife, Contessina dei Bardi, were born two sons; Piero in 1416 and Giovanni in 1421. The portrait derives from a painting by Alessandro Pieroni (inv. 1890, no. 2217), consigned to the Medici by the artist in 1585, and whose final payment dates from 1586; this work is a copy, smaller in size and seemingly made for a medallion, of the painting by Pontormo in the Uffizi. The latter is a slightly more then half-bust portrait of Cosimo, seated in an armchair; there is also a branch of laurel (the Broncone emblem), with a scroll around it, on which a motto taken from Virgil's *Eneid* is inscribed: "UNO AVULSO NON DEFICIT ALTER" (when a branch is broken, the other is not weakened). It may be deduced that the original by Pontormo is related to the birth of the future Cosimo I de' Medici, which took place on June 12, 1519. The numerous copies deriving from Pontormo's prototype, replicated many times as was common for early Medici portraits, testify to the popularity enjoyed by Cosimo the Elder. The replicas were either made for placement in the various seats and residences belonging to the Medici family, or were intended as offerings or official State gifts, or even as thanks for services rendered. Such a painting would therefore be included in each of the many galleries of illustrious personages to be found throughout Europe, all fashioned according to the model of Paolo Giovio's gallery in Florence. (M.B.)

Bibliography: Splendore dei Medici, Florence 1999, no. 1, p. 53; M. Tamassia in *Riflessi di una galleria*, 2001, no. 6, p. 28.

Lorenzo Ghiberti
(Florence 1378 - 1455)

DOOR OF A CIBORIUM WITH GOD THE FATHER
1450 - 1451

Cast and chiseled bronze, 34 x 20 cm
Florence, Ospedale di Santa Maria Nuova,
inv. no. S.B.A.S. 472- 09/00190158

The door once belonged to a tabernacle for the custody of the Holy Sacrament of the women's hospital, which was placed against the left wall of the choir in the church of the Florentine Arcispedale di Santa Maria Nuova; its marble part was commissioned from Bernardo Rossellino (1409-1464). The origin of this very ancient type of tabernacle, usually inserted into the wall, goes back to the Lateran Council IV, held in 1215: their function was to safely conserve the Eucharistic hosts. In the first half of the 15th century, many such tabernacles were commissioned from the principal sculptors of the time, some quite large. Later, they were also often the work of minor craftsmen, given the popularity of this type of liturgical object.

The door, for which Ghiberti was paid in 1450-51, was commissioned by an institution which held a place of great prestige in the history of Florence, the Hospital of Santa Maria Nuova was in fact founded in 1287 by Folco Portinari (father of Beatrice, source of Dante's poetic inspiration), together with the nearby Convent of the Oblate (for consecrated women who dedicated themselves to assisting others).

Although the work was carried out in the later years of Ghiberti's life, analogies can be discerned with the *Gates of Paradise*. An Eastern influence may be recognized in the style of the head gear worn by God the Father, traceable to the 1439 Council of Florence at which eminent Byzantines figures were present. Ghiberti had made in that period a similar figure of a blessing Christ for the lost "button" which fastened the

cope worn by Pope Martino V. Lorenzo Ghiberti, goldsmith, sculptor, architect, writer and theoretician on Italian art, was one of the great figures of the Florentine Renaissance. He started as a goldsmith, and in 1401, his panel with the *Sacrifice of Isaac* won the contest with Brunelleschi for the second set of bronze doors of the Florentine Baptistery. The second doors (1403-24) were commissioned by the guild of the *Mercanzia* (Merchants') with *Stories of the Life of Christ, the Evangelists* and the *Fathers of the Church*. He also sculpted three statues for Orsanmichele – symbol of the merchant and ecclesiastic power of Florence – as well as the baptismal font of Siena (1417-27). After a brief sojourn in Venice (1424) he received the commission for the third set of doors of the Baptistery that Michelangelo would later call the *Gates of Paradise*. Concluded in 1452, they represent biblical scenes divided among the ten parts, following a scheme elaborated by the humanist, Leonardo Bruni. Ghiberti was the major heir of the traditional art of the Tuscan goldsmiths, and ran a flourishing and very prosperous workshop in which his relatives also worked and where Donatello and other great Renaissance sculptors apprenticed. His *Commentaries*, begun in 1447, are an exceptionally important literary and art history source. (M.B.)

Bibliography: M. P. Vignolini in *Lorenzo Ghiberti materia e ragionamenti*, 1978, pp. 426-427; M. De Luca in *Florença: Tesouros do Renascimento*, Florence 1999-2000, pp. 49-56.

61

Donato de' Bardi called **Donatello** (attributed to)
(Florence 1386 - 1466)

MADONNA AND CHILD
CALLED "MADONNA DELLA MELA"
1420 - 1430
Polychrome terracotta, 90 x 64 cm
Florence, Museo Bardini, inv. no. 682/722

The Virgin, shown half-figure, seems to be trying to restrain the Child, who as if frightened, takes shelter near his mother, grasping the veil which covers her head. As she covers the Child's right leg with her mantle, she offers him an apple with a supremely natural gesture, as if to console or distract his attention from whatever has suddenly prompted his startled reaction.

The vertically constructed composition of the figuration now appears outlined and lacking a background, since the work was originally intended for placement in a niche, tabernacle or in any case, in a position permanently attached to the wall.

The sculpture is richly and accurately modeled, both in the anatomical parts and in the rendering of the drapery. The surface is very finely colored, with the apparent intention of bringing the divine image closer to reality, in order to increase its capacity to communicate the spiritual message.

This relief carving, the only example of the subject known to exist, comes from the town of Scarperia in the Province of Florence. When first published (Lensi 1923-24), the work was associated with the names of Donatello, Jacopo della Quercia, Luca della Robbia, as difficulty was encountered in understanding which of these artists' styles best

corresponded to that of the sculpture. Among the various ideas proposed by later historians, the most worthy of attention (Gentilini 1992) attributes it to the young Luca della Robbia, while the artist was still in very close contact with Donatello and Ghiberti, working themselves in the same period on compositions of a similar type in terracotta as in other materials.

Images of the Madonna and Child in terracotta or colored stucco were very widely diffused in 15th century Florence, testifying to the importance the city attributed to the cult of the Virgin. A single model was frequently reproduced in various exemplars, using molds taken from an original which might even be in marble. It was thus possible to achieve an easier and less costly production, destined for distribution among the churches, convents, city streets and private homes, while at the same time maintaining the works' high degree of excellence and expressive qualities. (M.G.V.)

Bibliography: A. Lensi, *Il Museo Bardini: stucchi e terrecotte* in "Dedalo", IV, 1923-24, p. 490; E. Neri Lusanna in *Il Museo Bardini*, Florence 1986, pp. 245-247; G. Gentilini, *I Della Robbia*, Florence 1998, pp. 42-43.

Francesco Granacci
(Florence 1477 -1543)

THE ENTRANCE OF CHARLES VIII TO FLORENCE
1494

Oil on panel, 81,5 x 68,5 cm
Florence, Galleria degli Uffizi, inv. 1890, no. 3908

The painting shows the solemn entrance of Charles VIII, King of France, to Florence on November 17, 1494, following the expulsion of the Medici which took place on November 9th, Holy Saviour's day, and the proclamation of the Republic. In fact, the stately procession passed along Via Larga, in front of the Medici Palace, proceeding from the Cathedral square towards San Marco and not viceversa as shown in the painting. Commissioned by Francesco Nasi, or by his father, Alessandro, republicans and supporters of the French, together with a matching painting showing the entrance of the King in Rome, the work was donated by the family to Cardinal Ferdinando de' Medici during the second half of the 16th century and was exhibited in his collection in Villa Medici in Rome. It was lost during the 17th century and was later acquired by the Italian State from the sale of the Crespi Collection in Milan. (A.C.)

Bibliography: A. Cecchi, *L'ingresso di Carlo VIII in Firenze* in "Paragone", no. 439, 1986, pp. 41-48; A. Natali in *Sandro Botticelli, pittore della Divina Commedia*, Milan 2000, no. 4.2, pp. 136-137.

Late Workshop of Michelozzo
(Giuliano and Benedetto da Maiano?)
(Maiano 1432 - Naples 1490)
(Maiano 1442 - Florence 1497)

FOUR PAIRS OF PANELS FROM A DOOR OF PALAZZO MEDICI ON VIA LARGA

After 1465
Carved wood with slight traces of painting,
47 x 47 cm each
Florence, Eredità Bardini,
inv. nos. 11492 AB, 11493 AB, 11506 AB, 11507 AB.

These eight panels are divided into four similar pairs of two, which show different heraldic types, all referring, however, to the Medici family: an emblem of Cosimo the Elder, grandfather of the Magnificent (three diamond points forming an equilateral triangle within a circle of rays); the Medici arms with seven bezants; a six-petal rose in the cente;, and a pomegranate. Discovered at different times, these elements have since been identified as belonging to the same door from the Medici Palace on Via Larga. The great refinement of the carving may be explained by the fact that the pieces were meant to be viewed close up rather than to be seen at a distance, as would have been the case if made for a ceiling, as has been instead hypothesized. Doors and portals played an important role in Renaissance palaces, either as a completion of the decoration of the external façade, or as a part of the fittings of the rooms inside. (E.C.)

Bibliography: M. G. Massafra, *Il portone in legno a Firenze nella seconda metà del XV secolo* in *Giuliano e la bottega dei Da Maiano*, Florence 1991, pp. 200-208; M. Ciatti in *Opere d'arte della famiglia Medici*, Florence 1997, p. 83; M. Scalini, *I tesori di un antiquario*, Florence 1998, pp. 60-61; M. Scalini in *Pulchritudo Amor Voluptas*, Florence 2001, pp. 76-77.

Florentine

STROZZI NUPTIAL CHEST
First half of the 15th century
Wood and painted parchment, 45 x 160 x 47 cm
Florence, Carlotta Bruschi Collection

The generic term *cassone* (chest) is used to define a type of furnishing which has the form of a rectangular case. Often present in private houses already in the Middle Ages (when it was more commonly referred to as a strong box or coffer), its function would later be taken over by wardrobes. The nuptial chest was designed to contain a bride's entire dowry, and was carried through the streets behind the nuptial procession, often together with that of the bridegroom. Chests designed for this purpose are usually more decorative than others; they might be carved, gilded and painted, and would often bear the owner's family arms. The example presented here has the Strozzi emblems, those of one of the noblest families in Florence (eagle and waxing moons). It is not unusual to find that the painted parts of such chests have been separated from the rest and used as actual paintings. (E.C.)

Bibliography: M. P. Masini, D. Salvadori *Museo di Palazzo Davanzati*, Florence 1991, pp. 7-10; G. Cantelli *La vita sociale e la nuova dimensione dell'abitare* in *L'architettura civile in Toscana*, Milan 1997, p. 354.

Central Italian

POLYGONAL-SHAPED CHAIR
End of 15th, beginning of the 16th century
Pine wood with walnut framework, 70 x 60 x 50 cm
Florence, Museo Horne, inv. no. 695

The chair has a back formed of seven rectangular segments and a drawer beneath the seat. It has been fashioned in a style typical of the 14th century, although it dates from a century later, and was evidently intended for use by a someone of a certain importance. It might be an abbot's seat coming from a monastery, or perhaps a piece of furniture from a wealthy private home. (E.C.)

Bibliography: F. Rossi, *Il Museo Horne a Firenze*, Florence 1966, p. 158;
Il Museo Horne, Florence 2001, p. 73.

Florentine

SMALL CREDENZA "MADE WITHOUT CORNERS"
16th century
Inlaid walnut, 105 x 97 x 40 cm
Florence, Eredità Bardini, inv. no. 9126

The credenza was a type of domestic furnishing widely diffused in 15th century private homes: this one, made of walnut, is of the type said to be "made without corners", and has a decorative inlaid frame which exalts the refined structure of the entire piece. The style is typically Florentine, characterized by generally horizontal lines and spacious areas whose smooth surfaces are delineated by simple intarsia ornamentation. Furniture-making in Florence was under the control of the Woodworkers' Guild which imposed precise standards in order to maintain the high quality of production. It was compulsory to employ only one species of wood, and it was forbidden to insert strips or frames with the intent of hiding the use of wood of a lesser quality. (E.C.)

Bibliography: M. Gregori, R. Ruotolo, L. Bandera Gregori, *I quaderni dell'antiquariato*, Milan 1981, pp. 3-13.

Tuscan

CHEST WITH FOOTBOARD
Beginning of the 16th century
Wood, 100 x 238 x 91 cm
Florence, Eredità Bardini, inv. no. 9113

Vasari himself, in the life of Dello Delli (15th century Florentine painter, sculptor and architect), mentions the splendors of Florentine houses during the Renaissance, with their abundance of various sorts of chests playing a fundamental role as clothing containers. This chest exhibits a back and a footboard, for as we know from contemporary painting, this sort of furniture was fitted against the wall so it could also be used as a seat. Elegant, geometrically-shaped intarsia decorations enhance its otherwise very somber forms, calling to mind the excellent production of several woodcarving workshops of this period, for example that of the da Maiano, which held a prominent place and was called upon to work for some of the noblest families of the times. (E.C.)

Bibliography: M. Gregori, R. Ruotolo, L. Bandera Gregori, *I quaderni dell'antiquariato*, Milan 1981, pp. 3-13.

French

SMALL STRONG BOX COFFER
15th century
Wood covered with stamped leather, 39 x 21 x 15 cm
Florence, Museo di Palazzo Davanzati, inv. Bg. Mobili 181 no. 184

This small coffer, whose inner surface is lined with thick, red-colored rag paper, has an iron handle on the lid and simple knobs, also of iron, on the lid and sides that terminate in lobes and notches. The iron lock is also original, but has no key and is incomplete internally. Such small strong boxes were already common in the Middle Ages, mostly for the safekeeping of brides' jewelry. Made of iron, they were sometimes covered with leather to protect their security and solidity during travel. (E.C.)

Bibliography: L. Berti, *Palazzo Davanzati a Firenze*, Florence 1958, p. 206.

Tuscan

STOOL WITH STROZZI COAT OF ARMS
Beginning of the 16th century
Carved and inlaid walnut, height 128 cm
Florence, Museo Horne, inv. no. 983

The stool has an octagonal-shaped seat over a trestle of three square-shaped legs, a feature which made it usable on the imperfect floor surfaces of the times, and a high back terminating in a medallion carved with the Strozzi coat of arms (the eagle on the recto and the waxing moons on the verso). The Horne Museum in Florence has two stools with the Strozzi arms, a third is conserved in the Metropolitan Museum in New York, while another ten or so are dispersed among various collections. The stools were originally in Palazzo Strozzi, and may have been the work of Benedetto da Maiano, architect of the palace itself and charged with designing the furnishings as well. This type of stool was particularly sought after during the 19th and 20th centuries, resulting in the production of numerous imitations and fakes. (E.C.)

Bibliography: F. Rossi, *Il Museo Horne*, Florence 1966, p. 159; F. Botticelli, *Rifacimenti e falsificazioni* in *L' architettura civile in Toscana*, Milan 1997 p. 398; C. Paolini, *Della sedia e dell'arte di sedersi* in *Il Museo Horne*, 2001, pp. 63, 82-83.

Fra' Giovanni da Fiesole called **Fra' Angelico**
(Vicchio di Mugello 1398 ca. - Rome 1455)

VIRGIN AND CHILD
1435 ca.
Detached sinopia, 116 x 76 cm
Fiesole, Convento di San Domenico

A fresco of *Virgin and Child* is mentioned in historic sources such as the Anonymous Author of the Magliabechian collection (1536-46) and Vasari, as being one of the works painted by Fra' Angelico in the monastery at San Domenico, "above the doorway of that church". The only existing painting that approaches the style and period of the artist was above a doorway of the new Novitiate of the monastery, transferred there centuries earlier from its original location on a wall of stone blocks. In 1960 the fresco underwent scrupulous restoration; the original surface reappeared from beneath a poor 19th century attempt at repainting, and to ensure its conservation was removed, allowing this splendid sinopia to re-emerge. While the quality of the painting of the fresco itself does not allow an unqualified attribution to Fra' Angelico, the confident and direct hand evident in the sinopia reveals the unmistakable style of the painter-priest, perfectly combining the spirituality of the religious message with particular attention to man and his dimension, characteristic of Renaissance art. Clearly visible in the sinopia is the close link that Angelico maintained culturally with the art of Giotto whose simple, yet monumental figures continued to inspire his work. Yet there is a new self-confidence in their contextual setting that makes their movements appear entirely natural, even in conventional situations such as the Child portrayed in a solemn gesture while the little feet are left with a freedom of movement. The tender face of the Virgin is typical of many paintings produced in the third decade of Angelico's busy workshop at San Domenico but is particularly close to two much larger paintings, now in the museum of San Marco, the *Tabernacolo dei Linaioli* (*Linen drapers' tabernacle*) of 1433, which made Angelico's reputation as one of the most important painters in the city, and the *Sacra conversazione* (*Holy conversation*) in the Annalena Convent. (M.S.)

Bibliography: M. Scudieri, *Miniatura del '400 a San Marco*, Florence 2003, p. 145.

Anonymous
("Master of the Sistine Apostles"?)

GIULIANO DE' MEDICI
1480 ca.
Marble, height 63 cm
Florence, Museo Nazionale del Bargello, inv. no. 360 S

Giuliano de' Medici, son of Piero and brother of Lorenzo the Magnificent, died at only twenty five years of age in the Pazzi Conspiracy on April, 26, 1478. The bust, slightly larger than real life, reproduces Giuliano's appearance in a realistic way. From both painted and sculpted portraits and from Bertoldo's medal, we know him to have been a handsome young man with thick hair and strongly marked features. The sculptor, who portrayed Giuliano after his death, perhaps for a funeral monument, probably had available not only painted effigies of his subject, but also a death cast, as was common in this period.
The work is exhibited in the museum together with the portraits of Lorenzo, Piero and his uncle, Giovanni de' Medici. (M.G.V.)

Bibliography: F. Caglioti in *L'eredità di Lorenzo il Magnifico*, Florence 1992, pp. 57-59.

Follower of Verrocchio

BUST OF LORENZO THE MAGNIFICENT
First quarter of the 16th century
Polichrome terracotta, 80 x 80 cm
Florence, Salvadori Carnevali Collection

The bust, noted since the 1920's, has enjoyed opposing opinions from critics over time; in an early period it was referred to as the work of Andrea del Verrochio or possibly even of Leonardo. It was later de-classified as probably an imitation of the 1800's.
The re-evaluation of Middeldorf (1976) and the presence of the bust at the Lorenzo the Magnificent exhibition of 1992 re-directed attention to the work, considered now to be among the most interesting of the various clay portraits of the Magnificent left to us. This direction has also

been expressed by G. Gentilini (who has now verbally reconfirmed his opinion to me) at a conference held in Washington in 1996, during which it was proposed to date the chronology of the bust towards the second decade of the 1500's as already hypothesized by Middledorf. Thus we're talking about a post-mortem bust of Lorenzo, who died in 1492, marked by the prevailing preconception of physical characteristics that were generated by other portraits or perhaps even the funeral mask itself of the Magnificent, already conserved at the time. The author of this vivid and all considered, monumental portrait might possibly be identified, as suggested by Gentilini, as Pietro Torrigiano, who exercised his abilities as a portraitist in the service of the King of England and who from 1515 and 1520 interrupted his travels for a sojourn in Florence. (A.G.)

Bibliography: K. Langedijk, *The portraits of the Medici*, Vol. II, Florence 1983, p. 1162, nos. 74, 28, (with previous bibliography); *L'Architettura di Lorenzo il Magnifico*, Milan 1992, p. 125.

Angelo Fabbrini
(San Giovanni Valdarno 1830 - Florence 1889)

THE PAZZI CONSPIRACY
1855 or 1862
Oil on canvas, 138 x 175 cm
Florence, Galleria d'Arte Moderna, inv. no. 373

The painting represents the Archbishop Salviati showing the dagger, blessed by Sixtus IV, to Guglielmo de' Pazzi, for him to use in the conspiracy against the Medici. Francesco della Rovere, who had become Pope in 1471 under the name of Sixtus IV, wished to expand his dominion in Romagna, which was contrary to the interests of Lorenzo de' Medici; furthermore, the Pope's nephew, Girolamo Riario, was pressing him towards the conquest of Florence, as he desired to make the city a personal possession. The two were supported by the Pazzi family, whose ancient prestige had been lost with the rise of the Medici. Disputes between the two families had never entirely ceased, despite the marriage of Bianca, sister of Lorenzo and Giuliano, to Guglielmo de' Pazzi. The Archbishop of Pisa, Francesco Salviati, joined the conspiracy, perhaps because Lorenzo had hindered his nomination as Archbishop of Florence. This re-evocation, painted four centuries after the event by Angelo Fabbrini, an artist representative of 19th century "historical" painting, confirms how indelible a mark such a momentous event as this conspiracy, which caused the death of Giuliano de' Medici, had left on Florentine history. (E.C.)

Bibliography: S. Pinto, *Romanticismo storico*, Florence 1974, p. 371; A. P. Torresi, *Neo-Medicei*, Ferrara 1996, p. 104.

German or Austrian

DAGGER
15th century

Chiseled and gilded bronze and steel, lenght 64 cm
Florence, Eredità Bardini, inv. no. 2445

This example of a 15th century dagger, of German origin, has been fashioned in the style typical of the period, and is perhaps not dissimilar from that used by the Pazzi in the conspiracy against the Medici. This type of short arm, which was used taking advantage of the blade-point to pierce even the most solid of protections, was already carried during the 13th and 14th centuries, on the side of the body opposite to that on which the sword was hung, and was used to stab the adversary in combat at close range. Starting in the 15th and continuing in the 16th century, the dagger also began to be used in a defensive role, helping the sword to parry the enemy's thrusts. As it was held in the left hand during fighting, changes in its shape tended to take place over time. Daggers were constructed with symmetrical, double-edged blades, similar to those of swords, or with three or four-sided blades, that although lacked cutting edges, succeeded in being very penetrating. (E.C.)

Bibliography: L. Salvatici in *Posate, pugnali e coltelli da caccia*, Florence 1991, pp. 10-12.

FRAGMENT OF THE BLOODIED SHIRT OF GIULIANO DE' MEDICI
15th century

Florence, Provincia di Firenze

The assassination of Giuliano de' Medici and his brother Lorenzo was planned for Holy Saturday, April, 25, 1478, but Giuliano's unexpected absence from the banquet where the evil deed was supposed to be perpetrated, convinced the conspirators to postpone it to the following day. On April 26, the assassins flung themselves upon the two brothers as Easter Sunday mass was being celebrated in the Cathedral. While Lorenzo sought refuge in the New Sacristy, numerous blows delivered by the hand of Francesco de' Pazzi succeeded in stabbing Giuliano to death (up to 19 stab wounds may be counted on his shirt). The crowd, witness to the assault, helped to capture the conspirators, and the failure of the attempt on the lives of the two brothers concluded in the hanging of the Archibishop Salviati and the others. The only member of the conspiracy to receive pardon was Guglielmo de' Pazzi, husband of Bianca de' Medici, sister of the slain Giuliano. (E.C.)

Bibliography: O. Gori, M. Sbrilli *Due famiglie implicate nella congiura del 1478: i Pazzi e i Salviati* in *Consorterie politiche e mutamenti istituzionali in età laurenziana*, Florence 1992, pp. 168-176.

Bertoldo di Giovanni
(Florence 1420 ca. - Poggio a Caiano 1491)

MEDAL COMMEMORATING THE PAZZI CONSPIRACY
1478

Bronze, diameter 6,5 cm
Florence, Museo Nazionale del Bargello, inv. no. 5956

This medal was coined following the Pazzi conspiracy.
The two faces give a detailed representation of the various phases of this attempt on the lives of the Medici brothers; the same scene is shown twice in a mirror image, above which the heads of the two brothers are placed. On the obverse, Lorenzo appears outside the chancel, protecting himself with his mantle as he flees towards the New Sacristy; on the reverse, Giuliano, already lies wounded on the ground, dying beneath the conspirators' blows.
Differently from other commemorative medals, in this case the chronicle of this criminal deed is precisely told in order to preserve and hand down the memory of the event as it actually happened. (M.G.V.)

Bibliography: J. G. Pollard, *Medaglie italiane del Rinascimento*, Florence 1984, Vol. I, p. 406; F. Vannel, G. Toderi in *L'eredità di Lorenzo il Magnifico*, Florence 1992, p. 62.

Italian (?)

BUST OF A BACCHANTE CROWNED WITH IVY
End of the 15th century
Chalcedony cameo, 5,8 x 5,1 cm
Florence, Museo Archeologico Nazionale, inv. no. 14504

This figure, often identified in the Medici inventories as a Bacchante crowned with ivy, has also been associated with Bacchus dressed in female clothing and adorned with a necklace, because of the affinity with a group of cameos portraying Mithridates VI in the guise of Dionysius.

This lovely stone, traces of which may be found in the Medici inventories since 1736, has five different layers of colors from which the cameo has been carved: the ivy crown, the head, the neck, the peplum, and the necklace are of a bluish white shade, while the tunic has a green tonality, lighter however than the background. While the style is Hellenistic Greek, the workmanship seems to indicate that the gem was made at the end of the 15th century. (M.Sf.)

Bibliography: M. E. Micheli in A. Giuliano, *I cammei della Collezione Medicea nel Museo Archeologico di Firenze*, Rome 1989, p. 182, no. 71; L. Tondo in L. Tondo, F. M. Vanni, *Le gemme dei Medici e dei Lorena al Museo Archeologico di Firenze*, Florence 1990, p. 41, no. 106.

Italian (?)

CROWNED FEMALE BUST
End of the 15th century
Chalcedony cameo, 4,9 x 3,6 cm
Florence, Museo Archeologico Nazionale, inv. no. 14553

Descriptions of the cameo are to be found in the inventories of the Medici possessions since 1635. In the past, it was held to be a work "very unique not so much for its fine style and workmanship", as the 1799 inventory recites, but rather "for the ornament of garnets, which do not seem to be modern replacements". In fact, the female head, finely carved from the solid white layer of stone, slightly bluish in tone and in sharp contrast with the ruby-colored background, wears a crown derived from a lighter-shaded part of the stone (as are the pendant and the peplum), into which are set six garnets, while another garnet adorns the pendant. This detail has brought the cameo to be dated at the end of the *Quattrocento* (1400's); this receives further support today from the fact that its proposed derivation from the statue of Hera at Argos no longer seems acceptable, while the identification with Antonia must be rejected because the type of crown has been recognized as typically late Medieval, rather than classical. (M.Sf.)

Bibliography: M. E. Micheli in A. Giuliano, *I cammei della Collezione Medicea nel Museo Archeologico di Firenze*, Rome 1989, p. 266, no. 214; L. Tondo in L. Tondo, F. M. Vanni, *Le gemme dei Medici e dei Lorena al Museo Archeologico di Firenze*, Florence 1990, p. 41, no.107

Anonymous

CUP
15th century
Red, brown and yellowish jasper, with large white streaks,
5,5 x 10,7 cm
Florence, Museo di Storia Naturale, Sezione Mineralogia, inv. 1947, no. 13504/209

The letters "LAU. R. MED." inscribed on the cup testify to Lorenzo the Magnificent's ownership. Lorenzo was the first Medici who truly cultivated a passion for vases and carvings made of semiprecious stones, which appear in great number in the inventory made at the moment of his death (1492).
A "small faceted cup", which may perhaps be identified as the one exhibited here, is cited among those received by the administrators of Lorenzo's inheritance, in the inventory of vases dated September 30, 1495. It was probably later donated to the Basilica of San Lorenzo by one of the Medici Popes (either Leo X, or Clement VII in 1532). In 1785 it was transferred to the museum of Natural History. (M.Sf.)

Bibliography: D. Heikamp in *Il tesoro di Lorenzo il Magnifico, II I vasi*, Florence 1972, pp. 153-154, no. 54.

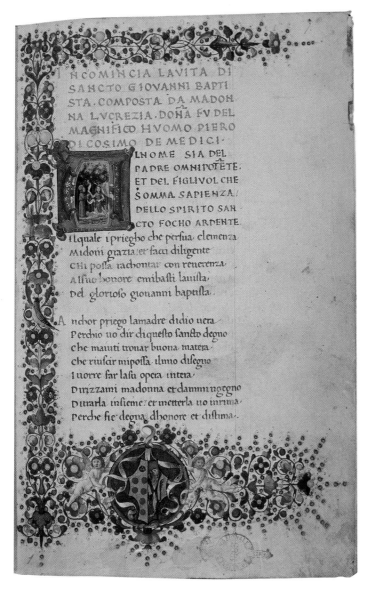

Anonymous
(Gherardo di Giovanni ?)
(Florence 1444 - 1497)

ILLUMINATED MANUSCRIPT WITH POEMS BY LUCREZIA TORNABUONI
After 1469
Parchment manuscript with miniatures, 22,1 x 14,3 cm
Florence, Biblioteca Nazionale Centrale, Magl. VII, 338

This codex is considered the basic textual source for editions of the literary works by Lucrezia Tornabuoni, wife of Piero di Cosimo from 1444 and mother of Lorenzo the Magnificent. Lucrezia, who had received a solid cultural education, contributed in her own right to the tradition of patronage practiced by the Medici family, thus assuming an absolutely exceptional role for a lady of her time. As evidenced in her letters, she maintained direct contacts and exchanged verses with the poets and bards hosted in the palace on Via Larga. Her writings also include brief religious poems, inspired in a very personal way by the Holy Scriptures. Precious miniatures attributed to Gherardo di Giovanni (Florence 1444-1497) illuminate the manuscript, greatly enriching a work meant after all for a close circle of family members and friends. (E.C.)

Bibliography: F. Pezzarossa, *I poemetti sacri di Lucrezia Tornabuoni*, Florence 1978, pp. 7-65; C. Di Domenico in *Lorenzo dopo Lorenzo*, Florence 1992, pp. 30, 193-194; D. Kent, *Women in Renaissance Florence* in *Virtue and Beauty*, Washington 2001, pp. 35-39.

Lorenzo The Magnificent
(Florence 1449 - 1492)

SONNET "MERITA PIÙ QUEL CUOR"
Second half of the 15th century
Paper manuscript, the two tercets are by Lorenzo's own hand, the two quatrains are by Niccolò Michelozzi; 5,8 x 11,8 cm
Florence, Biblioteca Nazionale Centrale, Palatino da ordinare 1190 (striscia 1355)

This sonnet's pair of tercets, which follow the two quatrains written by Niccolò Michelozzi (perhaps under dictation or copying from a former draft), may actually be ascribed to the hand of Lorenzo himself. Lorenzo the Magnificent, patron of all the arts, was in fact directly engaged in the art of poetry, and with the best of results. The early years of his literary career still seem to reflect the works of such contemporary poets as Luigi Pulci, while afterwards the major influence was that of the Neoplatonic philosopher Marsilio Ficino, founder of the Neoplatonic Academy. In the later years of his life, perhaps under the influence of the Dominican friar Gerolamo Savonarola, Lorenzo's literary efforts tended to reflect a more traditional religious sentiment. (E.C.)

Bibliography: P. Viti in *Lorenzo dopo Lorenzo*, Florence 1992, pp. 116-117; E. Bigi, *Lorenzo de' Medici e la letteratura* in *La Toscana al tempo di Lorenzo il Magnifico*, Pisa 1996, pp. 341-355.

Giovanni Stradano (Bruges 1523 - Florence 1605)
(cartoon)
Benedetto di Michele Squilli (active Florence 1555 - 1588)
(textile)

LORENZO DE' MEDICI AND HIS ARTISTS IN THE SCULPTURE GARDEN
1571

Wall tapestry, warp and weft, wool, 425 x 455 cm
Pisa, Museo Nazionale di San Matteo, inv. no.1516

This tapestry is part of a series of seven, consigned to the *Guardaroba* of the Medici in February-May, 1571, for hanging in the hall of Lorenzo the Magnificent in Palazzo Vecchio. They were woven from cartoons prepared by the painter Giovanni Stradano, under the supervision of Giorgio Vasari;

the one exhibited here should be the third of the series woven in order of time. The central part of the tapestry shows the Garden of San Marco, where the collection of antiquities belonging to the Medici family was kept under the custody of the sculptor Bertoldo; the border of the tapestry is instead decorated with masks and allegorical figures. The Sculpture Garden, defined by Vasari as a "school and academy", was opened by Lorenzo the Magnificent in the 1480's to encourage the study of sculpture of antiquity on the part of young artists. Among them we find Michelangelo himself, who seems to have sculpted in the Garden, the famous head of a Faun, passed off as an authentic antiquity. The importance of the Garden concluded its decline under Cosimo I, who founded the grand ducal tapestry manufactory there in 1545. (E.C.)

Bibliography: C. Elam in *Il Giardino di San Marco*, Florence 1992, pp. 157-170; M. Stefanini Sorrentino, *Arazzi medicei a Pisa*, Florence 1993, p. 60.

Andrea Sansovino (?)
(Monte San Savino 1460 - 1529) or
Bertoldo di Giovanni
(and workshop)
(Florence 1420 ca. - Poggio a Caiano 1491)

THE NIGHT AND THE CHARIOT OF THE SUN (OR TRIUMPH OF THE RIGHTEOUS SOUL)
End of the 15th century
Part of the relief frieze in glazed terracotta, 58 x 190 cm
Poggio a Caiano, Villa Medicea

The frieze, today substituted by a copy for conservation reasons, until only a few years ago adorned the exterior of the villa at Poggio a Caiano, constructed according to the design of Giuliano da Sangallo for Lorenzo the Magnificent, beginning in 1485.

The lively, shiny white and blue glazed surface, with its details in yellow to suggest the effect of gold, animates the otherwise severe facade of the building inspired by the pronaos of an Etruscan temple.

The theme developed along the frieze, with evident references to the place in which the villa is located, is that of the months and of the country labors typical of each of the different seasons, accompanied by allegorical figures derived from mythical and Neoplatonic philosophical sources, very well-known and widely studied in the Florentine cultural environment of the time.

The frieze is composed of numerous elements; the five scenes, each of which contains various episodes, are divided by herma. The meaning of the unusual figurations remains unclear and has been variously interpreted, although making constant reference to the philosophical culture of the humanists gravitating around the Medici court. Among the various possible interpretations, we may cite that according to which the frieze is an allegorical exaltation of the good government practiced by

Lorenzo. A more in-depth analysis of the philosophical textual evidence which may be the inspiration for the scenes, has instead led to the conviction that the relief actually narrates the story of the soul and its voyage from creation until it returns to heaven (Acidini 1991). Following this key to interpretation, the scene presented here would symbolize the immortality of the soul represented in the form of a chariot rising upwards in the sky.

The fact that various collaborators were probably required for such a large undertaking may be sufficient to explain the different modeling of the scenes. The overall planning of the work, attributed among others to Andrea Sansovino, may mostly likely be referred to another sculptor quite close to Lorenzo, Bertoldo di Giovanni, who actually died in the villa in December, 1491. Other artists were evidently involved in the carrying out of the project, while firing was likely done in the Della Robbia workshop, well-equipped and specialized in making this type of object. (M.G.V.)

Bibliography: C. Acidini Luchinat, *La scelta dell'anima* in "Artista", 1991, pp. 16-25; G. Gentilini, *I Della Robbia*, Florence 1992, pp. 483-485; A. Bellandi in *I Della Robbia*, Florence 1998, p. 369; L. Medri in *I Della Robbia*, Florence 1998, pp. 370-372.

Andrea di Francesco di Cione called **Andrea del Verrocchio**
(attributed to)
(Florence 1435 - Venice 1488)

IDEAL PORTRAIT OF ALEXANDER THE GREAT
Ninth decade of the 15th century
Marble relief, 42,9 x 32,6 cm
Italy, Private Collection

A previously unpublished 15th century Florentine work, recently discovered in a private collection in Italy, is presented for the first time in this exhibition and related catalogue. In fact, the subject and style of this exquisite head in profile were not altogether unknown as it may be linked to a reference in Vasari's *Lives of the Artists* and to a series of similar reliefs, although the present piece is of higher quality and more coherent in style.

In part of the text that Vasari dedicates to the life of Andrea Verrocchio, he mentions that the sculptor made two relief heads in profile of armed warriors with crested helmets conceived as idealized portraits of two warrior kings, Alexander the Great and Darius of Persia. Again according to Vasari, the two works were given by Lorenzo the Magnificent to Matthias Corvinus, King of Hungary and a cultured humanist who was fascinated by Italian art. Vasari states that the reliefs are "in metal", or rather in bronze, a metal that Verrocchio often used, but until now the reliefs linked to those referred to by Vasari, are in marble, plaster, or glazed terracotta.

Moreover, the two other works that critics have judged not to be later derivations (such as the plaster reliefs of the Victoria and Albert Museum), and that are generally accepted to be Verrocchio's, or at least his prototype, are both in marble and are in the Louvre and in the National Gallery of Washington. It has already been observed that quite possibly Vasari, writing some 80 years after the reliefs had been sent from Florence to Hungary, mistakenly believed them to be in bronze, while it is more probable that they were in marble, as were most of Verrocchio's works.

This complex issue is further complicated by a famous drawing by Leonardo da Vinci in the British Museum, London, also inspired by Verrocchio's model, where the warrior faces left, as in the relief exhibited here in Memphis, compared to the other two marbles that are facing to the right. Evidently Verrocchio's two reliefs, were conceived as a specular pair.

This is also confirmed by a fourth marble relief, identifiable with the series, at the Chicago Art Institute, in which Alessandro, in profile, faces the left. Art historians have debated this question at length, especially between the 1920's and 1940's, alternately attributing either the Washington marble to Verrocchio, or, though less insistently, the Paris relief. More recent studies tend to exclude both as works by Verrocchio; the Louvre marble is slightly weak in style, and the Washington one reveals certain inconsistencies in the creative and sculptural technique. Could this recently discovered marble not, therefore, be one of the two originals? The creative quality of the noble warrior's head, shadowed by the rim of the helmet, the skill of the spatial arrangement, the smoothness of the modeling and flow from one level to another, the delicacy of the decorative details which recall the bodyguards in the *Decollation of St. John the Baptist* made in silver by Verrocchio for the altar of the Florentine Baptistery, all suggest that this could be the case. Even some of the details that could seem more "mechanical", such as the curls, pierced by the point of the drill, are found elsewhere in Verrocchio's works as, for example, in the angels of the Forteguerri Monument in the Pistoia Cathedral. Not least, the relief is the only one to be oval in shape, daringly outlining the form of the helmet, while all the other known reliefs have a more banal and regular square form, more appropriate to a derivation. Most certainly, this newly discovered relief in marble of the ancient warrior, identifiable as Alessandro from the Gorgon that decorates the breastplate, is sure to stimulate much debate among experts. The questions posed cannot be answered in this brief note, but promise an in-depth study of the work that whatever its origin, is another precious addition to our knowledge of Renaissance sculpture in Florence. (A.G.)

Unpublished.

Alessandro di Mariano Filipepi called **Sandro Botticelli**
(Florence 1445 - 1510)

MADONNA AND CHILD,
CALLED "MADONNA DELLA LOGGIA"
1466 - 1467 ca.

Tempera on panel, 72 x 50 cm
Florence, Galleria degli Uffizi, inv. Depositi, no. 8

The painting was removed from a carved tabernacle which had been painted and gilded by a different and more fluid hand, with the inscription "Ave Gratia Plena D[o]m[inu]s". It probably belonged to one of the guilds or public authorities installed in the Uffizi during the second half of the 16th century by Cosimo I and was subsequently transferred with other furnishings to the Chamber of Commerce. When the Chamber closed, and sometime before 1784, the painting became part of the collections of the Lorraine family during the rule of Grand Duke Pietro Leopoldo.

Earlier attributed to the Florentine school (Morelli, 1890; Venturi, 1925; Mesnil, 1938), and then to the "Amico di Sandro", the young Filippino Lippi (Van Marle, 1931), it was attributed by Gamba to Botticelli (1932, 1936) followed by Berenson (1932, 1963, partial responsibility), as well as Bettini (1942), Salvini (1958), Mandel (1967), Lightbown (1978), Salvini again (1979), Pons (1989) and Caneva (1990).

The doubts regarding its attribution are due to the difficulties of valuation caused by the poor state of preservation and, in particular, the extensive and mortifying repainting that almost entirely covered the Virgin and Child in an attempt to hide the damage caused by drastic cleaning in the past that had particularly affected the skin tones and areas painted with shading and layers.

The restoration, carried out for this exhibition, arranged by Alfio del Serra, succeeded in removing layers of repainting, revealing, on the one hand, better preserved areas such as the red dress of the Virgin and the scenery visible in the background behind the arches, and unfortunately on the other hand, areas that are more worn and damaged such as the blue cloak lined with green and the flesh tones of the Child and Virgin. Though still with some reservations, after this restoration the work appears to be that of the young Sandro Botticelli, still greatly influenced by the approach and style of his master, Filippo Lippi, and with all the imperfections of drawing and painting and the changes and alterations inevitable, given the precocity of the work and youth of the artist. The work could be dated a year or two earlier than the existing critical chronology, which oscillates around 1467 as proposed by Salvini and accepted by Caneva (1990), and 1467-1470 as proposed by Gamba (1932, 1936) and accepted by Bettini (1942, 1947), and more recently by Pons (1989), and Mandel's suggested 1468 (1967). (A.C.)

Bibliography: R. Lightbown, *Sandro Botticelli*, London 1978, Vol. II, no. A9, p. 15 (with previous bibliography); R. Salvini in *Gli Uffizi*, Florence 1979, no. P224, p. 174; N. Pons, *Botticelli*, Milan 1989, no.10, p. 55; C. Caneva, *Botticelli*, Florence 1990, no. 3, p. 22.

Domenico Bigordi called **Domenico Ghirlandaio**
(Florence 1449 - 1494)

SAINT JEROME IN HIS STUDY
Dated 1480
Detached fresco, 184 x 119 cm
Florence, Chiesa di Ognissanti

The traditional iconography of Saint Jerome in his study is adapted in this fresco to a contemporary setting thus providing us with a detailed image of a late 15th century interior. The painting synthesizes many fundamental elements of the artistic culture and Renaissance fashion. These can be identified starting with the architectural forms consisting of decorative and structural elements – the fluted column, the composite capital, the molded lintel with an inscription in capital letters, the beaded frame – all derived from a classical repertory. This structure provides us with a perspective view of the study, where the portrait of the saint is composed with great simplicity and naturalness. This naturalness achieves a sense of intense psychological penetration seen in the expression of the face which shows concentration, but also doubt, uncertainty and perhaps curiosity for the world, represented by the viewer who the saint is observing. The fresco is therefore completely different to Sandro Botticelli's *Saint Augustine in his Study* painted for the same church and located on the opposite side of the choir. This shows the saint in ecstasy, during a vision of Saint Jerome himself, and involving no relationship at all with the viewer. Also entirely natural is the representation of objects that cover the table, desk and shelves, communicating an atmosphere of everyday activity that could refer indirectly to the study of Giorgio Antonio Vespucci who probably commissioned the work. The objects are depicted with a precision that is typical of Flemish art, which certainly influenced the artist. It is in fact possible that Ghirlandaio based this work on a similar painting by Jan Van Eyck and Petrus Christus, at the time owned by the Medici and now identified as a panel painting in the Detroit Institute of Art. However, it should be noted that, with the use of light and especially the choice of viewpoint and arrangement of the items, Ghirlandaio goes beyond the objective treatment of Flemish artists, relating them to the activity and life of the subject. (M.S.)

Bibliography: R. G. Kecks, *Ghirlandaio*, Florence 1995, pp. 111-112; J. Cadogan, *Domenico Ghirlandaio*, Florence 2000, pp. 216-218.

Piero di Lorenzo called **Piero di Cosimo**
(Florence 1461/62 - 1522)

ADORATION OF THE CHILD
1510 ca.
Oil on panel, carved and gilded wood frame, diameter 116 cm, diameter with the frame 164 cm
Florence, Museo di Palazzo Martelli, inv. Dipinti, no 170

This painting, which has been in the Martelli home since 1648, is one of the most important works of art in the collection of this ancient Florentine family, tied to the Medici by bonds of business and friendship, as well as being related to them by marriage (Camilla Martelli in fact married Cosimo I de' Medici). The painting, in its lovely, "antique"-style 19th century frame, still occupies the place of honor in the "yellow drawing-room". It reflects the widely diffused taste of private owners (from the late15th through the first decade of the 16th century) for images of sacred subjects painted on round panels, designed to be placed often very prominently in an ample setting, for example the center of a nuptial chamber.

This splendid painting by Piero di Cosimo, restored especially for this exhibition, is a *tondo* replica of the lost *Adoration of the Pastors* previously in Berlin. It reflects the art of Ridolfo del Ghirlandaio, with which it has many similarities (see, for example, the *Incarnation of Christ with Saints* in the Uffizi), making probable a date of around 1510. The eye of the observer is guided towards the focal point of the composition, the Holy Child seen lying on a mantle against a travel sack in the foreground, aided by the figures of the Virgin and St. Joseph, which together with the landscape in the background, help to converge vision on the work's central point. The evident taste for color and landscape has Flemish derivations, as was particularly popular among certain Florentine painters at the end of the 1400's and the first decade of the 1500's. Such characteristics reflected the influence of the altar piece (today in the Uffizi), painted by Hugo van de Goes for Tommaso Portinari, representative of the Medici in Bruges. The panel arrived in Florence in 1475-77, intended by Portinari

for the church of Sant'Egidio in the Hospital of Santa Maria Nuova. The Florentine painters, first of all Botticelli, but also Ghirlandaio and Piero di Cosimo, greeted this arrival by enriching their palettes, and dedicating themselves to the minute and graphic rendering of detail. The vividly bright and lively descriptive nature of this work confirms Piero's embracing of the northern modes then so much in vogue in Florence.

Besides their actual furnishings, the nuptial chambers of wealthy Florentines during the Renaissance were also full of easel paintings and relief carvings, usually of a religious nature; the Madonna and Child was the preferred subject, but figures of Saints and Crucifixes were also very popular. For example, the full-scale sculpture of St. John the Baptist now in the Bargello, formerly attributed to Donatello, was once in the Martelli Palace, as were the *David* and the bust of *St. John the Baptist as a Child* today in the National Gallery in Washington, and also two round panels with the *Virgin and Child*. Although the *tondo* format required more complex carpentry than that of rectangular panels, which also made them cost more, a great number of such round paintings were to be found in the rich Florentine homes of the 15th century. Luigi di Luigi Martelli acquired one of these from Botticelli in 1489 (now lost), while the patron who engaged Piero di Cosimo to paint the panel exhibited here remains unknown. Old inventories reveal that *tondi* were mainly kept in the chamber or its anteroom, usually placed high up on the wall. (M.B.)

Bibliography: E. Capretti in *L'Officina della Maniera*, Florence 1996, no. 108, p. 308.

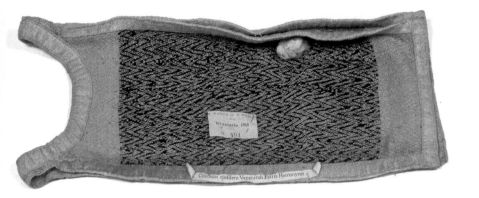

Francesco Della Robbia
(Florence 1477 - Macerata 1527/28)

PORTRAIT OF GIROLAMO SAVONAROLA
1498 - 1502
Relief medallion of colored plaster in painted maplewood box,
diameter 8,7 cm, box 10,5 x 5
Florence, Museo di San Marco, inv. 1915, no. 483

Savonarola, the priest who inflamed Florentine public opinion during the last decade of the 15th century with his passionate preaching is portrayed in this medallion with great immediacy and expressive skill. The high quality and the inscription in gold capital letters that runs around the edge of the medallion - "venie(n)t ad te q(ui)detrahebant tibi et adorabu(n)t vestigia pedum tuor(um)" - place the work immediately after the execution of the priest in 1498 and before the proclamation of 1502 by which the General of the Order banned all forms of glorification of Savonarola as the circulation of images was quite widespread at the time. Giorgio Vasari affirms that certain medals bearing images of this kind were made from a terracotta mold attributed to the two sons of Andrea Della Robbia, Francesco and Marco. As well as being skilled in modeling and relief, the Della Robbia had also followed a religious vocation and were Dominican monks at San Marco at the same time as Savonarola from 1495-96. The lineaments seen in the medallion are almost identical to those of a bronze medal in the Bargello museum (no. 6022), supporting the theory that the medallion and the medal were made from the same terracotta prototype identifiable as being the work of Francesco Della Robbia. (M.S.)

Bibliography: M. Scudieri in *Savonarola e le sue reliquie a San Marco*, Florence 1998, pp. 65-66.

Florentine

HAIRCLOTH JACKET
1490 ca.
Dark haircloth and white hemp, 55,5 x 26,5 cm
Florence, Museo di San Marco, inv. San Marco no. 491

This haircloth jacket is one of the relics of Girolamo Savonarola which were carefully preserved for centuries and transferred to the museum from the monastery of San Marco in the 19th century when historic recognition of the priest began to take on a more concrete form. Savonarola was one of the most important historic figures of the Dominican order and in the history of Florence during the late 15th century. Until his execution in 1498 he lived in the order at San Marco for many years.

The jacket is sleeveless and open at the sides with a particularly rough central panel where the haircloth is woven with untreated wool, intended to be worn next to the skin as a form of penitence. The kind and rarity of the garment make it of great interest, both for its manufacture and for its symbolic significance as a cult object. It is representative of an asceticism that would continue to have a strong power of attraction for many centuries. For Savonarola clothes had a much greater importance than their ordinary external purpose and they became the tangible symbol of his interior choice, his quest for simplicity and purity and his desire for penitence. Used as an everyday garment, he sorely regretted that this haircloth jacket was taken from him at the time of his execution at the stake. (M.S.)

Bibliography: G. Rasario in *Savonarola e le sue reliquie a San Marco*, Florence 1998, pp. 58-59.

Anonymous
(Florentine)

ORDEAL OF GIROLAMO SAVONAROLA
IN PIAZZA SIGNORIA
1498 - 1500
Oil on panel, 38 x 58 cm
Florence, Museo di San Marco, inv. 1915, no. 479

This small painting, similar to a much larger one providing a complete view of Piazza Signoria during the trial and execution of Savonarola and his two companions, also presents two other prominent moments in the drama that increase its documentary and symbolic importance. The sequence of events that preceded the ordeal - hanging and burning on a pyre - is depicted in the foreground of the main scene with the arrival of

the priests with their hands bound, pushed in the direction of Palazzo della Signoria by a group of soldiers. On the left, in the background, the beatific end to the ordeal of that tragic day - recorded in an inscription in the center of the piazza - with the ascension of the three priests to heaven enclosed in a cusp of light. Painted in a simple and popular, but effective style the terrible event remains impressed on the mind of the viewer, achieving exactly the commemorative intention of the work intended by the unknown client, clearly a follower of Savonarola. The attention to detail and the movement of the figures reflect the tendency towards description, especially in mural painting, that developed in Florence with Domenico Ghirlandaio and his workshop and to which, very probably, this unknown artist belonged. (M.S.)

Bibliography: M. Scudieri in *Savonarola e le sue reliquie in San Marco,* Florence 1998, pp. 84-85.

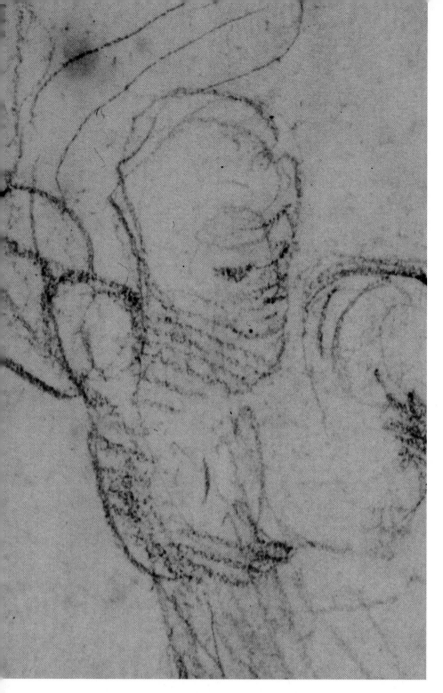

Michelangelo Buonarroti
(Caprese 1475 - Rome 1564)

STUDY FOR THE RESURRECTION OF CHRIST
1532 - 1533 ca.
Black pencil, 38,1 x 25,2 cm
Florence, Casa Buonarroti, inv. no. 61 F

The brisk and concise style of this drawing represents one of the most typical examples of the rapid and fluid technique of Michelangelo's first creative phase. The sketch is on the back of a piece of paper on the other side of which is another study for the same figure of the resurrected Christ, but reversed and surrounded by a series of lightly sketched heads. As in drawing no. 66 F, also in Casa Buonarroti, here too the artist has quickly outlined several legs in various positions. Both were preparatory drawings for a figure of Christ the Redeemer and are most probably related to a *Resurrection of Christ,* for which many other drawings were made (Tolnay, 1975-1980, II, nos. 252-265), believed to be for a lunette above the tombs of Lorenzo and Giuliano de' Medici in the Medici Chapels or for an altarpiece which Sebastiano del Piombo should have painted for the Chigi Chapel in Santa Maria del Popolo in Rome, or indeed perhaps originally intended for the altar wall in the Sistine Chapel instead of the *Last Judgement.*

Michelangelo must have worked enthusiastically and at length on this composition as can also be seen in the more general studies in the British Museum, London, where Christ is seen freeing himself into the air, amidst the amazement and dismay of the soldiers who flee as if pushed outward by a relentless thrust of energy, and in the Royal Library, Windsor (inv. no. 12767, cf. Tolnay, 1975-1980, II, no. 255 recto). This latter study, preceded by a more concise version in red pencil, in the Louvre (inv. no. 691 bis, cf. Tolbay, 1975-1980, II, no. 253 recto), shows the Redeemer emerging from the tomb with hands raised towards heaven, surrounded by sleeping soldiers in forced, Mannerist poses similar to that seen in the study for a soldier who is raising the tombstone, also housed in the Casa Buonarroti (inv. no. 32F, cf. Tolnay, 1975-1980, II, no. 254 recto) and related to a figure in the drawing at Windsor.

Though the *Resurrection* was never realized, all these drawings are generally accepted to be dated around 1532-1533. (A.C.)

Bibliography: C. Tolnay, *Corpus dei disegni di Michelangelo,* Novara 1975-1980, Vol. II, no. 261 recto (with previous bibliography); L. Berti, A. Cecchi, A. Natali, *Michelangelo: i disegni di Casa Buonarroti,* Florence 1985, no. 61 F recto and verso, pp. 187-189.

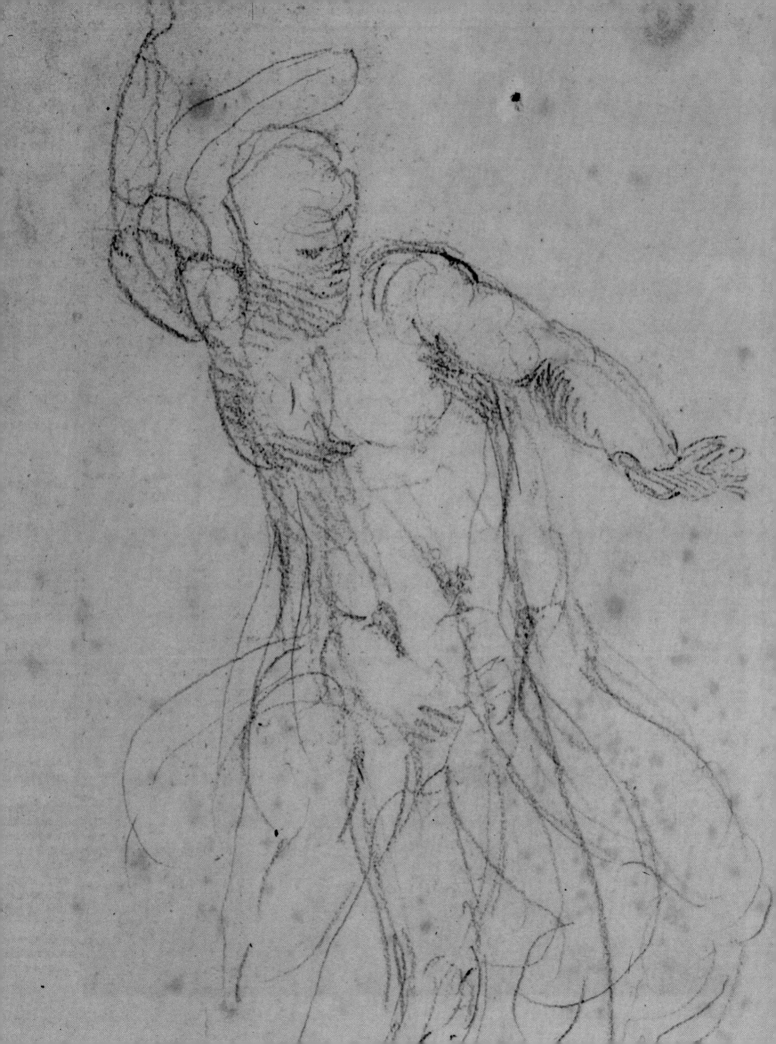

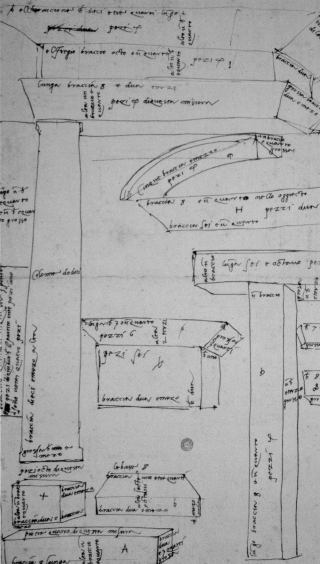

Michelangelo Buonarroti
(Caprese 1475 - Rome 1564)

STUDY FOR PORTA PIA
1560 ca.
Black pencil, pen and brown watercolor with touches of white lead on brown paper, 47 x 28 cm
Florence, Casa Buonarroti, inv. no. 102 A

Though some critics still have doubts, most now generally accept Michelangelo's authorship of the study, identifying it as a project for the renovation of the gates in the Roman walls, which Pope Pius IV commissioned from Michelangelo in 1560. The design is notable for its creativity and skill in combining curved elements with squared blocks, evident in Michelangelo's plan (inv. no. 106 A), with irregular and curved lintels, one of the most progressive of those preserved in Casa Buonarroti (nos. 73 A bis, 84 A, 97 A, 99 A). (A.C.)

Bibliography: C. Tolnay, *Corpus dei disegni di Michelangelo*, Novara 1975-1980, Vol. IV, no. 618 recto, pp. 111-112.

Michelangelo Buonarroti
(Caprese 1475 - Rome 1564)

SKETCHES OF MARBLE BLOCKS
1518
Pen and brown ink, 44,1 x 31,8 cm
Florence, Archivio Buonarroti I, 144-145, foll. 260v-261r 102 A

The drawing is part of a series of many sketches for marble blocks, some already shaped, in the Buonarroti Archive, showing details of measurements in Florentine *braccia* (a *braccio* was 58.3 cm.). The sketches were made for the marble cutters in the Apuan Alps and the blocks were intended for the structural framework of the façade of the Church of San Lorenzo in Florence which was never actually begun. The façade was commissioned from Michelangelo in January 1518 by Leo X, after he had won the competition of two years earlier in which the greatest artists of the day had participated (Giuliano and Antonio da Sangallo il Vecchio, Raphael, Baccio d'Agnolo, Andrea and Jacopo Sansovino). (A.C.)

Bibliography: C.Tolnay, *Corpus dei disegni di Michelangelo*, Novara 1975-1980, Vol. III, nos. 450 verso-451 recto, p. 93.

SLIPPERS
16th century
Leather, length 24,6 cm
Florence, Casa Buonarroti

The slippers come from the Florentine Casa Buonarroti, the house which was the property of and was lived in by Michelangelo's descendents. It has always been thought that they belonged to the great master himself, or at least to some member of his family. This type of foot wear was actually quite common in the 16th century, as may be clearly evinced from contemporary painted representations of the clothing worn at the time. Casa Buonarroti was built on the site of three houses purchased by Michelangelo in 1508, and lived in between 1516 and 1525 by his great-nephew, Michelangelo the Younger (1568-1647), who took great care in gathering numerous objects once the property of the master. (E.C.)

Bibliography: P. Ragionieri, *Casa Buonarroti*, Florence 1987.

Florentine

COMPASS WITH CASE
16th Century
Brass and steel, length 30 cm
Florence, Istituto e Museo di Storia della Scienza, inv. no. 1357

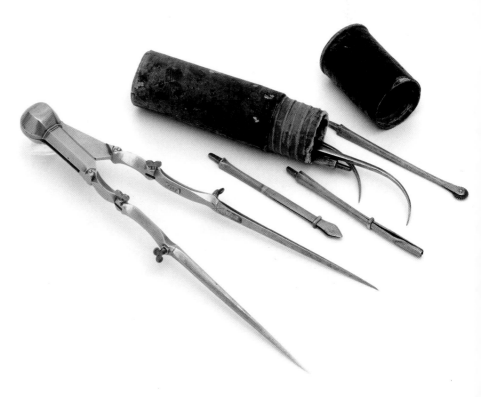

The compass is displayed together with its steel accessories (two points, two curved points, a pincer, a toothed cog-wheel), inside a cylindrical container made of black cardboard, in which there is also an antique note which attributes the instrument to Michelangelo. The compass is composed of two shaped arms of brass, attached to a slightly faceted spherical top piece. The adjustable arms may be held in the desired position by turning two little steel keys. The compass is one of the most ancient of all drawing instruments, and had a vast diffusion throughout the Renaissance thanks to its many, yet simple utilizations. (E.C.)

Bibliography: M. Miniati, *Il Museo di Storia della Scienza*, Florence 1991, p. 16; H. Millon, V. Magnago Lampugnani in *Rinascimento da Brunelleschi a Michelangelo*, Milan 1994, p. 478.

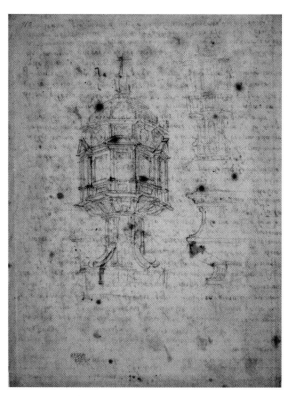

Michelangelo Buonarroti
(Caprese 1475 - Rome 1564)

DRAFT OF A LETTER (RECTO) AND STUDY FOR A TABERNACLE WITH A NICHE (VERSO)
Pen and brown ink (recto), red chalk (verso), 20,8 x 21 cm
Florence, Casa Buonarroti, inv. no. 112 A recto.

The recto of this sheet contains a letter written by Michelangelo to Piero Gondi on January 26, 1524, with which he informs the noble citizen, probably one of those among the *Provveditori* or *Operai* charged with overseeing work on the New Sacristy of San Lorenzo, about the situation of a man named Stefano, who was working with him on this job. Michelangelo informs Gondi that he had hired this person although holding him in scarce esteem, almost for charity's sake, and that he could not fire him, even though Stefano had proved to be ungrateful and unappreciative towards him, because otherwise he risked being "placed among the *piagnoni* and judged as the worst of traitors in the entire world, even if I was right". This Stefano, who remains unidentified in Tolnay's *Corpus*, may be recognized, following Barocchi and Ristori (Barocchi-Ristori, 1973, no. DCVIII, pp. 27-28), as the manuscript illuminator, Stefano di Tommaso Lunetti, cited on more than one occasion in various letters of Michelangelo's correspondence.

The study for a tabernacle and the partial studies of a tympanum-shaped crowning for it, on the verso of the drawing, were probably a first idea of Buonarroti for the door-tabernacles actually in the Medici Chapel. They may be dated around 1524, on the basis of the letter on the front of the sheet, and on the work schedule deducible from known documentation. (A.C.)

Bibliography: C. Tolnay, *Corpus dei disegni di Michelangelo*, Novara, 1975-1980, Vol. II, no.197 recto and verso, p. 36.

Michelangelo Buonarroti
(Caprese 1475 - Rome 1564)

STUDIES FOR TWO CIBORIUMS AND A SARCOPHAGUS
Black charcoal, 27,5 x 20,5 cm
Florence, Casa Buonarroti, inv. no. 110 A recto.

In the center of the recto of this drawing, we may see a study for an octagonal-shaped ciborium, surmounted by a cupola on a drum similar to that of the Florentine Cathedral of Santa Maria del Fiore, with aedicules alternating triangular and curvilinear tympanums. Another charcoal sketch of a second, slimmer ciborium appears on the upper right; its more slender main part is arranged in niches on top of a base. Still further down on the sheet, a barely suggested sketch for the molding of a sarcophagus may be observed. On the verso we find *ricordi* or remembrances of the artist relative to the period between December 5, 1516, and February 25, 1518, which therefore furnishes a "terminus post quem" for dating the drawings, and permits their association to a commission made by Pier Soderini for a reliquary of the head of St. John the Baptist and for two sarcophagi. Soderini, the old, life-time *gonfaloniere* of the Republic who had commissioned Leonardo and Michelangelo to paint the *Battles* in the Great Hall of Palazzo Vecchio, never actually done, and who had been living exiled in Rome since 1512, in fact requested Michelangelo to prepare several projects for a funeral chapel he wanted to have built for himself in San Silvestro in Capite in Rome. Correspondence between Soderini and Piero Rosselli starting in May, 1518, documents that the latter was charged with carrying out work from the drawings, and in general for the work to be done on the chapel. Only the altar of the chapel had been actually carried out in 1524, but this has nothing whatsoever to do with Michelangelo's inventions; we may take this as further confirmation of the usual unsuccess of Soderini's commissions. (A.C.)

Bibliography: C. Tolnay, *Corpus dei disegni di Michelangelo*, Novara, 1975-1980, Vol. II, no. 175 recto, p. 21; L. Berti, A. Cecchi, A. Natali, *Michelangelo: i disegni di Casa Buonarroti*, Florence 1985, p. 89.

Michelangelo Buonarroti
(Caprese 1475 - Rome 1564)

STUDY OF NUDE FIGURES

Black chalk, pen and brown ink, 18 x 21 cm
Florence, Casa Buonarroti, inv. no. 38 F

This drawing presents various sketches of male nudes, shown lifting their hands towards the sky as if to protect themselves from a dazzling light. Most of the figures have been drawn with black chalk and are barely visible; only three in the lower right have also been gone over with pen and brown ink, with the rapid, darting marks typical of Michelangelo when doing this type of drawing.

The drawing is part of a group conserved in the Casa Buonarroti, four of which (nos. 17F, 67F, 68F recto, 18F recto) have the same three figures rapidly sketched in by pen, while a fifth (no. 58 F) represents a Transfiguration (Tolnay, 1975-1980, I, nos. 78 recto, 79 recto, 80 recto, 81 recto, 82 recto). From this Tolnay deduced, although somewhat doubtfully, that the entire series could have been drawn by Buonarroti for a Transfiguration, such as the one frescoed between 1517 and 1520 by Sebastiano del Piombo in the apse of the Borgherini Chapel in San Pietro in Montorio in Rome.

While Robinson (1870) mistakenly thought of these sketches as being studies for the merchants of an *Expulsion from the Temple*, and Ferri considered them *38 Ideas for the Expulsion of Adam and Eve in the Sistine Chapel*, thus erroneously holding them to be studies for the progenitors of the Sistine fresco, Wilde (1953) associated these little figures to the related ones in the *Martyrdom of St. Catherine*, painted by Giuliano Bugiardini in the Rucellai Chapel in Santa Maria Novella, according to Vasari, from drawings supplied by his friend Michelangelo.

As far as present knowledge allows us to understand, this drawing together with the rest of the series might well be related to a Transfiguration scene, perhaps one never actually carried out by Buonarroti; it is in any case certain, however, that this minute "corpus" does not refer to the *Transfiguration* painted by the friar in Rome, since this was designed for a conch and therefore necessarily required the Apostles to be shown lying on their sides, or at least reclining, rather than in rapid movement as they are to be seen in the drawings under examination. (A.C.)

Bibliography: C.Tolnay, *Corpus dei disegni di Michelangelo*, Novara 1975-1980, Vol. I, no. 83 recto, p. 77; L. Berti, A. Cecchi, A. Natali, *Michelangelo: i disegni di Casa Buonarroti*, Florence 1985, p. 85.

Leonardo da Vinci
(Vinci 1452 - Amboise 1519)

FEMALE HEAD, CALLED **"LA SCAPIGLIATA"**
OR **"DAMA SCAPIGLIATA"**
Early 16th century
Tracing color, green amber and white lead on panel, 24,7 x 21 cm
Parma, Galleria Nazionale, inv. no. 362

Acquired by the Galleria Nazionale of Parma in 1839 as a work by Leonardo, over the years critics have frequently doubted the attribution both for the unusual technique and the characteristics of an unfinished draft. Ricci, in 1896, considered it to be false and perhaps the work of the painter Gaetano Callani, from whose collection it came. Accepted as part of Leonardo's body of work by Venturi (1924), Quintavalle (1939) and Bottari (1942), the work has had a particularly difficult critical history, believed by Suida to be, at the very most, by a follower of Leonardo (1929) until Ottino (1967) reinstated it, though with some hesitation, as a work by the master. Pedretti, however, has never doubted its paternity and has frequently reconfirmed the painting as genuine (1953, 1974, 1977, 1983 and 1985) and this acceptance is included in the most recent guide to the Gallery (Fornari Schianchi s.d., but 1983).

The attribution finds authoritative documentary confirmation if the painting can be identified with the "*quadro dipintovi la testa di una donna scapiliata, bozzata...opera di Leonardo da Vinci*" ("picture painted with the tousled head of a woman, a draft ... the work of Leonardo da Vinci"), described in an inventory of the Gonzaga household, dated 1627, year of the unfortunate sale of the collection to the King of England. If, indeed, it can be identified with the painting mentioned in 1531 as one of those in the appartment of Margherita Paleologa, wife of Federico Gonzaga, son of Isabella d'Este, it could, as Pedretti believes, have been part of Isabella's collection as she had never been able to obtain a finished work from Leonardo, despite continual and repeated requests.

Marani, author of the critical catalogue entry for the work (1989) suggests there are stylistic and technical similarities with the head of the angel in the second version of the *Virgin of the Rocks*, probably begun in the early 1490s and completed between 1506-1508. He therefore dates the work to the early 16th century, especially if *La Scapigliata* could be considered a rough draft for a Virgin, a request made by Isabella d'Este in 1501 and never fulfilled by Leonardo. (A.C.)

Bibliography: P. C. Marani, *Leonardo. Catalogo completo*, Florence 1989, no. 22, p. 110; P. C. Marani, *Leonardo. Una carriera di pittore*, Milan 1999, pp. 145, 340.

The Zenith of the Dynasty

Pontiffs

Annamaria Giusti

The fortunes of the Medici family, which at the end of the 15th century seemed miserably on the decline, found renewed and lasting strength in the 16th century. Florence had again become a free Republic in 1494, but it no longer enjoyed the international reputation it once had at the time of Lorenzo the Magnificent. Moreover, all of Italy had suffered a general political decline and become the battleground between the two powers of France and Spain.

In Florence, however, the arts maintained a very high level due to the presence of prestigious artists such as Michelangelo, Leonardo and Raphael. They were in turn surrounded by a multi-faceted and lively artistic environment.

In Rome, Cardinal Giovanni de' Medici who had a strong influence on the Pope, occupied himself with securing the return of the Medici to Florence. Due to an alliance between the Pope and Spain, the Florentine Republic had to capitulate and accept the return of the Medici to their palace on Via Larga. Their supremacy became even more guaranteed when Giovanni de' Medici became Pontiff a year later.

In 1513, Giovanni de' Medici became Pope Leo X. Like his predecessors, Leo X took an active part in the military and political conflicts that afflicted Italy, but at the same time, continuing the family tradition, he was animated by a great passion for art and culture which translated into a princely patronage. In fact it was under his pontificate that Rome consolidated its pivotal artistic position in Italy and that Raphael completed the decoration of the *Stanze* at the Vatican. To fund the completion of St. Peter's Basilica, Leo X issued indulgences that promised in exchange for gifts of charity to the church, the years of penalty in purgatory after death would either be reduced or abolished altogether. The reaction against the sale of these indulgences culminated in the Reformation in Germany and its separation from the Church of Rome in 1517 led by Martin Luther, who Leo X attempted to oppose through excommunication and charges of heresy.

In 1521, Leo X died, and after a brief Flemish papacy, it would be another Medici to assume the pontificate: Leo X's cousin, Cardinal Giulio became Pope Clement VII in 1523. He too became involved in the hostilities between France and the Hapsburg Emperor Charles V. The latter successfully advanced his troops towards Rome, despite the efforts of Giovanni dalle Bande Nere, a Medici himself, who died in battle. In 1527, Rome was sacked and occupied by the Imperial Army; even the goldsmith, Benvenuto Cellini, made his services available to the Pope for the defense of Rome. Florence, meanwhile, had taken advantage of the papal misfortune in Rome and again distanced the Medici, however in 1529, Pope Clement VII reached an accord with the Emperor that would lay siege to Florence. Michelangelo participated in the defense of Florence, but the city capitulated after 10 months and the Medici were reinstated. In the meantime, Clement VII had approached the French king and in 1533, the alliance was ratified, again with a personal benefit to the Medici, through the marriage of Clement VII's niece, Caterina de' Medici with the second son of Francis I, Henry of Orleans. Clement VII died the following year shortly after the schism between Rome and the Church of England under Henry VIII.

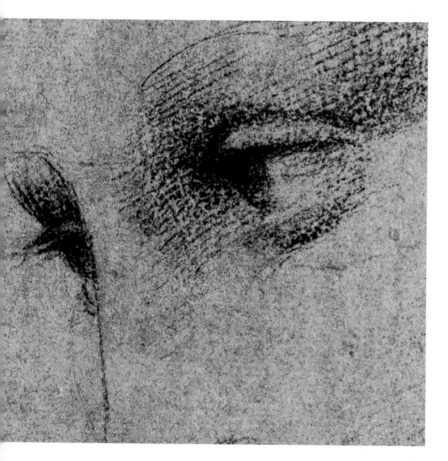

Raffaello Sanzio
(Urbino 1483 - Rome 1520)

STUDY OF A FEMALE HEAD
1509 - 1511 ca.
Black pencil, 26,7 x 20,9 cm
Florence, Museo Horne, inv. no. 5643

The drawing is unanimously recognized as a preparatory study for the head of Clio, the Muse of History and Fame, painted with her sisters seated around Apollo, who is playing a modern lyre, in the *Parnassus* fresco in the Room of the Apostolic Signature in the Vatican Apartments, originally the private library of Pope Julius II, painted between 1509 and 1511.

The original use of the room is evident in the decorative scheme that links Parnassus, where ancient and modern poets are portrayed such as Homer and Sappho, Virgil and Dante, Petrarch and Boccaccio, and the *Disputation of the Blessed Sacrament* with its reference to theology and the *School of Athens*, a potent and magnificent evocation of classical thought and philosophy.

While several of the poses of the Muses clearly seem to be influenced by classical statuary, the female face here, although idealized, is drawn with skillful hatching creating a chiaroscuro that models the form seeking a sculptural effect, and seems to have been drawn from life. It is in fact quite different from the head in the final fresco which has a sharper and more stylized outline, while the hair looped in a knot in the drawing, is tied with a ribbon in the fresco.

The work is authentic evidence of Raphael's wonderful ability to bring the glories of classical art back to life in his work with an understanding of philological relationships and, at the same time, an interpretative skill that made him the favorite artist of Julius II and Leo X.

So pleased was Raphael with this study that he re-used it, as noted by Shearman, in the face of a mother with a child in the *Miracle of the Lame Man* in one of the cartoons for the tapestries of the *Acts of the Apostles* housed in the Victoria and Albert Museum in London. (A.C.)

Bibliography: A. Petrioli Tofani in *Raffaello a Firenze*, Florence 1984, no. 32, p. 340 (with previous bibliography).

Domenico Casini (Florence 1580 - 1660)
Valore Casini (Florence 1590 - 1660)

PORTRAIT OF LEO X
1628
Oil on canvas, 230 x 168 cm
Cerreto Guidi, Museo Storico della Caccia e del Territorio, inv. no. 4258

In the month of April, 1628, the two brothers, Domenico and Valore Casini, consigned five portraits of personages belonging to the Medici family to the *Guardaroba*, for placement in a hall in the Pitti Palace. The portrait of Leo X is essentially derived from that painted by Raphael in 1518, now conserved in the Uffizi. Cardinal Giovanni de' Medici, son of the Magnificent, attained the papal throne under the name of Leo X on March 11, 1513. The Medici, who had regained rule of Florence in 1512, could hardly have wished for anything better, and the city celebrated the

event with great enthusiasm. Leo X proved to be an enlightened patron both in Rome, where he had Raphael working for him, and in Florence, where he demonstrated particular interest in the Church of San Lorenzo and in the family villa at Poggio a Caiano. The need to raise money to finance the great artistic undertakings in Rome, induced the Pope in 1515 to issue the famous bull on indulgences (according to which the faithful would receive a reduction of punishment for their sins in exchange for their confession and a sum of money). This resulted in the harsh reaction of Martin Luther, to which Leo X replied in 1520 with a threat of excommunication. The Pope's death by pneumonia in 1521 left the difficult inheritance of the war against Protestant reform to his successor. (E.C.)

Bibliography: K. Langedijk, *The portraits of the Medici*, Vol. II, Florence 1983, p. 1402; A. Cecchi, A. Natali, C. Sisi in *L'officina della maniera*, Florence 1994, pp. 32-36; S. Bertelli in *Leone X e Clemente VII* in *Giovanni dalle Bande Nere*, Florence 2001, pp. 43-101.

Luca di Andrea della Robbia
called **Della Robbia the Younger**
(Florence 1475 - 1548?)

EMBLEM OF LEO X
1520 ca.
Glazed terracotta, diameter 120 cm
Rome, Museo Nazionale di Castel Sant' Angelo,
inv. no. 563/IV

The terracotta panel is part of a series of "devices" of Cardinal Giovanni de' Medici (Florence, 1475-1521), son of Lorenzo the Magnificent, who became Pope in 1513 with the name of Leo X. The papal name is referred to by the grand lion's head, framed by the Medici symbol of a large ring with a diamond, the family device adopted by the Medici since the time of Cosimo the Elder. Although Luca della Robbia had often worked in the Vatican for the pope, this terracotta was commissioned by a member of the curia, monsignor Eurialo Silvestri da Cingoli, who used it to decorate a wall in the garden of his Roman villa near the Basilica of Maxentius. (A.C.)

Bibliography: F. Petrucci in *L'Officina della Maniera*, Florence 1996, no. 61, pp. 202-203.

Italian

RING OF LEO X
16th century
Silver, diameter 2,1 cm, height 3,5 cm, weight 23 gr
Iscribed: "LEO. X. P. M."
Rome, Vatican City, Biblioteca Apostolica, Museo Sacro,
inv. no. 2094

This large silver ring bears the Medici arms on one side, and the inscription "LEO.X.P.M." on the other, thus suggesting its connection to Pope Leo X. Presumably it was once enriched by a now missing stone. Despite the fact of its unknown origin, the ring may be identified as a type diffused throughout Italy since the 15th century, although the usage of a ring as symbol of papal dignity goes back to the first centuries of Church history. Papal rings were not obliged to follow any fixed pattern, although they were usually mounted with gems different from those found on bishops' or cardinals' rings, and were inscribed with symbols allusive to the pontifical heraldry, for example St. Peter's keys. (E.C.)

Bibliography: F. Kampf, *Hochrenaissance im Vatikan*, Bonn 1998, p. 445.

Lucas Cranach the Elder (and workshop)
(Kronach 1472 - Weimar 1553)

PORTRAIT OF MARTIN LUTHER
PORTRAIT OF CATERINA VON BORA
1529
Oil on panel, 36,5 x 23 cm each
Florence, Galleria degli Uffizi, inv. no. 1160

The initials and date on the work are proof that the Uffizi portrait of Martin Luther is one of the many made in the workshop of the famous German painter and engraver, Lucas Cranach, who arrived at the court of the Saxon princes from Wittenberg in 1505. Working for his entire life at

the service of the newly reformed ideas, he made numerous portraits such as this of Martin Luther (1483-1546), seen here with the portrait of his wife, Caterina von Bora. Doctor of Theology and Professor of Biblical exegesis at the University of Wittenberg, Luther, through the development of the concept that mankind cannot achieve salvation by good actions but only through Divine Providence, also arrived at invalidating the principle behind the selling of indulgences, excogitated by Pope Leo X mainly for financial purposes. Leaving aside the theological and doctrinal aspects, the result was that opposition to the Reformation took on a prevalently political nature, in the form of a clash between Pope and Emperor, with Clement VII and Charles V as protagonists. (E.C.)

Bibliography: Gli Uffizi, Florence 1979, p. 229.

Bulla contra errores Martini Lutheri z sequacium.

Pope Leo X
(Florence 1475 - Rome 1521)

BULLA CONTRA ERRORES MARTINI LUTHERI ET SEQUACIUM
1520

Paper manuscript, 4°, cc. (11), 20,5 x 14 cm
Florence, Biblioteca Nazionale Centrale, Palatino Misc. 4.E.I.16

The bull issued by Pope Leo X against Martin Luther attests to the discord between Lutheran reformists and papal authority.
The Lutheran doctrine soon was known in Florence. In fact, already at the beginning of the 1520's, Cardinal Giulio de' Medici, afterwards Pope Clement VII, was aware of what was happening in the north through the exchange of frequent correspondence with a legate to the Diet of Worms. Considering the close ties between the Medici and the papal court, Florence mainly feared the political consequences of the diffusion of Luther's ideas, while tending to consider the theological questions secondary. In Florence, the doctrines proclaimed by Luther were often connected to the austerity of the followers of Fra' Savonarola, although historically no such connection ever really existed between these essentially different experiences. Even Clemente VII, in a bull of October 27,1530, associated Savonarola and his followers to the Saxon monk and to the religious movement which was causing the schism of the German territories. (E.C.)

Bibliography: M. Firpo, *Gli affreschi di Pontormo a San Lorenzo,* Turin 1997, pp. 339-349.

Florentine or Milanese

CHALICE WITH MEDICI ARMS AND CARDINAL'S HAT
Early 16th century
Gilt copper and silver, embossed, chiseled and decorated with niello
ornaments, height 22 cm, base diameter 13,8 cm
Iscribed on the node "HOC FACITE IN MEAM COMMEMORATIONEM"
Florence, Museo dell'Opera di Santa Maria del Fiore,
inv. no. S.B.A.S. FI 09/00227651

Domenico Casini (Florence 1580 - 1660)
Valore Casini (Florence 1590 - 1660)

PORTRAIT OF CLEMENT VII
1628
Oil on canvas, 230 x 168 cm
Cerreto Guidi, Museo Storico della Caccia e del Territorio
inv. no. 4257

The chalice, whose style still refers to Gothic models, was previously
attributed to a Florentine goldsmith; recently, instead, on the basis of the
shape of the cup, the decorations and the type of *niello*, it has been
connected to a Milanese workshop. The Medici arms, showing traces of
enamel, appear surmounted by a cardinal's hat on one of the medallions on
the base (the other two represent a half figure of the Virgin and Child and
a *Pietà*). This indicates that the chalice was commissioned by Giulio de'
Medici, at the time of his bishopric in Florence between 1513 and 1523.
Cardinal Giulio, very closely bound to his cousin Leo X, took care of the
pontiff's financial and judicial interests in Florence and succeeded in
regaining the friendships lost by the Medici at the time of the nephew of
the Magnificent. Cardinal Giulio gained the papal throne as Clement VII in
the month of November, 1523. (E.C.)

The openly anti-Medici faction which arose in the Roman pontifical curia
after the death of Leo X, tried with determination to impede the election
of Cardinal Giulio, cousin of Leo X and natural son of the brother of the
Magnificent, Giuliano. Only on November 17, 1523, after the brief papacy
of Adriano VI, did Giulio succeed in becoming pontiff under the name of
Clement VII. As Pope, he was determined to maintain the conquests made
in the name of the State of the Church by his predecessors, while also
favoring his family's interests in Florence. Although he had claimed being
Charles V's candidate for election to the papacy, he did not hesitate in later
betraying the Emperor, by siding against him with Francis I, King of
France, in the Holy League of 1526. The conquest and sack of Rome
carried out by Charles V in 1527, forced Clement VII to recognize the
Emperor's authority, although in exchange he succeeded in obtaining the
return to Florence of the Medici, who had been previously driven out of
the city by the Imperial allies. (E.C.)

Bibliography: L. Becherucci, G. Brunetti, *Il Museo dell'Opera del Duomo a
Firenze*, Milan 1969-70, p. 225; G. Cantelli, *Storia dell'oreficeria e dell'arte
tessile in Toscana dal Medioevo all'età moderna*, Florence 1996, pp. 164,
188; D. Liscia Bemporad, *Gli Orafi di Santa Maria del Fiore* in *Alla
riscoperta di piazza del Duomo in Firenze*, Florence 1997, Vol. VI, p. 104.

Bibliography: K. Langedijk, *The Portraits of the Medici*, Vol. II, Florence
1983, pp. 1364-1365.

Casa Pirota, Faenza

PLATE WITH CLEMENT VII CROWNING THE EMPEROR CHARLES V
1530 ca.

Majolica, diameter 26,4 cm, height 5,5 cm
Bologna, Museo Civico, inv. no. 984

The verso of the plate is decorated with a grotesque motif traced only with an orange outline. A turquoise-colored inscription on the base reads: "FATO IN FA/ENZA IN CAXA/ PIROTA".
On the recto is the crowning of Charles V by Pope Clement VII, an event which took place in Bologna in 1530. The iconography derives from a

drawing by Domenico Beccafumi, which has in turn been taken from the fresco painted by Pinturicchio between 1502 and 1506 in the Piccolomini Library in the Duomo of Siena, representing *Enea Silvio Piccolomini kneeling before Pope Eugenio IV.* Charles V, betrayed by the Pope's alliance with Francis I and the Holy League, who made war against him in 1525, decided to attack Rome, setting the city under siege which culminated in the devastating Sack of 1527, while the consequence of these events in Florence was the expulsion of the Medici. Only in exchange for aid in bringing the Medici back to Florence, did Clement VII finally consent in 1530 to crown Charles V Emperor of Italy, following an agreement reached in Barcellona in the month of June, 1529. (E.C.)

Bibliography: C. Ravanelli Guidotti, *Ceramiche occidentali del Museo Civico Medievale di Bologna,* Bologna 1985, p. 76.

Benvenuto Cellini
(Florence 1500 - 1571)

COIN WITH ALESSANDRO DE' MEDICI
("Testone" worth 40 soldi)
1535
Gilded silver, diameter 4 cm
Florence, Museo Nazionale del Bargello, inv. no. 378

This coin minted by Cellini manifests Alessandro de' Medici's desire to render the power he held over the city evident to all through the diffusion of his portrait. The profile of the Duke, shown beardless and with short, curly hair, appears on the front; on the rear, no longer is St. John the Baptist represented as on previous coins, but rather Sts. Cosma and Damiano, protectors of the Medici. According to Cellini, the coin met with the approval of the Duke, who had turned to the artist for models of highly artistic coins and medals able to correspond to the new heroic style in which Alessandro wished his image to be presented. (M.G.V.)

Bibliography: D. Trento, *Benvenuto Cellini*, Florence 1984, pp. 16-17; B. Paolozzi Strozzi, *Monete fiorentine dalla Repubblica ai Medici*, Florence 1984, p. 55, no. 104.

Benvenuto Cellini
(Florence 1500 - 1571)

AUTOGRAPH PAGE OF THE "LIFE" OF BENVENUTO CELLINI
1557 - 59
Paper manuscript, 31 x 24 x 13 cm
Florence, Biblioteca Laurenziana, Mediceo Palatino 2342

The original manuscript of the *Life,* partially written by Benvenuto Cellini's own hand and for the rest the work of two different copyists, is to be found in the Mediceo-Palatino Codex 2342, conserved in the Biblioteca Laurenziana. It is composed of 520 sheets, bound together subsequently. The artist's autograph pages include parts of folios 1a-10a and 464b-520, while all the others were dictated by Cellini to the young Michele di Goro, except for 461a-464a written by an unidentified hand. The work was begun in July, 1557, and Cellini himself gave the manuscript to his friend Benedetto Varchi, illustrious man of letters of the time, in April or May, 1559, while the first complete publication of the *Vita,* edited by Antonio Cocchi, dates from 1728. This autobiography of Cellini is complete up to the moment of its writing, and still remains an incomparable source of information, not only about the artist, but also about the period in which he lived and about his contemporaries, even though the author tends to present a quite biased version of facts, the truth of which remains highly questionable. The work's informal style, justified by the fact that it was dictated orally, lends a vivid flavor to the narrative even beyond its content already rich in anecdotes. (E.C.)

Bibliography: E. Camesasca, *Vita di B. Cellini,* Milan 1985; J. Pope-Hennessy, *Cellini,* Milan 1986, pp. 11-16.

Spanish

CASE BELONGING TO CLEMENT VII, CONTAINING TWO KNIVES, A SCRAPER, SCISSORS
16th century
Case: wood, parchment and leather; utensils: burnished steel, lenght of the case 17,3 cm
Rome, Vatican City, Musei Vaticani, inv. no. 1114

A scroll bearing the arms of the Medici combined with crossed pontifical keys may be seen on the main part of this cylindrical case, while "CLEMENS VII" and "PONT MAX" may be read on the edge of the lid.
The decorative elements and fragmentary inscription all point to Clement VII de' Medici as the owner of this case, a small practical item containing cutting instruments which the Pope probably carried with him during his travels. (E.C.)

Bibliography: F. Kampf, *Hochrenaissance im Vatikan,* Bonn 1998, p. 453.

Benvenuto Cellini
(Florence 1500 - 1571)

MEDAL OF CLEMENT VII
1534
Gilt silver, diameter 4 cm
Florence, Museo Nazionale del Bargello, inv. no. 6215

The medal portrays Pope Clement VII, shown in profile and clad in a richly embroidered cope closed with an oval button. The verso bears a female figure impersonating Peace, holding a cornucopia in her left hand and a torch in the right, as she is about to set fire to the arms placed before the temple dedicated to Janis, to which a male figure representing Fury is enchained.

The many documents pertaining to this medal testify to its importance and to the value attributed to it by the artist himself. Benvenuto Cellini narrates in his *Life* and in the *Treatises*, the story of its preparation and the technical details of its making. Coining was prepared in complete secrecy, after which the medal was stamped in gold, silver and brass. Cellini used a mechanical system of mintage which he called "by screw", capable of producing a very precise and uniform relief which greatly enhanced the refined modeling of the figures and the richness of detail. The artistic quality of the resulting medal was so high that it succeeded in exalting both the personage portrayed and his deeds; for this the Pope accepted it with great satisfaction and enthusiasm, and requested the artist to do another example with a different reverse, this time representing the episode of Moses drawing water from the rock. This medal with the new version on the reverse, which alludes to the digging of a well in Orvieto ordered by the Pope, was presented to Clemente VII in 1534, shortly before he died.

The making of the Clement VII medal is subsequent to Benvenuto Cellini's earliest work experiences with the papal mint, for which he had prepared dies for three coins between 1529 and 1530.

The fame acquired through these undertakings later brought Cellini to be engaged by Alessandro de' Medici in Florence, and by the King of France, Francis I. (M.G.V.)

Bibliography: A. Armand, *Les Medailleurs Italien des quinzième et seizième siecles*, Paris 1883, Vol. I, p. 149, no. 9; S. Barbaglia, *L'opera completa di Cellini*, Milan 1981, pp. 87-88, no. 9; J. G. Pollard, *Medaglie italiane del Rinascimento*, Florence 1984, p. 10; D. Trento, *Benvenuto Cellini*, Florence 1984, pp. 10-14.

113

Venetian

RELIQUARY OF THE SAINTS COSMA AND DAMIANO
1400 ca.
Carved and faceted rock crystal, gilt silver, enamel, 44,4 cm
Florence, Museo delle Cappelle Medicee, inv. no. 95

The reliquary, which belongs to the treasury of the Basilica of San Lorenzo, has been deposited in the museum of the *Cappelle Medicee* (Medici Chapel) since 1945.

The exquisite rock crystal vase is faceted and slightly flared; two dragons form the handles, and on its top an eagle with spread wings is posed on the vegetable knot which terminates the little cupola. The mounting is similar to that of other precious objects which emerged from the manufactory operating in Venice around the year 1400.

The reliquary was donated to the Basilica in 1532 by Pope Clement VII, born Giulio de' Medici (1478-1534) following his decision to transfer all the relics gathered by Pope Leo X (Giovanni de' Medici, 1475-1521) during the second decade of the 16th century, to the Church of San Lorenzo in Florence. Leo X had acquired numerous relics in Greece and Constantinople, and had left some of them in the Florentine church during his visits to the city, enclosed in four precious rock crystal, amethyst and jasper vases. At least some of these vases, transformed for the occasion into reliquaries, were previously part of the treasury of Lorenzo the Magnificent (1449-1492), whose surviving pieces had come into the hands of Giovanni when he was Cardinal.

Clement VII also commissioned Michelangelo Buonarroti to make the ciborium for exhibiting the precious reliquaries, carried out in 1531 on the inner façade of the Basilica of San Lorenzo.

The passion of Lorenzo the Magnificent for stones, gems and cameos brought him to put together an immense collection of these objects, an actual treasure, which was unfortunately partially dispersed with the expulsion of the Medici from Florence. He desired having the most important pieces inscribed with his own name, showing both an extraordinary personal touch and a remarkable sense of history. His successors also cultivated this enthusiasm for "stones", culminating in the

opening of an actual manufactory dedicated to them, capable of reaching unrivaled heights: the Opificio delle Pietre Dure or semiprecious stone workshop – founded by Ferdinando I in 1588 – royal manufactory for producing works destined not only to the Florentine court, but also to be sent as precious gifts to courts throughout Italy and Europe. The workshop was called to carry out the monumental mausoleum for the Medici, with the purpose of amplifying the celebrative and dynastic aspects of the project initiated by Cosimo I. The chapel, conceived for a special site in one of the most important of the city's monuments, reserved a surprise for those who entered; that of being entirely covered with semiprecious stones. This place of mortality could thus also testify with unaltered splendor to the perpetual magnificence of the Medici dynasty. Francesco I had already been known to consider semiprecious stones, thanks to their vast range of "fantastic" and "magical" qualities, a perfect representation of that union between nature, art and science, towards which the late Mannerist cultural environment was always striving. Rock crystal, whose purity and transparency had made it one of the most esteemed materials since the Middles Ages, undoubtedly partook of this. Its rarity, capable of accentuating its symbolic valence, combined with its beauty and transparency made this material a preferred choice also throughout the 15th century. A material, therefore, whose very nature rendered it perfectly suitable for making vases designed to contain relics, or for the creation of other sorts of preciously and elegantly refined containers, of which the object exhibited here, designed for Lorenzo the Magnificent to use in a secular context, is an excellent example. (M.B.)

Bibliography: E. Nardinocchi in L. Bertani, E. Nardinocchi, *I Tesori di San Lorenzo*, Livorno 1995, p. 26.

The Zenith of the Dynasty

Queens of France

Annamaria Giusti

Caterina, born in Florence from the main branch of the family, was orphaned at a very young age and at the age of fourteen, was married to the second son of the King of France. Shortly after, the Dauphin died, and her husband became heir to the French throne. At the French court, Caterina enjoyed the support of the French king, but encountered much hostility towards her too, especially when the beautiful Diane de Poitiers, although twenty years his senior, became Henry's mistress. Henry tried to repudiate Caterina as sterile, although she had born 10 children. In 1547, upon the death of Francis I, she became Queen of France, although her husband Henry II was so involved in his love affair with Diane de Poitiers that Caterina was largely marginalized and mostly dedicated herself to her children. In 1559, at a tournament which was part of the wedding festivities of one of their daughters, Henry was pierced in the eye by a lance and died, leaving Caterina a widow at the age of forty. From then on until her death in 1589, Caterina exercised great influence in the affairs of France through her regencies of three sons, Francis II, Charles IX and Henry III who would all be king throughout a period of great internal strife and bloody battles between Catholics and Protestant Calvinists known as the Huguenots. If the energy and political wisdom of Caterina could not resolve the difficulties of France, the Queen did succeed in bringing to her adopted homeland benefits in the field of culture, fashion and art, proving herself a true Medici and dignified heir to her ancestors, Cosimo the Elder and the Magnificent.

Maria de' Medici was born in 1575 in Florence, daughter of Francesco I, second Grand Duke of Tuscany and Joanna of Austria. It was her uncle, Ferdinand I who in 1600, arranged her marriage with the French king Henry IV as part of a clever act of foreign politics linking the little Tuscan Grand Duchy to the major European centers of power. After the wedding by proxy, Maria set sail from Livorno with a huge dowry and many gifts for the French court which would testify to the magnificence of Florence. The ten years of her marriage were marked by the frequent and open infidelities of the King, whom Maria sincerely loved and to whom she had born five children. In 1610, when the King was murdered by a religious fanatic, Maria became regent for her young son, the future King Louis XIII. She was not particularly gifted as a regent and in fact was exiled by her son, once he had ascended to the throne. Her presence in France, however, was important to the arts which Maria, as a true Medici, loved and supported. She modernized the Parisian tapestry factory, which as the "Gobelins" reached its zenith during the subsequent reign of the Sun King, Louis XIV. She also expanded the Louvre and enriched its interiors. She engaged many artists for the decoration of the Palais du Luxembourg, particularly Pieter Paul Rubens, who remembering the favors granted to him by Maria, offered her hospitality during her last melancholic years of exile from France.

Anonymous

Portrait of Caterina de' Medici
1600 - 1610 ca.

Oil on canvas, 222 x 109 cm
Florence, Galleria degli Uffizi, inv. 1890, no. 4301

Caterina was born in Florence on April 13, 1519, the only daughter of the Duke of Urbino Lorenzo and Maddalena de la Tour d'Auvergne. Orphaned very young, she was educated by her paternal grandmother, Alfonsina Orsini, who took her to Rome in October, 1519, and by her uncle, Giulio, later to become Pope Clement VII. In 1525, she was sent back to Florence, and after the expulsion of the Medici (1527) was entrusted to the care of the nuns of the Murate convent. In 1533, she married Henry of Valois, who received the throne of his father (Francis I of France) in 1547, and died from wounds suffered in a joust in 1559. Following the death in 1560 of her first son, Francis II, Caterina assumed the regency in the name of her second-born son, Charles IX, maintaining her influence throughout his entire reign. She died on January 5, 1589, just a few months before the death of her third son, Henry III (1574-1589), last of the Valois kings.

This painting is a copy of another portrait of Caterina conserved in the Uffizi collection (inv. 1890, no. 2448), which in turn derives from an original made in France, today unidentified, and was presumably painted in Italy at the beginning of the 17th century. (M.B.)

Bibliography: S. Meloni Trkulja in *Gli Uffizi*, Florence 1980, Ic 937 p. 746; K. Langedijk, *The portraits of the Medici*, Vol. I, 1981, p. 350 nos. 17, 3a.

Florentine (?)

CATERINA DE' MEDICI, QUEEN OF FRANCE
1533 ca.

Onyx cameo mounted in gold and rubies; 3,1 x 2,6 cm (4 x 3,5 with frame)
Florence, Museo degli Argenti, inv. Gemme 1921, no. 116

Martha McCrory (1979) recognized in this cameo the likeness of Caterina, only daughter of Lorenzo de' Medici, Duke of Urbino and Maddalena de la Tour d'Auvergne, at fourteen years of age, that is at the moment of her marriage to Henry of Valois (1533). The young Caterina is dressed according to the fashion of her time: hair gathered back, and dress open at the neck to reveal a necklace of pearls. The profile is extraordinarily similar to the effigy of the French queen in a painting still to be found deposited in the Florentine Galleries (inv. 1890, no. 2448), in which she is portrayed in a sumptuous ceremonial dress, studded with pearls and diamonds and over-abundantly adorned with jewels and trimmings of lace and fur. Mario Scalini has recently made an observation which also corroborates the identification with Caterina; the bodice of the young lady displays a medallion with the image of St. Michael, emblem of the knightly Order founded by the Valois, which only a few elect members were permitted to wear.

Furthermore, the cameo arrived in Florence in the dowry of Cristina of Lorraine, grandchild of Caterina wed to Ferdinando I de' Medici in 1589. Various cameos are mentioned among the possessions inherited by Cristina, one of which is said to bear the "portrait of the queen Caterina as a young girl, with gold adornment", which might indeed be the one we see here, enclosed in an elegant gold frame enhanced by 29 rubies mounted with a "closed" setting. (M.Sf.)

Bibliography: C. Contu in *I gioielli dei Medici*, Florence 2003, p. 118, no. 57 (with previous bibliography).

119

Saracchi Workshop, Milan

JASPER FLASK IN THE FORM OF A SEASHELL, WITH THE HEAD OF A FEMALE MOOR IN THE CENTER
Before 1559
Jasper, sardonic, pearls, rubies, gold, enamel, and gilded metal (spout), 27,6 x 24,3 cm
Florence, Museo degli Argenti, inv. Gemme 1921, no. 705

The flask is in the form of a pair of coupled seashells, fastened together by a wide band of gold decorated with acanthus leaves and pearls; a cameo representing the head of a female Moor is set centrally, in a gold mount of scroll motifs with enamel decorations and rubies. The precious object appears for the first time in written documents in a list of Cristina of Lorraine's belongings dated 1600, together with four other vases for a total value amounting to 2050 *scudi*. It is subsequently easy to trace the object in the Medici inventories: we know that on November 23, 1609, after the death of Ferdinando, the flask was brought into the Galleria and then formally donated by Cristina in 1635, to her grandson and heir to the grand ducal throne of Tuscany, Ferdinando II.

The main theme of the piece is that of the seashell, connected with the French Royal House from an heraldic point of view, and present in the chain of the Order of St. Michael, founded by Louis XI in 1469, and further strengthened by Francis I and Henry II. This has been used in the past to support the hypothesis that it was a member of the French royalty to originally commission this luxurious object, perhaps Caterina herself or more likely her husband Henry of Valois. The date of the flask would have to be placed, however, before the French sovereign died from the injuries suffered in a jousting tournament in 1559. Mario Scalini has recently suggested that the double seashell form of the flask, which in the collar of the Order alludes to the parity between two knights, may be here re-interpreted in association with nuptial iconography, since Cristina of Lorraine made a gift of it to her grandson Ferdinando II, shortly after his marriage to Vittoria della Rovere (1634). (M.Sf.)

Bibliography: M. Scalini, in *Magnificenza alla corte dei Medici*, Florence 1997, p. 157, no. 118 (with previous bibliography).

AUTOGRAPH LETTER OF MARIA DE' MEDICI TO HER SISTER ELEONORA GONZAGA
1585

Ink on paper, 42 x 28,2 cm (opened)
Mantua, Archivio di Stato, Archivio Gonzaga,
Busta 1089, cc. 429, 430

The second Grand Duke of Florence, Francesco I de' Medici, arranged illustrious marriages for his daughters: Maria (1573-1642) actually became Queen of France by marrying Henry IV, while Eleonora (1567-1611) wed Vincenzo Gonzaga, Duke of Mantua. This letter confirms the lasting warmth the two sisters felt for each other: Maria, still unmarried in 1585, sends her best wishes to Eleonora for the birth of her first son Francesco, adding her own little affectionate and ingenuous sketch of a newborn baby. (E.C.)

Bibliography: K. Simon, *I Gonzaga*, Rome 1990, pp. 289-290.

Grand Ducal Workshops

DRAWINGS FOR JEWELS BELONGING TO MARIA DE' MEDICI, QUEEN OF FRANCE
End of the 16th century (?)

Pen and bistro on paper, 14, 4 x 20; 21,1 x 20,7;
30 x 21,2; 30 x 21,2 cm
Florence, Archivio di Stato, Miscellanea Medicea 18,
ins. 5, cc. 20-23

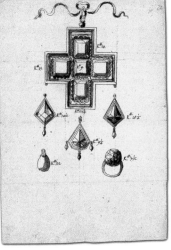

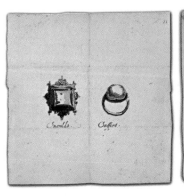

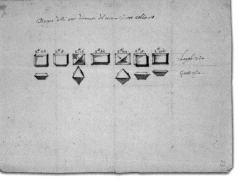

The drawings are inserted in a dossier which refers to the wedding of the daughter of Francesco I de' Medici, Maria, to Henry IV of Bourbon, celebrated in the month of October, 1600; it unites documents relative to negotiations, dowry agreements, preparations and celebrations, and chronicles of the event.
In the first drawing, the following pieces of jewelry are represented: a cross to be worn on the chest, composed of five different size diamonds - ranging from 9 to 21,3/4 carats - within an outline of semicircular motifs whose touches of color would derive from enamel inserts; three cut diamonds - two of which could be hooked to the cross - with small pearl pendants; a pendant with a pear-shaped pearl; a ring with a diamond in the form of a faceted sphere, set completely open to exalt its brilliance. The other two sheets show, respectively: the first, seven diamonds varying in size from 8 to 22 carats, two of which are cut to a point, the other five flat; in the second drawing, we see a pendant with an emerald set according to the taste typical of the 16th century, and a cabochon sapphire mounted in a ring.
All the gems have characteristics common to Florentine jewelry of the late 1500's, and since the court jeweler was then Jaques Bylivelt, it may not be excluded that he was also the author of these extraordinary drawings. (M.Sf.)

Bibliography: C. Contu, A. Martelli in *I gioielli dei Medici*, Florence 2003, pp. 122-123, no. 60 (with previous bibliography).

Santi di Tito (attributed to)
(Sansepolcro 1536 - Florence 1603)

PORTRAIT OF THE YOUNG MARIA DE' MEDICI
End of the 16th century
Oil on canvas, 60,5 x 45 cm
Florence, Museo dell'Opificio delle Pietre Dure, inv. no. 1033

This painting, mentioned generically as a portrait of "a Princess" is in an inventory of the Opificio collections dated 1789; the image is recognizable as that of the Princess Maria de' Medici, daughter of the Grand Duke Francesco I and Joanna of Austria. Her uncle, the Grand

Duke Ferdinando I, succeeded in arranging an illustrious marriage for this niece, wedding her to the King of France, Henry IV in the year 1600.
No regal attributes are represented, making it certain that Maria has been portrayed before her marriage. The young Princess is clad in a sumptuous brocade gown, embroidered with pearls and trimmed with the finest ornate lace. This type of dress was customary in the late 1500's, a period in which the stitched lace collar became fashionable in Florence, as did the hairstyle gathered up from the nape of the neck and crowned with a twig of pearls. (A.G.)

Bibliography: A. Giusti in A. Giusti, P. Mazzoni, A. Pampaloni Martelli, *Il Museo dell'Opificio delle Pietre Dure a Firenze*, Florence 1978, p. 333.

Santi di Tito
(Sansepolcro 1536 - Florence 1603)

PORTRAIT OF HENRY IV OF FRANCE
1600
Oil on canvas, 66,5 x 53 cm
Florence, Museo dell'Opificio delle Pietre Dure, inv. no. 1034

The painter Santi di Tito consigned this canvas in July, 1600, to the creator of polychrome stone inlays for the grand ducal workshop, Francesco Ferrucci, as a model for making a portrait in the semiprecious stone technique known as *commesso in pietre dure*. Ferrucci, who had already produced a similar portrait of Cosimo I de' Medici two years

earlier (see page 144), completed the task of portraying Henry IV in three months' time. Maria de' Medici was thus able to bring it with her as a gift for her promised husband when she left for France in the month of October, as an example of the rare capabilites of the Florentine semiprecious stone manufactory.

While the inlaid stone portrait of the King of France has since been lost, we still are able to admire its painted model, conserved as was customary in the grand ducal workshop. (A.G.)

Bibliography: A. Giusti in A. Giusti, P. Mazzoni, A. Pampaloni Martelli, *Il Museo dell'Opificio delle Pietre Dure a Firenze*, Florence 1978, p. 317; A. Gonzàlez Palacios, *Il gusto dei Principi*, Milan 1993, p. 303; A. Giusti, *Guida al Museo dell'Opificio delle Pietre Dure di Firenze*, Venice 1995, p. 24.

Follower of Santi di Tito

PORTRAIT OF MARIA DE' MEDICI
1601ca.

Oil on canvas, 192 x 109 cm
Florence, Galleria Palatina, inv. 1890, no. 2421

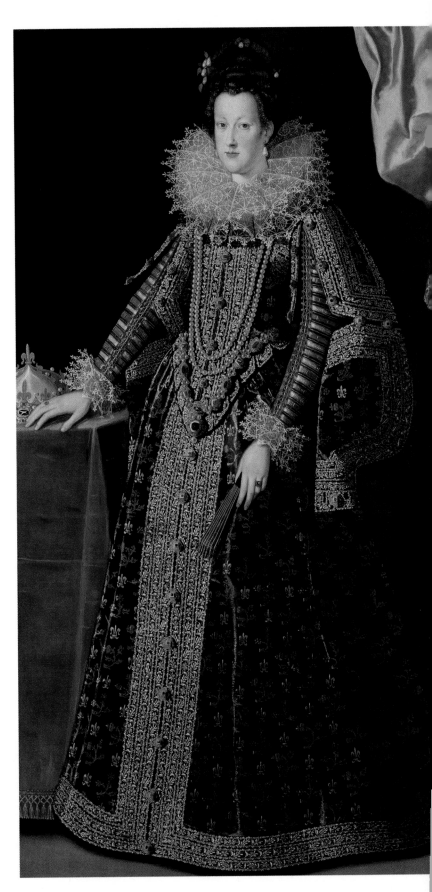

Maria de' Medici, daughter of Grand Duke Francesco I and Joanna of Austria, was born on April 26, 1575. After she was orphaned by the death of her mother in 1578 and that of her father in 1587, Maria's education was taken over by her uncle, Ferdinando de' Medici and aunt, Cristina of Lorraine. The negotiations for marrying her to Henry IV of Bourbon, King of France and of Navarra, were concluded in 1600 and on November 17th of that year, Maria embarked on a ship in Livorno towards Marseilles from where she proceeded to Lyons to meet her future husband. Six children were born from this union. After the death of her husband, who was assassinated in Paris on May 13, 1610, Maria was nominated guardian of her first-born child, the future King Louis XIII. After many episodes of contrast between mother and son, Maria was expelled from Paris in 1631, and first went in exile to Belgium, then to England from 1638 to 1641, and lastly, to Köln where she died on July 4, 1642.

This portrait has been identified by Karla Langedijk as the one for which Santi di Tito received payment on September 6, 1601: "A natural-size painting on canvas portraying Queen Maria of France by Santi di Tito" (ASF, *Gurdaroba medicea* 236, ins.4, c. 325), inside a frame made by Matteo Nigetti, for which he seems to have been paid on the following 18th of January: "for the making of a walnut ornament with its poplar framework of the same size and quality as the ones in the gallery fitted on the big paintings of the House of the Medici, putting into it the portrait of the Queen Maria de' Medici of France, painted by Santi di Tito, to be hung in the Gallery, together with the others" (ASF, *Guardaroba medicea* 228 ins. 6, c. 589). While it is certain this portrait is the painting referred to, it is also certain that it was the done in the workshop, as Lisa Goldenberg Stoppato has communicated orally to me. In any case Maria was portrayed at a moment very close to her royal wedding (1600): she in fact appears clothed in regal garments, wearing a rich dress decorated with the fleurs-de-lis of France and with the crown placed on a table to her right. The jewelry worn by the queen is exquisitely fashioned: a long double necklace of pearls, pear-shaped pearl earrings, pearls to ornament her hairdo, together with an unusual "little plume" (a cluster of pear-shaped pearls fastened to a gold twig), two rings, a sumptuous belt or collar of gold with precious stones set into it. The presence here of pearls, a gem always linked to the feminine universe and womanly virtues, and which in later portraits of the Queen would tend to increase in number (see those painted by Frans Pourbus II), seems to suggest that the jewelry itself might have been part of the dowry given by the family to the young bride. Even more so because many other ladies of the Medici house were portrayed in the same years or immediately afterwards with similar adornments. It is also known that Ferdinando I gave to his niece Maria, as a gift for her marriage, a collar composed of fourteen enameled parts decorated with diamonds, perhaps similar to the one she is seen wearing in this portrait. (M.B.)

Bibliography: K. Langedijk, *The Portraits of the Medici*, Vol. II, Florence 1983, pp. 1248-1249, nos. 86,16; for comparison, see M. Sframeli in *I gioielli dei Medici dal vero e in ritratto*, Florence 2003, pp. 120-127, 146-151.

Torrini Jewelery

FORK WITH MEDICI COAT OF ARMS
Modern

Silver, AR 0018
Florence, Torrini Collection

Caterina de' Medici, wedded to Henry of Orleans in 1533, is traditionally thought to have been the first to introduce the use of the fork in the banquets held at the French court. The fork shown here, decorated with a Medici coat of arms, represents a modern hypothesis about what forks probably looked like in Florence at the time of Caterina. It has been handmade in Florence by the Torrini Jewellers, on the basis of various period models, several of which are conserved in the national museum of the Bargello. (E.C.)

Anonymous
(French or Florentine?)

OUTDOOR BANQUET FOR HENRY IV OF FRANCE AND HIS FAMILY
1610 ca.
Oil on canvas, 97 x 102 cm
Nantes, Musée des Beaux Arts, inv. no. 755

Described in the catalogues published by the museum of Nantes as by an unknown 17th century French artist, and attributed by Benoist (1953) to the descendant of Niccolò dell'Abate, Nicolas Labbé, who died in 1637, the painting testifies to the usage common in Florence during the 16th and 17th centuries, to represent salient moments or episodes relative to the families of important personages connected to the Medici for political reasons. The canvases painted for funerals, marriages and baptismal events, which used to adorn the Medici parish church (in other words the Basilica of San Lorenzo) or the Duomo of Florence during celebration of religious rites, should be interpreted in this key. There are still numerous surviving examples of paintings coming from this type of pictorial cycle, such as the monochromes painted for the funerals of Philip II of Spain (1598), of Henry IV of France (1610), and of Margherita of Austria (1612); or the polychrome ones done for the matrimony of Cristina of Lorraine and Ferdinando I de' Medici (1589), and still others of the same

sort designed to foster the idea of the wedding as a significant aspect of Medici dynastic politics.

Not only may we not exclude, but it is even probable that Maria de' Medici exported this usage to France when she became the wife of Henry IV in 1600. In this painting, she is portrayed with her husband, the Dauphin (the future Louis XIII, who died in 1643), and her daughter Elisabeth of Bourbon, Princess of France (1602-1644), attending an outdoor banquet together with the court, perhaps in the forest of Fontainebleau, where elegantly dressed gentlemen may be seen as they bear silver plates to the table. The scene, of which two other small versions are known (Merson, p. 67, no. 6), testifies to the refined life led by Queen Maria de' Medici at the court of France, into which she had introduced chefs and servants brought with her from Florence, thus expanding Florentine tastes beyond the Alps (see for this the volume by Sara Mamone, *Firenze e Parigi due capitali dello spettacolo per la Regina Maria de' Medici*, Milan 1987). (M.B.)

Bibliography: O. Merson, *Inventaire général des richesses d'art de la France*, Paris, n.d (1883); *Catalogue des objets composant le Musée Municipal des Beaux-Arts*, Nantes 1876, no. 977; *Ville de Nantes. Musée Municipal des Beaux-Arts*, Paris, 1903, no. 167, p. 56 ; M. Nicolle, *Ville de Nantes. Musée Municipal des Beaux-Arts. Catalogue*, Nantes 1913, pp. 281-282; L. Benoist, *Ville de Nantes. Musée des Beaux-Arts*, Nantes 1953, p.128 no. 755; *Les Français et la table*, Paris 1986, no. 164, p. 193.

The Zenith of the Dynasty

Grand Dukes of Tuscany

Annamaria Giusti

Cosimo I, Founder of the Dynasty.

In 1529, the Medici had returned to Florence due to the alliance between the Pope and the Hapsburg Emperor, and in 1531, the illegitimate son of Pope Clement VII, Alessandro came to power. In 1532, Alessandro obtained absolute power after he was able to abolish the institutions of the Republic by a special Imperial order.

In 1537 however, Alessandro was murdered by his cousin Lorenzino, who had tricked him into an ambush on the pretext of an amorous encounter. The Florentine supporters of the Medici called for the young son of Giovanni dalle Bande Nere, Cosimo, descendant of a secondary branch of the Medici family which stems from the brother of Cosimo the Elder. The ascent to power of Cosimo is of fundamental importance to the history of the family, but also to the history of Florence. Under Cosimo, the republican institutions disappear completely while the family becomes a hereditary monarchy.

The oppostion to the Medici from a number of illustrious Florentine families was swiftly silenced, and in 1530 Cosimo re-enforced his power through his arranged marriage with Eleonora of Toledo, daughter of the Viceroy of Naples and Deputy of the Emperor Charles V. Through this important liaison, Cosimo intended to realize some of his own ambitions. In fact, one of his plans was to gradually conquer all of Tuscany, in which he was successful through armed force and his alliance with the Emperor. In Florence, meanwhile, Cosimo moved from the Medici Palace on Via Larga to Palazzo Vecchio, historic symbol of the government of Florence. Soon however, Palazzo Vecchio turned out to be inadequate both as a residence for the large family of Cosimo (Eleonora had born ten children) or as a place for the international court to which Cosimo aspired. In the mid 16th century, the palace left incompleted by the Pitti family a century before, was purchased and regally restored. In 1570, Cosimo was able to realize his greatest ambition, receiving the title of Grand Duke granted to him by the Pope and recognized by the major states of Europe. In an attempt to further the link between the House of the Hapsburgs and the Medici, another political success was achieved through the marriage arranged in 1565 between his son and heir, Francesco and Joanna of Austria, daughter of the reigning Emperor and sister of the future one. During his last years, Cosimo I, who died in 1574, effectively handed power over to his son.

Francesco I, Prince of the Arts and Sciences.

More than for his government, which in fact was of little interest to Francesco I de' Medici, Francesco is remembered for his patronage of the arts and sciences and for his notorious love affair. Even prior to his marriage to Joanna of Austria, Francesco had fallen in love with the beautiful Venetian Bianca Cappello after once seeing her behind a window. She and her husband had fled Venice, escaping the opposition of her noble family to their marriage. The love affair between Francesco and Bianca Cappello began in 1563 and lasted for the rest of their lives. After the death of Joanna of Austria in 1578, Francesco officially married Bianca despite opposition from the court and in particular from his brother, Cardinal Ferdinando. So much so that Ferdinando, heir to the throne, was suspected in the death of the Grand Duke and Bianca; in October 1587 both died within eleven hours of each other at their preferred residence of Villa Poggio a Caiano.

GRAND DUKES OF TUSCANY

Raised at the refined court of his father, Francesco surpassed Cosimo in his passion as a patron and collector. In his private residence in San Marco, he received artists who often worked under his direction producing very sophisticated and exclusive works such as ceramics that rivaled Chinese porcelain, vases of the purest rock crystal, intarsia in a fantastic chromatic range of the rarest precious stones, chests decorated with gems, antique cameos and goldsmithery in which the ingenuity of invention equaled the technical and material quality. With Francesco, Florence reaffirmed its leading position in the field of the decorative arts, a distinction that would endure until the end of the Medici dynasty, becoming a model recognized and imitated internationally. Also under Francesco, a keen interest was established in research into the natural world which would bear rich and varied fruit in the next century.

Ferdinando I, Good Government, the Grand Duchy and the Arts.

In Ferdinando, the political calling of his father and the exquisite artistic taste of his brother seemed to merge. Of particular influence on Ferdinando for the arts was his stay in Rome as a cardinal, where he acquired a prestigious collection of antiquities and contemporary works for his residence at the Villa Medici. At the death of his brother in 1587, Ferdinando left his ecclesiastic career in order to ensure the continuity of the dynasty; he succeeded his brother in Florence and married Cristina of Lorraine, descendant from the French royal family with whom Ferdinando wanted to consolidate relations.

Upon the arrival in Florence of Cristina, favorite granddaughter of Caterina de' Medici, great festivities were held. Although the marriage was arranged, it was a happy union of which nine children were born. The economy was less flourishing than in the past, but Ferdinando turned out to be an excellent governor and was able to reinvigorate agriculture and textile manufacturing through various initiatives. He also empowered Livorno, which due to the Grand Duke's efforts became a cosmopolitan city and the largest harbor in Italy after Genova. From here the military fleet of the *Ordine dei Cavalieri di Santo Stefano* (Order of the Knights of St. Stephen), originally from Pisa, set sail with the mission to counter Turkish raids which constantly threatened commerce in the western world.

Government however, did not curb Ferdinando's passion for the arts; it was he who, in 1588, founded the famous grand ducal manufactory of hard stones, the Opificio delle Pietre Dure which turned Florence into the lasting and undisputed leader in the field. One of the objectives for which the manufactory was founded was the ambitious project to realize a grand, dynastic mausoleum, conceived as a jewel case covered in precious stones. Other treasures made at the manufactory or acquired by Ferdinando were exhibited at the Tribune, the octagonal room in the center of one of the long galleries in the Uffizi intended by Francesco I as a showroom for the most important items of the Medici collections.

DV·X·ALESADER·P·M·

Baccio d'Agnolo (Florence 1462 - 1543)
Giorgio Vasari (?) (Arezzo 1511 - Florence 1574)

COAT OF ARMS OF DUKE ALESSANDRO DE' MEDICI
1534 ca.
Carved wood, painted and gilded, 165 x 155 cm
Florence, Museo Nazionale del Bargello, inv. no. 13

The Medici arms, supported by two cupids with cornucopia, decorated with two cherubs' heads and surmounted by a ducal crown with three colored feathers, are those of Duke Alessandro de' Medici (Florence 1510-1537), as indicated by the painted inscription "Dux Alesander Primus". Alessandro was believed to be the natural son - later legitimized - of Lorenzo de' Medici, Duke of Urbino, though it is more likely he was the illegitimate son of Giulio de' Medici, the future Pope Clement VII. He ruled Florence for only six years from 1531 to 1537 when he was assassinated by his cousin, Lorenzino.
The arms can most probably be identified as those carved in 1534 by this famous wood sculptor with the collaboration of Vasari for the Great Hall of the Palazzo della Mercanzia (Merchants' Palace). (A.C.)

Bibliography: A. Cecchi in *L'Officina della maniera*, Florence 1996, no. 150, pp. 396-397.

Florentine

GOLD COIN OF COSIMO I
Mid- 16th century

Gold, diameter 4,1 cm
Florence, Museo Nazionale del Bargello, inv. no. 910

Cosimo I, subsequent to his conquest of power and after being nominated duke in 1537, strove to increment the Florentine economy through the creation of a modernized monetary system. A new gold *scudo* bearing the Medici arms substituted the previous one, and the gold *piastra*, valued ten *scudi*, was coined perhaps more for reasons of prestige than for commercial needs. The *piastra* presented here is an example of the second minting of the coin, with the right profile of Cosimo dressed in his armor on the obverse and a decorated cross on the reverse, which followed the first coin minted with only the shield and cross.

Coinage is attributed to Pietro Paolo Galeotti, pupil of Cellini who worked for the Florentine Mint. (M.G.V.)

Bibliography: B. Paolozzi Strozzi, *Monete fiorentine dalla Repubblica ai Medici*, Florence 1984, p. 63.

Anonymous
(Florentine)

VIEW OF PIAZZA SIGNORIA WITH FIREWORKS ON ST JOHN'S DAY
1605 - 1630

Detached fresco, 193 x 229 cm
Florence, Museo di San Marco, Cat. 1904, no. 16

The fresco shows a view of Piazza Signoria during the display of fireworks given to celebrate the festival of St. John the Baptist, patron saint of the city. As well as illustrating the kinds of entertainment held for the occasion (still celebrated today, though with different events) the fresco provides important documentary evidence of the arrangement of the piazza at the beginning of the 17th century. The same viewpoint as that of the famous *Ordeal of Savonarola*, painted at the close of the 15th century, is used showing the relevant changes to the piazza. At the back

of the square, paved in terracotta, the Tribunale della Mercanzia (Merchants' Court) can be seen, with Palazzo Uguccione on the left, and the Loggia dei Lanzi and the Uffizi on the right. As well as the monument to Cosimo I by Giambologna, in front of Palazzo Vecchio are Michelangelo's *David*, the *Neptune Fountain* by Bartolomeo Ammannati, *Hercules and Cacus* by Bandinelli and, below the Loggia, *Perseus* by Benvenuto Cellini and the *Rape of the Sabine Women* by Giambologna. This last statue was placed in the Loggia in 1582 thus giving us a preliminary dating for the fresco, though it could be dated between 1605-30, when Alessandro Marzi Medici was Archbishop of Florence as his coat of arms once surmounted the fresco. It was originally located above the fireplace in the main hall on the first floor of the Archbishop's Palace, which stands behind St. John's Baptistery. It was removed in 1894 before the palace was partially demolished as part of a ruinous program for the renovation of Florence's old center which was completed that year. (M.S.)

Bibliography: M. Sframeli, *Il centro di Firenze restituito*, Florence 1989, p. 409.

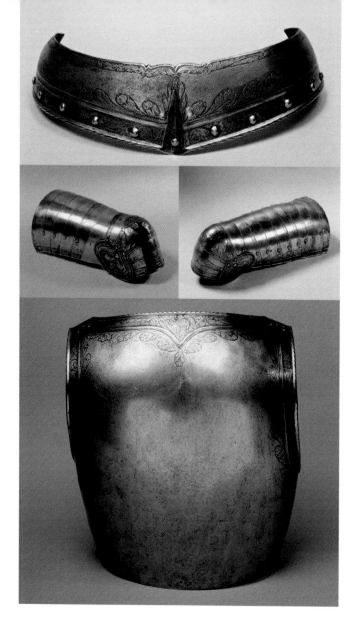

Jorg Seusenhofer (armorer)
(Innsbruck, documented between 1528 and 1580)
Leonhard Meurl (engraver)
(Innsbruck d. 1547)

FOUR ELEMENTS OF THE LIGHT HORSEBACK CORSELET OF COSIMO I DE' MEDICI: FAULD PLATE, BRASSARDS WITH CUBITIERES, BACK PLATE

Steel
Museo Nazionale del Bargello, inv. nos. M 972 and M 1489-1490, M 1570

The objects exhibited are part of the suit of armor worn by Cosimo I in the half-figure portrait painted by Bronzino in 1539. This soberly refined suit of armor was suitable for use both on foot and on horseback, thanks not only to its light weight but also to technical features which allowed adjustment of the length of the tasset plates. It was the result of the skilled work of the famous armorer Seusehenofer of Innsbruck, who had already worked for the Imperial court of the Hapsburgs, while its decoration was the work of the engraver Meurl (see the angel heads on the elbow pieces), who used methods usually encountered only in the Tyrolese milieu. The most illustrious predecessor of Cosimo I as a man of arms and warrior, was undoubtedly his father, Giovanni dalle Bande Nere, the renowned military leader who requested to be buried in just such a light weight corselet. (E.C.)

Bibliography: M. Scalini, *Armature da Cosimo I a Cosimo III de' Medici*, Florence 1990, pp. 14, 16; M. Scalini in *Opere d'arte della famiglia Medici*, Milan 1997, pp. 111-112.

Baccio Bandinelli
(Florence 1493 - 1560)

EQUESTRIAN STATUE OF COSIMO
1545 ca.
Bronze, base in walnut with gilded profiles and hard stone inlays, heigth 27,5 cm
Florence, Museo Nazionale del Bargello, inv. no. 275 B

The bronze statuette represents an equestrian figure of Cosimo I, holding the rod of command in his right hand. Horseman and horse both turn their heads toward the right; the rider in a martial pose upon the horse which proceeds in a tranquil way.

This small sculpture may perhaps be connected in some way to a project for an equestrian monument which the artist supposedly proposed to the attention of Duke Cosimo. The project however seems to have never been carried out, apparently to avoid the reaction of those among the Florentine citizens still favorable to the Republic, who would not have appreciated such a self-celebrative gesture on the part of the Duke of Florence. Brought to the Bargello in 1865 from the Medici collections, this sculpture with its wooden base inlaid with hard stones reveals the taste typical of the collections of bronze statuettes belonging to Cosimo I, later inherited by Francesco I, who moved them to the Casino of San Marco. The passion for this type of sculpture "in miniature", which the princes greatly appreciated and sought after for their private collections, actually dates from an earlier period, that of Lorenzo the Magnificent.

As far as the artist responsible for this work, an attribution to Giambologna, although recently re-proposed (Becker 1995, pp. 60-61), does not seem entirely convincing. His style, rich instead in references to classical statuary - as can be seen in the bronze monument to Marcus Aurelius - and the pose chosen for this statuette of the prince, which is that of his official portrait, seem closer to the work of an artist such as Baccio Bandinelli. This sculptor was employed at length by Cosimo, not only in the making of bronze portraits, but also on larger, more important marble sculptures, such as the equestrian statue of Giovanni dalle Bande Nere in piazza San Lorenzo in Florence. Bandinelli seems to have been in the habit of modeling small figures for casting in bronze, in order to try them out before actually undertaking the final large-scale sculptures. (M.G.V.)

Bibliography: U. Becker in *Von allen Seiten Schon*, Bonn 1995, pp. 60-61; F. Vossilla in *Magnificenza alla corte dei Medici*, Florence 1997, p. 148; D. Heikamp in *Magnificenza alla corte dei Medici*, Florence 1997, pp. 347-348.

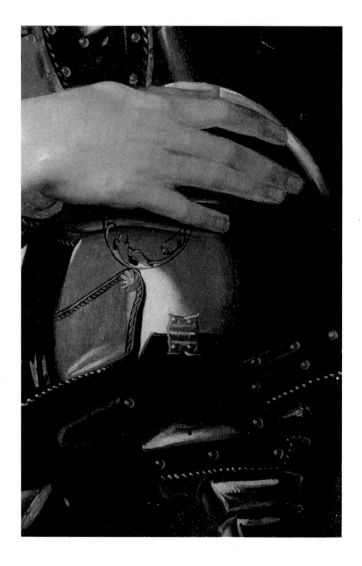

Agnolo di Cosimo called **Agnolo Bronzino**
(and workshop)
(Florence 1503 - 1572)

PORTRAIT OF COSIMO I IN ARMOR
1550 ca.
Oil on panel, 114 x 89 cm
Florence, Museo degli Argenti, inv. 1890, no. 8739

The painting is one of some twenty-five similar works mainly produced by Bronzino's workshop to be used as state portraits, based on a prototype, now in Sydney, dated 1544. This showed a three-quarters figure of the Duke "*armato tutto d'arme bianche e con una mano sull'elmo*" ("fully armed with swords and with his hand resting on a helmet") (Vasari, 1878-1885, Vol. VII, p. 598) standing by a trunk from which springs a laurel branch, an emblem of the Medici, with the motto "Uno avulso non deficit alter" (Though one is removed, there is yet another) signifying that the continuity of Medici governance of Florence was ensured by Cosimo after the assassination of Duke Alessandro in 1537.

Here and in the portrait now in the Tribune in the Uffizi, the Duke is portrayed armed to emphasize his committment to defend the state from external enemies, in the conflict that would only end with the fall of Siena in 1555. (A.C.)

Bibliography: E. Baccheschi in *L'opera completa del Bronzino*, Milan 1973, no. 54; K. Langedijk, *The portraits of the Medici*, Vol. I, Florence 1981, p. 417, nos. 27, 28.

Giovanni Maria Butteri
(active Florence, second half of the 16th century)

VIRGIN AND CHILD WITH SAINT ANNE AND MEMBERS OF THE MEDICI FAMILY AS SAINTS
1575

Oil on panel, 192 x 140 cm
On the scroll held by Saint John: "Ecce Agnus Dei"; inscribed on Saint Catherine's book is the date "AD/MCL/XX/V"
Florence, Cenacolo di Andrea del Sarto, inv. 1890, no. 3402

Acquired by the State from the collection of Prince Odescalchi, this unusual painting portrays a *Sacra Conversazione* (Holy Conversation), in which members of the grand ducal family represent the various saints. This includes personages who had died some time earlier, such as Eleonora of Toledo who died in 1562, here portrayed as the Virgin, or Saint Cosmas, interpreted by Grand Duke Cosimo I who had died a year before the painting was undertaken. Others were still alive, such as Grand Duke Francesco I who succeeded his father in 1574, here seen as Saint George, Cardinal Ferdinando is Saint Damian, and their sister, Isabella de' Medici, who would die a year later on July 16, 1576 at the Medici villa of Cerreto Guidi, is Saint Catherine of Alexandria. Her husband, Paolo Giordano Orsini, Duke of Bracciano, is perhaps Saint Torpè bearing a standard with the cross of Pisa (?).

The attribution of the painting to Butteri, suggested by Langedijk (1968 and 1980), is reliably based on comparisons with other works known to be by the same artist, such as *Christ with the Centurion,* one of the few paintings of Vasari's circle to have survived the fire in Santa Maria del Carmine, and *The Discovery of Glass* belonging to Francesco de' Medici's *Studiolo* (Study). It is more difficult however to establish who commissioned this rare and unusual Medici *Sacra Conversazione.* The pre-eminence of Isabella in the foreground as Saint Catherine would suggest she was the client, also as her husband, Paolo Giordano Orsini, would have had little interest in requesting a painting with the portraits of his wife's relatives, either alive or dead. (A.C.)

Bibliography: L. Berti, *Il principe dello studiolo*, Florence 1967, no. 5; L. Bertani Bigagli in *Gli Uffizi*, Florence 1979, no. P314, p. 192; K. Langedijk in *Palazzo Vecchio*, Florence 1980, no. 573, p. 289 (with previous bibliography).

Tuscan

DRESS OF ELEONORA OF TOLEDO
1550 - 60 ca.
Red silk velvet, 149 x 161,1 cm
Pisa, Museo Nazionale di Palazzo Reale, inv. no. 1545

Recovered only a few years ago from storage in the museum of San Matteo in Pisa, the dress has been identified as the one worn by Eleonora of Toledo in the famous painting in which Bronzino portrays her with her son, exhibited since 1995 in the national museum of the Palazzo Reale in Pisa. The conservation of the dress was assured by the fact that it was adapted for re-use, as frequently occurred, on a wood sculpture of an Annunciated Virgin, since lost but once in the Convent of San Matteo, adjacent to Cosimo de' Medici's earliest residence in the city of Pisa. After the initial restoration which involved only the fabric itself, conservation has been continued for this occasion on the dress itself, recovering the train which had been folded and stitched under the hem of the skirt during its adaptation for use on the religious statue. Further confirmation that the gown did indeed belong to Eleonora comes from the discovery of 16th century notes in the *Ricordanze Generali* of the *Guardaroba*, which list the purchase of crimson velvet and other materials which would have been necessary for its making. The dress is in fact made of crimson red silk velvet, a color which the sumptuary laws in effect in Florence in 1562, and in Pisa from the year after, reserved only for princes and nobility. The cut and materials are those used by the refined dressmakers working in Florence, while only after 1588, under the rule of the Grand Duke Ferdinando, did production of silk and other sorts of sophisticated textiles also develop in Pisa. Velvet was the cloth that tailors working for the ducal court used most, and the constant need for fabric resulted in significant purchases of it, which the court tried to distribute among the numerous Florentine manufactories, as a means of sustaining the city economy.

The brief annotations of the Medici *Guardaroba* demonstrate that Eleonora, who became Cosimo's wife in 1539, was particularly careful in choosing the textiles necessary for the family's clothing and for household fittings. Florence, one of the most important centers in Europe for clothing textiles, was certainly able to offer a selection of these capable of satisfying whatever might be the duchess' desire. Although her personal taste naturally inclined towards a certain degree of luxury, perhaps inherited from her Spanish origins, caution (reflected in Cosimo's emanation of the sumptuary laws) induced her to avoid exceeding in ostentation, especially in a moment when the principality was finally consolidating its power after years of crisis and republican government. It is difficult to imagine in what Eleonora's wardrobe exactly consisted, or how long she kept her clothes, or even how often she was in the habit of changing her dress. She seems to have possessed clothing suitable for any occasion, although in a rather limited range of colors, since she preferred tones that were neither too bright nor too somber: white, grey, a golden brown (tané). Red was definitely the brightest color she was known to wear. Embroidery (made by Antonio Bachiacca, brother of the painter Francesco), trimmings, and fringes of gold and silver thread enlivened the garments. We may thus deduce that this crimson red dress was meant to be worn on official occasions. (E.C.)

Bibliography: R. Landini, *L'amore del lusso e la necessità della modestia* in *Moda alla corte dei Medici*, Florence 1993, pp. 35-45; M. Burresi, *L'abito della Granduchessa*, Pisa 2000; K. Aschengreen Piacenti in *L'ombra del genio,* Florence 2002, pp. 37-38.

Agnolo Allori called **Agnolo Bronzino** (Workshop of)
(Florence 1503 - 1572)

THE AILING ELEONORA
1556
Oil on panel, diameter 75 cm
Florence, Museo Bardini, inv. no. 1476

There are numerous portraits of Eleonora (1522-1562) from Bronzino's workshop, often copies made by pupils from an original by the master, who had also frescoed the private chapel of the Duchess in Palazzo Vecchio. Eleonora had begun since the early 1550's to show signs of the

tuberculosis which would later be the cause of her death, but this did not stop her from continuing to be present at official events and from traveling at her husband's side. The 1562 inventory of the *Guardaroba* confirms the fact that during the later years of her life, Eleonora was accustomed to wearing dresses made of plain silk, adorned however with splendid decorations (in this case pearls), and although weakened by illness, she still appears in this portrait as elegant as ever. (E.C.)

Bibliography: K. Langedijk, *The Portraits of the Medici*, Vol. I, Florence 1981, pp. 693-694; G. Lazzi, *La moda alla corte di Cosimo I de' Medici* in *Moda alla corte de' Medici*, Florence 1993, p. 29; A. Petrioli Tofani in *Il primato del disegno*, Florence 1980, p. 85.

Domenico di Polo
(Florence 1480 ca. - 1547)

SEAL OF DUKE ALESSANDRO, LATER SEAL OF DUKE COSIMO I
1532 ca.

Quartz, partially gilded and enameled silver, height 9,1 cm
Inscribed on the mounting around the stone: "COSMUS. MED. R. P. FLOREN. DUX. ET. EIUS. CONSILIARII".
Florence, Museo degli Argenti, inv. Bargello, no.1917 (II) 30.

The quartz seal is engraved with a figure of Hercules, mythical hero symbolically associated with the Florentine council and republic since medieval times, and from the second half of the 15th century, the symbol of the Medici. The commission by Cosimo the Elder, or more probably his son, Piero the Gouty, for Antonio Pollaiolo to reproduce some of the *Labors of Hercules* is evidence of this, though they were later lost. The small panels by Pollaiolo in the Uffizi portraying *Hercules and the Hydra*, and *Hercules and Antaeus* recall the originals and were recorded in the Gondi Collection at the beginning of the 17th century.

Milanesi identifies it as the (in Vasari, 1568, ed.1878-1885, vol.V, p. 384, note 1) "quartz engraved with a Hercules for a seal of the palace", for which, on 27 October 1532, 105 *lire* were paid to the engraver and medal maker Domenico di Polo, official artist of the Florentine mint under Dukes Alessandro and Cosimo de' Medici (ASF, *Deliberazioni degli Operai di Palazzo,* 15, cc. 26v.-27r., cfr. Frey, 1909, p.137, nos. 257-258, which gives the inventory number as 25, and indicates sheets 26-28; see Fox, 1991 on Domenico di Polo).

The seal was made for Duke Alessandro (Florence 1512-1537), who ruled Florence briefly between 1531 and 1537. He was succeeded by Cosimo after his assassination in 1537, and the Medici emblem or ring with three colored feathers, repeated three times on the fine, elaborate handle refers to him. Engraved on the mounting are a yoke, emblem of Pope Leo X, the ring with a diamond and the three feathers again, and an emblem that is not identifiable as it is superimposed by a Medici coat of arms surmounted by a ducal crown. This was presumably done when the new Duke Cosimo adopted the seal as his own and had it inscribed as can still be seen today, though he also made use of other seals, identifiable in the wax stamps of Cosimo's documents housed in the Florentine State Archive. (A.C.)

Bibliography: G. Milanesi in *Vasari*, ed.1878-1885, vol. V, p. 384, note 1; K. Frey, *Studien zur Michelangelo Buonarroti und zur Kunst seiner Zeit* in "Jahrbuch der Koniglich Preussichen Kunstsammlungen", Beiheft, XXX, 1909, p.137, nos. 257-258; S. P. Fox, *Domenico di Polo* in *Dizionario Biografico degli italiani*, Rome 1991, 40, pp. 659-661 (with previous bibliography).

Francesco Ferrucci
(active Florence, late16th - early 17th century)

PORTRAIT OF COSIMO I DE' MEDICI
1598

Polychrome stone inlay, with wood and semiprecious stone frame, 50 x 65 cm
Florence, Museo dell'Opificio delle Pietre Dure, inv. no. 1370

The workshop specialized in making semiprecious stone inlays was founded in 1588 by Ferdinando I de' Medici, and from the start specialized in producing elaborate creations through the combination of various pieces of stone as if in a sort of puzzle. The resulting objects may almost be considered paintings made of stone, using a technique capable of rendering a great variety of themes, including portraits of important people. Among these, we find Pope Clement VIII, the King of France Henry IV (see page 124), and the founder of the Medici dynasty, Cosimo I, whose portrait we see here. The work, which is composed of different varieties of marble coming from various areas of the Tuscan Grand Duchy, was commissioned in 1598 by the son of Cosimo, Ferdinando I de' Medici. The artist called upon for this task was the specialist in inlaid stone, Francesco Ferrucci, who based his work on a model painted in oil for this purpose by Domenico Passignano, also conserved in the museum of the Opificio. The wooden frame with stone rosettes set in the corners is a 19th century addition. (A.G.)

Bibliography: A. Giusti in A. Giusti, P. Mazzoni, A. Pampaloni Martelli, *Il Museo dell'Opificio delle Pietre Dure a Firenze*, Florence 1978, p. 282; A. Gonzàlez Palacios, *Il gusto dei Principi*, Milan 1993, p. 303.

Florentine

CAMEO WITH A PROFILE OF COSIMO I DE' MEDICI
After 1546?

Agate, enameled gold, copper, 4,24 x 3,2 cm (with mount)
Florence, Museo degli Argenti, inv. Gemme 1921, no. 117

Cosimo is portrayed in profile, dressed in a suit of armor and with a mantle tied at the shoulder. The Duke is shown wearing the collar of the Order of the Golden Fleece, conferred to him by Charles V in 1546, which consecrated the authority of the Duke of Tuscany in his relations with foreign diplomacy, and was a form of recognition of the close ties maintained with Spain and the importance of his financial relationships.

The object comes from the Medici collections, where it was listed in inventories at the start of the 18th century. The gem is set in its splendid original enameled and pearled mount, with a pod motif ornamented strip. (M.Sf.)

Bibliography: C. Contu in *I gioielli dei Medici*, Florence 2003, p. 63, no. 4 (with previous bibliography).

Anonymous
(Florentine)

COSIMO I, SEATED IN GRAND DUCAL ROBE
16th - 17th century
Oil on canvas, 218 x 144 cm
Pisa, Museo di Palazzo Reale, inv. no. 4508

This painting is one of the many portraits, in this case posthumous, of Cosimo I de' Medici represented as Grand Duke, crowned and with the scepter in his left hand. Pope Pius V conceded the title of Grand Duke to Cosimo on August 27, 1569, an event that was formalized in a solemn investiture ceremony held in Rome on March 5, 1570. The ceremony took place in the Hall of the Consistory with thirty-three cardinals present and Cosimo clad in a gold-cloth garment and crimson mantle, ermine cape, and black velvet cap on his head. A crown was placed upon his head; given the newness of the title of Grand Duke, it had been specially made in Florence according to the Pope's precise indications (seventeen rays with the fleur-de-lis of Florence in the middle, and one of every two rays terminating in a smaller fleur-de-lis). This event marked the high point of the political success which Cosimo had constructed with such great ability over the years, and signified precedence over the other Italian states. After his death, which took place on April 21, 1574, the Emperor Maximilian signed the license which conceded the title of Grand Duke to the Medici dynasty. (E.C.)

Bibliography: K. Langedijk, *The portraits of the Medici*, Vol. I, Florence 1981, p. 410; K. Aschengreen Piacenti in *L'ombra del genio*, Florence 2002, pp. 33-41.

Giorgio Vasari
(Arezzo 1511 - Florence 1574)

VULCAN'S FORGE
1567 - 1568 ca.
Oil on copper, 38 x 28 cm
Florence, Galleria degli Uffizi, inv. 1890, no. 1558

This small painting on copper shows Minerva with compass and sextant in her right hand, presenting a design to Vulcan who is engraving Archelaus' shield with the zodiac signs of Capricorn, also the emblem of Duke Cosimo de' Medici, and Aries which refers instead to Prince Francesco, his son. In the background, on the left, rows of young men, protected by the Three Graces representing the Arts of drawing, painting, sculpture and architecture for which the *Accademia del Disegno* was founded in 1563, are intently copying from statues, vases and other drawings. On the right, others are following Vulcan's example of working metal. The composition is clearly intended to symbolize the close relationship between Invention - the outcome of intelligence translated into design - and Art in its technical and practical sense.

The painting was commissioned, with other small pieces by Prince Francesco de' Medici around 1567-1568 based on a series of "Inventions" by Vincenzo Borghini, the learned director of the *Ospedale degli Innocenti* (Hospital of the Innocent) and close friend of Giorgio Vasari, found in a manuscript preserved in the national library of Florence, and published by Scoti-Bertinelli (Cecchi, 1982).

A splendid preparatory drawing by Vasari of *Vulcan's Forge* is in the Louvre and a variation on the theme by Zucchi is in the Royal Library of Windsor. In the same series as this painting are the drawing for the *Age of Gold* by Vasari, also in the Louvre, and the painting of the same subject, realized at a later date by Poppi (Edimburgh, National Gallery of Scotland); a study by Vasari for *Cupid Hunting* (Louvre); the *Judgement of Paris* of which preparatory drawings by Naldini are in the Louvre and the Siena city library; a *Picture of Virtue and Fortune*, a bizzare and whimsical drawing by Zucchi in the Louvre; and lastly the *Allegory of Happiness* by Bronzino and *Hercules and the Muses* by Alessandro Allori, both in the Uffizi.

All these works, whether completed or only in the preparatory stage, are part of a program celebrating the Medici (the *Age of Gold* and *Hercules and the Muses*) and in particular extolling the virtues of Prince Francesco as in the *Judgement of Paris, Cupid Hunting, Virtue and Fortune* and also partly *Vulcan's Forge*, which exalts the patronage of Cosimo I of the arts, that his son would continue on coming to rule in 1564. (A.C.)

Bibliography: A. Cecchi, "*Invenzioni per quadri*" di Don Vincenzo Borghini in "Paragone", nos. 383-385, 1982, pp. 89-96; L. Privitera in *Magnificenza alla corte dei Medici*, Florence 1997, no. 147, p. 191, (with previous bibliography).

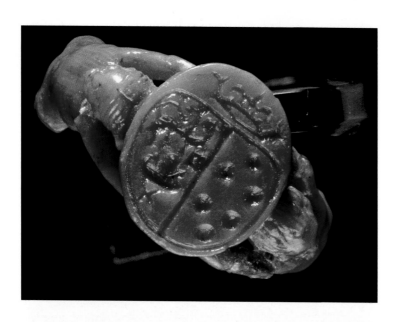

RING WITH THE ARMS OF THE MEDICI AND CAPPELLO FAMILIES
Second half of the 16th century
Coral, diameter 2,7; arms 1,45 x 1,25 cm
Florence, Museo degli Argenti, inv. Gemme 1921, no. 350

The joined arms of the Medici and the Cappello families, surmounted by the grand-ducal crown and held up by a pair of telamons, is proof that the ring belonged to Bianca Cappello, the beautiful Venetian lady beloved by Francesco I de' Medici, who he married in 1578 after the death of his wife Joanna of Austria. The ring has always been conserved in the Medici collections, and is cited in documents since 1638, year in which it was in one of the closets in the Tribune of the Uffizi. (M.Sf.)

Bibliography: C. Contu in *I gioielli dei Medici*, Florence 2003, p. 95, no. 28 (with previous bibliography).

Tommaso d'Antonio Manzuoli called Maso da San Friano
(San Friano 1536 - Florence 1571)

PORTRAIT OF FRANCESCO I
1570
Oil on panel, 176 x 129 cm
Prato, Museo Civico, inv. no. 1747

Payments to Maso tell us that he made this painting in Buontalenti's workshop, where he worked. A preparatory drawing for this panel, with the detail of the head of Francesco, is also known. Francesco I is portrayed full-length seated in an armchair, while a scepter, crown and a female allegorical figure (Tuscany?) may be seen on a table in the background. This portrait conveys a personal and intimate vision of Francesco, who is seen placing his right hand over his heart, which seems to reflect Francesco's personality to perfection. This son of Eleonora and Cosimo I, who took over a great part of internal affairs the same year his father was crowned Grand Duke (1570), had a temperament which was instead fundamentally that of a scientist and patron. He is in fact most well known for such undertakings as the creation of a foundry and other artistic laboratories; the most celebrated of his initiatives is the *Studiolo* (Study) in Palazzo Vecchio. (E.C.)

Bibliography: K. Langedijk, *The portraits of the Medici*, Vol. II, Florence 1983, p. 869; L. Berti, *Il principe dello studiolo*, Florence 1967, p 36.

Florentine

VENUS
Second half of the 16th century
Bronze, height without the base 60 cm
Florence, Museo di Palazzo Davanzati, inv. no. 60

This bronze statuette recalls a marble Venus with a putto - the so-called Medici Venus - exhibited in the Tribune in the Uffizi. Already referred to as modern in the inventory of 1574, the statuette may have been the work of the sculptor Valerio Cioli, done in the year 1561.

Bronze statuettes, small bronze sculptures inspired by classical statuary, were widely diffused during the Italian Renaissance, and were sought after by collectors in Florence, as in northern Italy. The antique works of art and the numerous curiosities collected by Duke Cosimo I and his offspring were reproduced in numerous versions by Florentine artists of the period. This small *Venus* from Palazzo Davanzati is an example of this type of work. (E.C.)

Bibliography: L. Berti, *Palazzo Davanzati a Firenze*, Florence 1958, p. 215; F. Haskell, N. Penny, *Taste and the Antique*, London 1981, p. 325; A. M. Massinelli, *Bronzi e anticaglie nella Guardaroba di Cosimo I*, Florence 1991, pp. 100-106.

Anonymous
(Girolamo Macchietti ?)
(Florence 1535 - 1592)

PORTRAIT OF BIANCA CAPPELLO
1579 - 83 ca.
Oil on panel, 99 x 73 cm
Lucca, Museo Nazionale di Palazzo Mansi inv. no. 102

Bianca Cappello, first lover and then second wife of Francesco I de' Medici, was born in Venice in 1548. Upon arrival in Florence, she openly accompanied Francesco I — who was married to Joanna of Austria - bearing him a son, Antonio de' Medici, in 1576. The Grand Duke married Bianca in secret after the death of Joanna in 1578; this wedding was repeated in public in October, 1579. The Grand Duchess died on October 20, 1587, only one day after the death of Francesco I, both from a malarial fever they had contracted together.

In this portrait which derives from the grand ducal collections in Florence, Bianca appears wearing her wedding rings: it was therefore most likely made after her official wedding, but perhaps before the famous portrait conserved in Vienna (1585).

The painting has been recently associated with Alessandro Allori, and subsequently also to the Florentine artist Girolamo Macchietti, noted for having worked in the *Studiolo* (Study) of Francesco I de' Medici. Macchietti's style does in fact have noticeable affinities with this portrait from Lucca. (M.B.)

Bibliography: S. Lecchini Giovannoni in *Magnificenza alla corte dei Medici*, Florence 1997, p. 95, no. 54; L. Goldenberg Stoppato in *I gioielli dei Medici dal vero e in ritratto*, Florence 2003, pp. 91-93, no. 25.

Jean de Boulogne called **Giambologna**
(Douai 1529 - Florence 1608)

MERCURY
1563 - 1564
Bronze, height 56,2 cm
Bologna, Museo Civico, inv. no. 68

This figure of Mercury is universally attributed to Giambologna, supposedly made during the period when the artist was working in Bologna on the Neptune fountain; it is considered the model for a larger bronze statue, perhaps never made.

Pier Donato Cesi, Bishop of Narni and Nuncio in Bologna between 1560 and 1565, mentions the bronze statuette in a description of the Palazzo dell'Archiginnasio, seat of the University of Bologna, without making any reference to an author. The sculpture, which was most likely placed in the center of the palace courtyard, does not represent the running Mercury, as was usual when represented as a messenger of the gods, but is rather placed in a suspended, upwards-moving pose that concludes with the forefinger pointed towards the heavens.

This was the first version of a theme destined to have great fortune, and which Giambologna re-proposed in numerous variations and dimensions. A flying Mercury, ordered from Giambologna by Cosimo I de' Medici as a gift for the Emperor Maximilian II, brother of the intended bride of prince Francesco, his son, Joanna of Austria, has since been lost. Still existing, instead, is one of the most beautiful bronze statuettes of the subject, conserved in the state collections in Dresden (h. cm 61.9); it is mentioned

in an inventory of the Kunstkammer of Christian I in the year 1587, as a gift of Francesco I de' Medici. Other examples in Naples and Vienna are similar to this in style. Such works of art were often reproductions of famous originals on a smaller scale, but could also be totally original small sculptures. The princes commissioned them for their *studioli* (studies), particularly suited to housing collections of rarities and precious objects such as bronze statuettes.

One of the most lovely among the larger examples is that conserved in the Bargello. This sculpture derives from the Medici collections, and was used to decorate the fountain at Villa Medici in Rome until 1780. In comparison to this exemplar, the Bologna Mercury lacks the head of Zephyr, emerging as he blows his vigorous gust of wind from beneath the figure of the god, as well as the minute wings on heels and hat. Also partially missing is the rod Mercury holds in his right hand, of which only the handle remains. (M.G.V.)

Bibliography: H. Keutner, *Giambologna*, 1978, pp. 112-113; C. Avery, *Giambologna*, Florence 1987, p. 125; D. Pegazzano in *Magnificenza alla corte dei Medici*, Florence 1997, p. 151.

Egnatio Danti
(Perugia 1536 - Alatri 1586)

INSTRUMENT OF THE PRIMO MOBILE
1586
Brass, height 27,9 cm
Florence, Istituto e Museo di Storia della Scienza, inv. no. 2643

This instrument, otherwise called "Pietro Apiano's quadrant" from the name of its inventor, was used to calculate sines and cosines. The coat of arms of the Grand Duke, to whom Egnatio Danti dedicated the instrument, and the initials "F.E.D.P.F." are placed in the center of the border, which is divided into 90°.
In 1562, the Dominican friar of the Order of the Preachers, Egnatio Danti, painted the geographical maps which decorate the closets of the so-called Map Room in Palazzo Vecchio, later finished by Stefano Buonsignori. Astronomer and mathematician (he was also lector of mathematics at the Florentine Studio), in 1580 Danti participated as pontifical cosmographer in the reforming of the calendar ordered by Gregorio XIII, and directed the making of the geographical maps of Italy in the Vatican Gallery. He produced publications of relevant scientific value, and was responsible for the astronomical quadrant and the armillary on the façade of Santa Maria Novella in Florence, as well as the church's gnomon. It must have been Cosimo who prompted Danti to insist upon the analogy between Cosimo and Kosmos, with the intent of self-attributing the merits for having widened the boundaries of the known world. (E.C.)

Bibliography: M. Miniati, *Il Museo di Storia della Scienza*, Florence 1991, pp. 39, 44.

Anonymous

ARMILLARY SPHERE
1575
Brass, wood, diameter 17 cm
Florence, Istituto e Museo di Storia della Scienza, inv. no. 1104

The armillary sphere is an astronomical instrument formed of partially fixed and partially mobile rings or armills, arranged so as to represent the principal orbits which the Sun and stars appear to make around the Earth, if the instrument is based on the earth-centered Ptolemaic-Aristotelian concept, or vice versa, if the basis is the heliocentric Copernican one. Already known to the ancient Alexandrian astronomers, it was again introduced into Europe by the Arabs. See, for example, the armillary sphere similar to this one, represented in Tito Lessi's portrait of Galileo present in the exhibition. (E.C.)

Bibliography: M. Miniati, *Il Museo di Storia della Scienza*, Florence 1991, p. 40.

Stefano Buonsignori
(active Florence, second half of the 16th century - 1589)

SUNDIAL
1587
Wood, height 17 cm
Florence, Istituto e Museo di Storia della Scienza, inv. no. 2459

This type of timepiece, which functions through the projection of
the shadow produced by the gnomon onto a surface marked
with hour lines, was widely diffused among the scientific objects
to be found in the Medici court. The example of a sundial
presented here, decorated with miniatures, may be ascribed to
Stefano Buonsignori, given its similarity with other instruments
whose attribution to him is certain. In 1584, this monk of the
Olivetano Order, who finished the work begun by Danti in the
Map Room in Palazzo Vecchio, also prepared the first map in
perspective of the city of Florence, widely known and used until
the 17th century. (E.C.)

Bibliography: M. Miniati, *Il Museo di Storia della Scienza*, 1991,
pp. 40, 50.

Grand Ducal Workshops

CUP
1582
Jasper, diameter 7,5 x15 cm
Florence, Museo di Storia Naturale, Sezione Mineralogia, inv. no. 13505/4

The initials "F M", together with the date "1582", and the grand ducal crown on the base indicate that the cup belonged to the collection of Francesco I de' Medici, who ten years earlier (1572) had called to the Florentine court two expert semiprecious stone cutters from Milan, Gian Ambrogio and Gian Stefano Caroni, joined three years later by Giorgio di Cristofano Gaffurri. Francesco himself participated in the activities carried out in the workshops of the Casino di San Marco, such as the melting of rock crystal and the cutting of semiprecious and precious stones. Francesco gathered together the most important rarities contained in his collection in the Tribune of the Uffizi, that marvelous octagonal room with its mother-of-pearl dome, walls the color of red lacquer, floor of semiprecious stones, and plinth representing a marine backdrop, symbolic of the cosmos and all of its elements. It seems possible to identify this cup for the first time in the Tribune inventory of 1589. (M.Sf.)

Grand Ducal Workshops

SMALL CUP
16th - 17th century
Borage agate mounted in gilt and engraved silver,
3.5 x 8,5 x 7 cm
Florence, Museo di Storia Naturale, Sezione Mineralogia, inv. no. 13439/4

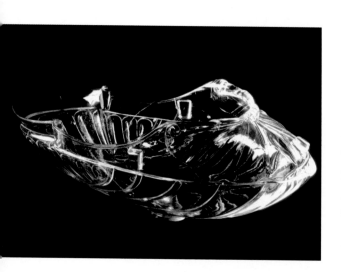

The cup, carved in an oval shape from a special variety of agate, was fitted with a gilt silver mounting in the middle of the 17th century; this adornment recalls and accentuates the form of the stone cup. The fretwork on the base and the foliage decorations on the handles, laced by cordon motifs, demonstrate the desire to update a certainly more antique semiprecious stone carving to a 17th century style. (M.Sf.)

Grand Ducal Workshops (?)

VASE
End of 16th century
Cut rock crystal, 12 x 35 x 21 cm
Florence, Museo dell'Opificio delle Pietre Dure, inv. O.D.A. Bargello cristalli, no. 19

Belonging to the Medici collections, this vase, without mounting, is one of numerous exemplars of vases in rock crystal, a material preferred by collectors of the 1500's and much appreciated for its clear transparency. Rock crystal is a quality of quartz that comes in hard and transparent blocks, often crisscrossed internally with whitish slivers. Artisans capable of working with it had to have the dual abilities to select pieces without imperfections and to cut and incise the resistant material. Workshops in Milan perfected the art of working with rock crystal, becoming in the 1500's the major suppliers of vases in elegant, bizarre forms, often enriched by opalescent incisions, commissioned by nobility and collectors throughout Europe. The Medici were also assiduous clients of the famed Milanese workshops of Saracchi, Miseroni and Annibale Fontana, but with the relocation to Florence of Caroni and Gaffurri, called to the court by Francesco I, the manufacture of vases in hard stones became a part of the production of the grand ducal workshops. Accordingly, it cannot be excluded that this vase, that through the simplicity of its modeling exalts the luminsoity of the material, was made in Florence. (A.G.)

Bibliography: A. Giusti in *Guida al Museo dell'Opificio delle Pietre Dure di Firenze*, Venice 1995, p. 22.

Opificio delle Pietre Dure, Florence

COPY OF AN INTERNAL ELEMENT OF A STIPO
Modern (1995)

Semiprecious stones, brass and wood, 34 x 74 cm
Florence, Museo dell'Opificio delle Pietre Dure, without inv. no.

The Florentine institution of the Opificio delle Pietre Dure as we know it today, is the direct descendent of the famous workshop founded by the Medici in the *Cinquecento* (1500's), dedicated to the production of imposing creations in semiprecious stones. This perfect copy reproduces an original work now in the museum of Mineralogy of Florence, dating from the second half of the 16th century. The copy was made in 1995, on the occasion of the renovation of the museum, and was meant to give an idea of the great manual dexterity involved, as well as of the reserves of rare and valuable stones still conserved today in the Opificio. The work is a flat rectangular piece originally fitted inside a now lost, free-standing *stipo* (cabinet), made of ebony and semiprecious stones. The taste expressed in the geometric outlay of this work, which is the only part of the cabinet still surviving, permits us to associate it to the period of Francesco I de' Medici. The evanescent luminosity of the background made of Oriental chalcedony, a translucent stone from India, enhances the bright colors of the semiprecious stone inlays. Fine strips of metal - gilt silver in the original and brass in the copy - function as a border and connecting element for the stone inserts. (A.G.)

Bibliography: A. Giusti, *Guida al Museo dell'Opificio delle Pietre Dure di Firenze*, Venice 1995, p. 22; A. Giusti in *Cristalli e Gemme*, Venice 1999, pp. 54-56.

Grand Ducal Workshops

COAT OF ARMS WITH THE FLEURS-DE-LIS OF FRANCE
16th century

Lapis lazuli and citrine quartz, 7 x 4,5 x 1 cm
Florence, Museo di Storia Naturale, Sezione Mineralogia, inv. no. 13149/4

Three fleurs-de-lis are set into an oval of splendid, intensely blue lapis lazuli. The yellow shade of the lilies made of citrine quartz is so bright that it suggests the use of an artificial means of obtaining it. It seems, in fact, that the stone may have been "heated" to achieve this golden tone.

The precious object must have been meant for one of the many Medici coats of arms made of semiprecious stones. The Medici arms were in fact modified in 1465 to include a sphere "of azure with three gold fleurs-de-lis", conceded by the King of France Louis XI to Piero de' Medici and to all his heirs and successors. This was an explicit recognition of the greatness of the Medici family on the part of the French royal house. Since then the heraldic iconography of the Medici coat of arms has been "gold, with five red balls, the upper one azure with three fleurs-de-lis of the prime sort added", as may be seen in all the arms made during the 16th century, the period to which this object belongs.

In 1704 this precious coat of arms was in the Tribune of the Uffizi, kept in one of the drawers of the cabinet of Ferdinando I, full of splendid objects - animal figurines, cups of semiprecious stones, scent-burners - each of which are described in the inventory of that year (Uffizi Library, Ms. 82). Entry no. 2192 of the inventory describes the coat of arms as "An oval of lapis lazuli s. 2.8 long and 1.8 wide into which three topaz lilies are set in relief, mounted in a copper setting, and with a strip of gold around it". (M.Sf.)

Bibliography: A. M. Massinelli, *Magnificenze medicee: gli stipi della Tribuna*, in "Antologia di Belle Arti", nos. 35-38 (*Studi sul Neoclassicismo II*), 1990, pp. 119, 131.

Anonymous (Florentine)

PORTRAIT OF FERDINANDO I DRESSED AS GRAN MAESTRO OF THE ORDER OF ST. STEPHEN
1608-1609 ca.

Oil on canvas, 201 x 115 cm
Pisa, Museo Nazionale di San Matteo, inv. no. 1499 (146)

Domenico Casini (Florence 1588 - 1660)
Valore Casini (Florence 1590 - 1660)

PORTRAIT OF CRISTINA OF LORRAINE
1620 ca.

Oil on canvas, 199 x 115 cm
Florence, Galleria degli Uffizi, inv. 1890, no. 2318

Ferdinando, born in 1549, was the ninth of the eleven children born to Cosimo and Eleonora of Toledo. Elected cardinal in 1563, he demonstrated great political capacities, as well as being a magnificent patron. It was he who constructed Villa Medici in Rome. Ferdinando was 38 years of age when Francesco I died, and since his brother had left no legitimate heirs, he then renounced the title of Cardinal to inherit that of Grand Duke as Ferdinando I. His marriage to Cristina of Lorraine in 1589 gave eight children to the dynasty. He founded the port of Livorno and increased the Tuscan naval forces, which under the *Ordine dei Cavalieri di Santo Stefano* (Order of the Knights of St. Stephen) freed the seas from the pirates which constituted a severe obstruction to maritime commerce.

He was a great and wise politician; he created the conditions by which Henry IV gained the French throne, and those for the matrimony of his niece Maria de' Medici (daughter of Francesco I) to the King of France.

Passionate lover of art and antiquities, he brought the pieces he had collected in Villa Medici in Rome with him to Florence, where he also founded the semiprecious stone workshop or Opificio delle Pietre Dure. He bought and renovated the Medici villas of Petraia, Artimino and Ambrogiana, before his death on February 7, 1609. Ferdinando I already appears quite old in this portrait, which probably depicts him near to the moment of his death; the Grand Duke was actually buried wearing the garments of *Gran Maestro* of the Order of St. Stephen. The work is by a Florentine painter of the early 17th century. According to Langedjk, the prototype of the painting may be identified in that numbered inv. 1890 no. 5104, although it seems more similar to an oval painting (published by the same historian) which was once the property of the Knights of St. Stephen, from which our painting seems to derive. (M.B.)

Cristina of Lorraine was born on August 6, 1565. Daughter of the Duke Charles II and Claudia of Valois, and grandchild of the Queen of France, Caterina de' Medici, she married the Grand Duke Ferdinando I de' Medici (1549-1609) on February 25, 1589, first by proxy in Blois, then making her solemn entry in Florence on April 30th. Great festivities celebrated this triumphal entrance, with decorative apparatus lining the streets of the city and in the principal churches, especially in the Duomo where the wedding took place (the original canvases used there still exist). Nine children were born from this marriage, five boys and four girls. After the death of her husband, she continued to be the wise advisor to her son, Grand Duke Cosimo II; upon his death (1621), she was named guardian, together with her daughter-in-law Maria Maddalena of Austria, of her grandson, Ferdinando II.

This full-length portrait derives from an original by Scipione Pulzone, in which the Grand Duchess is shown in a three-quarter representation down to her knees (inv. 1890 no. 9161). The painting is the work of Domenico and Valore Casini, painted in 1620, as Lisa Goldemberg Stoppato has kindly informed me. (M.B.)

Bibliography: A. Bellini Pietri, *Catalogo del Museo civico di Pisa*, Pisa 1906, p. 213, no. 8, K. Langedijk, *The Portraits of the Medici* Vol. II, 1983, pp. 722-723, no. 37, 11 c.

Bibliography: K. Langedijk, *The Portraits of the Medici*, Vol. I, Florence 1981, p. 660, no. 19 a; C. Caneva, R. Orsi Landini, M. Sframeli in *I volti del potere*, Florence 2002, pp. 44-46 no. 9; L. Goldemberg Stoppato, *Per Domenico e Valore Casini ritrattisti fiorentini* in "Mittelungen des Kunsthistorischen Insitutes in Florenz", 2004 (in print).

Florentine

"SAVONAROLA" CHAIR, WITH ARMS OF FERDINANDO DE' MEDICI AS CARDINAL
Second half of the 16th century
Carved walnut, partially restored, 68 x 68 x 58 cm
Florence, Museo Bardini, inv. no. 695

This chair, made according to the type called "Savonarola", has been connected to Ferdinando de' Medici (1549-1609), son of Cosimo I and Cardinal at only fourteen years of age, because of the presence on it of the Medici coat of arms surmounted by a Cardinal's hat. The "Savonarola" armchair, several examples of which date from the mid-1400's, reached a wide diffusion during the following century. Although in Florence it was usually rather severe in style, there are several examples, such as this one whose twelve slats meet in a rosette, which demonstrate refined, although sober decorations. "Savonarola" is a name invented in the 19th century, with the intention of underlining the Florentine nature of this piece of furniture. It seems in fact that several chairs of this sort were found in the cell of the monk, Savonarola.
This cardinal's chair comes from the collection of the antique dealer Bardini, and is not without restored parts, probably added in the 19th century. (E.C.)

Bibliography: M. Trionfi Honorati in *Palazzo Vecchio*, Florence 1980, pp. 211-212.

Ludovico Buti
(Florence 1550/60 ca. - 1606)

OPTICAL ILLUSION WITH PORTRAITS OF CHARLES II AND HIS DAUGHTER CRISTINA OF LORRAINE
1593
Oil on prismatic panels, glass, 81,5 x 112 cm
Florence, Istituto e Museo di Storia della Scienza, inv. no. 3197

This is one of the few known examples of a painted optical illusion, obtained by fastening a panel composed of painted triangular, prismatic strips of wood to a framework. The pieces are arranged so that a portrait of Charles II of Lorraine appears when the panel is observed from above, looking downwards, or one of his daughter, the Grand Duchess Cristina, wife of Ferdinando I de' Medici, if the object is viewed from below or using a special mirror. Karla Langedijk mentions a document which refers that Ludovico Buti received payment on February 26, 1592 (following the Florentine year, otherwise 1593; *Guardaroba Medicea 185,* ins.1, c. 54), for the painting of the portrait of Charles II on thirty seven strips of wood, and for that of Cristina of Lorraine done on paper (deriving the latter from the prototype in the series made by Scipione Pulzone for the court). The work was then consigned through the goldsmith, Jaques Bilivert to the Medici *Guardaroba*. This unusual object was evidently made after the sumptuous wedding between Cristina and Ferdinando I, which took place in 1589, perhaps ordered by Ferdinando I in honor of the Grand Duchess, who was distinguishing herself for her humanity and political ability. The painter, probably followed the instructions provided by the cartographer monk, Egnatio Danti, in his commentary on Vignola's work. (M.B.)

Bibliography: K. Langedijk, *The Portraits of the Medici* , Vol. I, Florence 1981, pp. 657-658, nos. 31, 14; M. Miniati, *Il Museo di Storia della Scienza*, 1991, p. 88, no. 53; S. Zanieri, *Un gioco ottico* in "Nuncius", 2000, pp. 665-670.

Grand Ducal Workshops

MEDICI-LORRAINE COAT OF ARMS
End of the 16th century
Polychrome marble inlay on white marble, 38 x 29 cm
Florence, Museo dell'Opificio delle Pietre Dure, inv. no. 262

This coat of arms in the form of a mosaic of precious polychrome marbles, is one of the first objects produced in the artistic workshop founded by Ferdinando I de' Medici in 1588. This type of workmanship was soon to become the pride and distinctive mark of the Florentine manufactory. Standing out vividly against the white marble oval, the lively colors of the inlaid stones form the coupled heraldic arms of the Medici and of the noble Lorraine family, to which belonged Cristina, wed to Ferdinando I in 1590. The relationship of Cristina to the French royal family is represented on the right by the royal arms of France, golden lilies in an azure field. Two cornucopias, a symbol of prosperity often connected to nuptial occasions, flank the couple's coat of arms, which is surmounted by the crown of the Grand Duchy of Tuscany.

The creation of this small, yet highly refined object was probably intended to celebrate a union destined to increase the prestige of the Medici family, and was perhaps designed for the altar of the family mausoleum planned by Ferdinando I towards the end of the 16th century, of which only a few dismembered pieces survive. (A.G.)

Bibliography: R. Przyborowski in *Splendori di pietre dure*, Florence 1988, p. 124; A. Giusti in *Magnificenza alla Corte dei Medici*, Florence 1997, p. 181; A. Giusti in *L'ombra del genio*, Florence 2002, p. 264

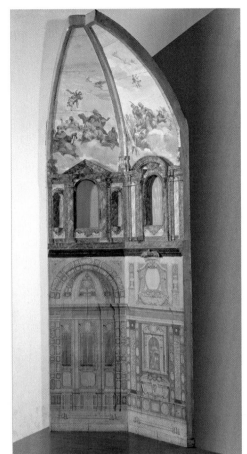

Matteo Nigetti
(Florence 1560/70 -1648)

PROJECT FOR THE ALTAR OF THE CAPPELLA DEI PRINCIPI
1602
Water color drawing on paper, 74,5 x 52 cm
Florence, Biblioteca Nazionale, Ms. Palatino 3.B.1.7, c. 57

Antonio Nicola Pillori
(Florence 1687 ca. - 1763)
Giovanni Filippo Giarrè
(active Florence, first half of the 18th century)

MODEL FOR TWO SIDES OF THE CAPPELLA DEI PRINCIPI
1743
Painting on wood and paper, 230 x 49 cm each side
Florence, Museo dell'Opificio delle Pietre Dure, inv. no. 2655

Ferdinando I de' Medici planned a small temple-shaped altar, entirely composed of semiprecious stones and precious metals to make it sparkle like a jewel, to be placed in the center of the precious treasure chest that was the Chapel of the Princes. This model drawn by Matteo Nigetti, who actually elaborated and directed the project although it had been formally assigned to the brother of the Grand Duke, Don Giovanni de' Medici, shows how this unique object was actually meant to appear. Although the idea for the altar had already commenced to be realized in 1598, even before the Chapel itself was constructed, and despite the great initial effort afforded on it, it was destined to remain incomplete. In the middle of the 17th century it was still to be found, in fact, in an only partially assembled form in the grand ducal workshop, where it remained for over a century. It was an object that astounded anyone who had the opportunity to view it, until the Grand Duke Pietro Leopoldo of the Hapsburg Lorraine family, which succeeded the extinct Medici dynasty, had it dismantled in order to have the most precious parts available for re-use. (A.G.)

The most important artistic enterprise undertaken by the Grand Duke Ferdinando I de' Medici was the construction of a mausoleum designed to contain the sepulchres of the Medici family members, known as the *Cappella dei Principi* or Chapel of the Princes, begun in 1604 and finally concluded two and a half centuries later. The most unique feature of this project was the plan for decorating its interior: it was to be entirely covered from floor to dome with shining semiprecious stones, prepared in the workshop founded by Ferdinando I in 1588. Being far too ambitious even for the Medici's ample financial possibilities, the project was still incomplete when the last descendent of the family, Anna Maria Luisa, commissioned this model in 1743. It shows the idea then formulated for completing the construction and pictorial decoration of the drum and dome, not yet built at the time. Death overtook the daughter of Cosimo III de' Medici that very same year, however, and the Chapel was finally finished a century later. (A.G.)

Bibliography: A. Pampaloni Martelli in A. Giusti, P. Mazzoni, A. Pampaloni Martelli, *Il Museo dell' Opificio delle Pietre Dure a Firenze*, Florence 1978, p. 287; C. Cresti, *La cappella dei Principi* in *Splendori di pietre dure*, Florence 1988, p. 68.

Bibliography: A. Giusti in *Il Museo dell' Opificio delle Pietre Dure a Firenze*, Florence 1978, p. 318; A. Giusti, *Guida al Museo dell'Opificio delle Pietre Dure di Firenze*, Venice 1995, p. 29.

Grand Ducal Workshops
(after a model by Bernardino Poccetti)
(San Martino di Valdelsa 1548 - Florence 1612)

TUSCAN LANDSCAPE
1608

Hard stone inlay, 15 x 51 cm
Florence, Museo dell'Opificio delle Pietre Dure, inv. no. 463

Ferdinando I de' Medici decided to compete with the art of painting - and actually succeeded in doing so - through the semiprecious stone inlays in which the workshop founded by him in 1588 was specialized. Until then, the mosaics fashioned in Rome and Florence composed of different colored pieces of stone, tended to display only geometric designs (see page 155), and even when more complex decorative motifs were undertaken, never contained figurative elements. Not long after, instead, the highly specialized workshops founded by Ferdinando I, proved to be capable of cutting the semiprecious stones along sinuous and complex contours, while still making the single pieces fit together so precisely as to make the joints between the various stones practically invisible. This perfect craftsmanship, together with an exquisite taste for the selection of the stone nuances capable of rendering the desired pictorial effects, permitted the Florentine semiprecious stone inlay masters to venture into an extremely vast repertory of images, rivaling that of painting. In fact, subject matter ranged from portraiture (see page 144) to still life, to sacred scenes and to landscapes.

An example of the landscape theme is this delightful view of the Tuscan hillsides; together with a similar panel, it originally formed a pair meant for the precious jeweled altar to be placed in the center of the never-finished Medici mausoleum (see page 159). The two landscape panels, already completed in 1608, were derived from painted models prepared expressly for the purpose as was customary in the grand ducal workshop. The painter in this case was the elderly Bernardino Poccetti, an affirmed artist with an already lengthy activity on behalf of the Medici, who elaborated the theme of landscape, conceived as the protagonist by itself of the representation, for use in stone inlay, something new at this time in Florence. The landscape view was therefore neither expected to divide the scene with persons or events, as was instead usual in Florentine painting at the time. Beyond the novelty and realism of the subject matter, however, we may admire this stone panel for the fanciful and intelligent choice of materials which succeed in creating a magical yet plausible landscape scene: Sicilian jasper for the rolling hills, in part in shadow and in part scorched by the sun; the spring green of the vegetation evoked by the Bohemian jasper; the effect of movement of the lapis lazuli sky dotted with light clouds. (A.G.)

Bibliography: A. Giusti in A. Giusti, P. Mazzoni, A. Pampaloni Martelli, *Il Museo dell'Opificio delle Pietre Dure a Firenze*, Florence 1978, pp. 288-289; R. Przyborowski in *Splendori di pietre dure*, Florence 1988, p. 120.

Grand Ducal Workshops

THE EVANGELISTS MATTHEW AND MARK
1605 ca.

Semiprecious stone inlay sculpture, height 32 cm each
Florence, Museo degli Argenti, inv. Gemme 1921, nos. 510, 765

The workshop founded by Ferdinando I de' Medici not only developed the technique of inlaying semiprecious stones on flat surfaces, but also a new method which used the same material to realize relief and free-standing sculpture. It thus became possible to make three-dimensional objects, such as these two small statuettes of St. Mark and St. Matthew, two of a series of four Evangelists made for the altar of the Chapel of the Princes (see page 159). The statuettes are composed of various pieces of different color semiprecious stones, each carved individually and then glued together, with the aid of tiny invisible pins, to form the finished object. The figures were thus conceived as a unit, meant to differ only in color. The skin tones are obtained with chalcedony, the robes from lapis lazuli, veined agate, and yellow or red jasper.

As was common for flat inlays, such sculptural works were preceded by a full-scale model, which a Medici court sculptor would in this case be commissioned to model in wax. Specialized craftsmen would then transform the model into semiprecious stone objects, demonstrating an extraordinary capability in achieving particularly soft effects of modeling, considering the intrinsically inflexible nature of the stones themselves. The

first example of this type of artistic work, absolutely new not only for Italy but for the rest of Europe as well, was a little temple shrine made in Florence, and now conserved in Vienna. Two statuettes of Christ and the Samaritan made of polychrome semiprecious stones are positioned in an inlaid landscape setting, on either side of a well which has been carved out of a large emerald. Another stunning creation of the grand ducal workshop, made thirty years after this, is the sculptural relief representing Cosimo II de' Medici, robed in regal jeweled vestments made of semiprecious stones, conserved in the Museo degli Argenti in Florence. After a period in the mid-17th century, characterized by a certain decline in the use of this three-dimensional technique and by a preference for flat mosaics with still life subjects, semiprecious stone sculpture flourished again in the late period of the Medici, in particular during the rule of Cosimo III (see page 219). At this time the manufactory was directed by the sculptor Giovan Battista Foggini, whose brilliant sculptural creations were transformed into semiprecious stone objects by specialists in the art of carving, with apparent ease, but in reality overcoming noticeable technical problems.

The still anonymous authors of these two Evangelists seem to have derived inspiration from such noble examples of Renaissance statuary as the marble *Habakkuk* by Donatello, an apparent source for the realism of the face and bald head of the St. Mark. (A.G.)

Bibliography: A. Giusti in U. Baldini, A. Giusti, A. Pampaloni Martelli, *La Cappella dei principi e le pietre dure a Firenze*, Milan 1979, pp. 263-265; R. Przyborowski in *Splendori di pietre dure*, Florence 1988, p.134; A. Giusti, *Pietre Dure*, Turin 1992, p. 79.

Grand Ducal Workshops

VASE OF FLOWERS
1615 ca.
Hard stone inlay, 29 x 18 cm
Florence, Museo dell'Opificio delle Pietre Dure, inv. no. 561

Girolamo della Valle

SUNFLOWER
1664
Hard stone inlay, 32 x 20 cm
Florence, Museo dell'Opificio delle Pietre Dure, inv. no. 560

While early 17th century Florentine painting hesitated in adopting the floral motifs becoming fashionable at the time, such themes had already gained the favor of the grand ducal semiprecious stone manufactory at the end of the 16th century. They were frequently repeated, each time in a different version, as in this pair of minute, exquisite panels designed for the altar of the Chapel of the Princes.

We see tulips, hyacinths and other spring flowers emerging bright with cheerful colors from the elegantly stylized forms of a double-handled vase, beautifully evoked with the jasper and chalcedony, chosen for this composition with great care among the vast variety of stones available.

It seems almost as if the workshop artists were trying to engage in a contest, and certainly not a losing one, with two of the most fascinating and various "palettes" nature has to offer, by fixing the beauty of flowers into the eternal brilliancy of semiprecious stones. (A.G.)

This panel offers a brilliant example of the floral repertory destined to become a predominant leit motiv, almost the distinctive mark, of mosaic production in Florence between the 17th and 19th centuries. Such themes, treated with scrupulous analysis and faithful depiction of the flowers or other subjects derived from nature, were rendered in the elegant and stylized style of drawing. This is enhanced, however, by the fanciful variety of colors offered by the semiprecious stones, patiently selected by the artisans according to an exquisite sense of chromatic nuances. This sunflower, signed and dated on the rear by Girolamo della Valle, is an admirable example of this technique from the speckled stone capable of suggesting the sunflower's large pistil to the variegated alabasters which make the wings of the butterflies seem almost to flutter. This floral motif, here shown stemming from an elegant pair of volutes, had such a great success that the workshop replicated it in numerous examples, among which we find a version in semiprecious stones also conserved in the museum of the Opificio. (A.G.)

Bibliography: A. Pampaloni Martelli in A. Giusti, P. Mazzoni, A. Pampaloni Martelli, *Il Museo dell'Opificio delle Pietre Dure a Firenze*, Florence 1978, p. 287; R. Przyborowski in *Splendori di pietre dure*, Florence 1988, p. 110.

Bibliography: A. Pampaloni Martelli in A. Giusti, P. Mazzoni, A. Pampaloni Martelli, *Il Museo dell'Opificio delle Pietre Dure a Firenze*, Florence 1978, p. 292; A. Giusti in *Splendori di pietre dure*, Florence 1988, p. 156.

Jacopo Ligozzi
(Verona 1547 ca. - Florence 1627)

MODEL FOR A PIETRE DURE TABLE TOP
Second decade of the 17th century
Oil on paper, 78 x 88 cm
Florence, Museo dell'Opificio delle Pietre Dure, without inv. no.

Ligozzi was renowned among the painters of the Medici entourage for his trait of being an attentive, yet poetic observer of nature, already made evident in the series of botanical and zoological drawings he had previously dedicated to Francesco I. He was initially charged by Grand Duke Ferdinando I to collaborate with the workshop specialized in semiprecious stone inlay. This association was destined to become closer and closer over time through the supplying of models for fascinating flower, fruit and bird subjects, which would long remain present in the thematic repertory of Florentine mosaic work.

This oil painting on paper may be recognized as a full scale model for one of the numerous table tops fashioned from semiprecious stones, representing floral compositions against a background of black marble. Such objects are frequently mentioned in the workshop's registers, especially during the second decade of the *Seicento* (1600's). (A.G.)

Bibliography: A. Giusti, *Guida al Museo dell'Opificio delle Pietre Dure di Firenze*, Venice 1995, p. 51; A. Giusti in *La Natura morta italiana*, Florence 2003, p. 258.

163

Grand Ducal Workshops

MEDICI COAT OF ARMS

Smoked quartz ("Spanish topaz"), 7,4 x 5 x 2 cm
Florence, Museo di Storia Naturale, Sezione Mineralogia,
 inv. no. 13201

This composition representing the Medici arms originally adorned the summit of the central niche of a cabinet belonging to Ferdinando I destined for the keeping of the refined objects belonging to the collection of the Grand Duke of Tuscany in the Tribune of the Uffizi. The cabinet with time and changes in taste was evidently no longer held to be appropriate, and was dismantled; only a few decorative elements were saved because of their fine craftsmanship and the precious materials of which they were made. Drawings and paintings depict the gem fastened to a frontal of lapis lazuli and surmounted by a gold grand ducal crown encrusted with a multitude of little diamonds. The accounts of travellers and the most authoritative guide books of Florence further inform us that the spheres of the Medici coat of arms were originally precious rubies. (M.Sf.)

Bibliography: D. Heikamp in *Magnificenza alla corte dei Medici*, Florence 1997, p. 82, no. 43 (with previous bibliography); M. Sframeli, in *Il Rinascimento in Italia*, Rome 2001, p. 247, no. IV. 50.

Grand Ducal Workshops

CUP INCISED "FM 1600"
1600

Lapis lazuli, 22 x 11 x 5 cm
Florence, Museo di Storia Naturale, Sezione Mineralogia,
inv. no. 13682/4

The cup, derived from a single piece of lapis lazuli of not exceptional quality because of the presence of iron, is carved with large pod motifs that form an asymmetrical ornamental design according to the craftsman's plan. The letters engraved on the base read "F M 1600", and are accompanied by the grand ducal crown. This proves that the object came from the court workshops after they had already been transferred by the Grand Duke Ferdinando I to the western wing of the Uffizi. This also provides the timeframe for identifying the initials themselves.
Lapis lazuli was one of the most highly appreciated semiprecious stones in the court of Tuscany, previously supplied to Florence by the Milanese workshops and used in the laboratories of the Casino di San Marco since the time of Ferdinando's brother and predecessor, Francesco. It is the latter we may thank for such masterpieces of lapis lazuli carving as the famous vase of the Museo degli Argenti, designed by Bernardo Buontalenti, the most ingenious of the Florentine Mannerists. The precious mounting in gold and precious stones, work of the court goldsmith, Jaques Bylivelt, further embellishes the object. (M.Sf.)

Orazio Migliorini and **Andrea Ferrucci**
(active second half of the 16th century)

MODEL FOR THE FAÇADE OF THE CHIESA DEI CAVALIERI DI SANTO STEFANO IN PISA
1593
Linden wood, 134 x 134,4 x 13 cm
Pisa, Museo Nazionale di San Matteo, inv. no. 4607

The church dedicated to the *Ordine dei Cavalieri di Santo Stefano* (Order of the Knights of St. Stephen), constructed between 1565 and 1569 by order of Cosimo I, according to a project by Giorgio Vasari, remained without a façade (already visible in Vasari's drawings) until 1593. At this time, Ferdinando I commissioned the plan for completing the façade from his step-brother Giovanni de' Medici, who worked in collaboration with the architect Alessandro Pieroni. The marble façade, initiated in 1593, remained quite faithful to its scale model, exhibited here. In 1562, Cosimo I instituted the *Sacro Militare Ordine Marittimo dei Cavalieri di Santo Stefano* in defense against the Turkish menace to commercial shipping in the Mediterranean and in Europe in general. The religious seat of the Order was Pisa, in homage to the city's marine traditions. Vasari was called to intervene on a site, now Piazza dei Cavalieri, where the most representative buildings of the ancient Pisan republic were once found. (E.C.)

Bibliography: C. Conforti, *Vasari architetto*, Milan 1993, pp. 191-208; S. Renzoni in *Pisa e Il Mediterraneo*, Milan 2003, p. 470.

Santi Santucci and **Andrea Mattei**
(active Pisa, late 17th - early 18th century)

PARTS OF THE STERN OF A PARADE GALLEY
17th - 18th century
Carved and partially painted wood, 80 x 265 cm
Pisa, Chiesa dei Cavalieri di Santo Stefano

The portions of high relief carving exhibited here, composed of eagles, coats of arms, heads of Turks, and having traces of color, may once have been part of the stern of the parade ship *Peota dorata*. This boat was used by Cosimo III for navigation on the Arno and for special occasions such as the transfer of the relics of St. Stephen from Trani to Pisa, which took place on April, 25, 1683. Although the ship was demolished at the end of the 18th century, its carvings continued to be used to decorate the boat used in the regatta for the feast of San Ranieri, patron saint of the city. Purchased by the State in 1846, they were transferred to the Church of Santo Stefano dei Cavalieri where they can still be admired today.

The three relief carvings are among the few surviving examples of the activity of woodcarvers in the Pisan arsenal. The craftsmen to whom the carvings were assigned, Santi Santucci, called Santino, and Andrea Mattei, are remembered as among the best then working in Pisa. Santucci received numerous other commissions from the Medici court, while Mattei was often called to decorate galley ships. Due to the scarce opportunities for expert woodcarvers to find work in Pisa, the arsenal usually resorted to calling in Florentine woodworkers, on purpose for the few, sporadically assigned jobs.

For example, in 1549-1550, Giovanni Battista del Tasso was engaged by Duke Cosimo and Andrea Doria to work on several galley sterns, while his son Marco was sent by the *Cavalieri di Santo Stefano* in 1564, first to Pisa and then to Livorno, to work on another two galley sterns; later on, in 1586, Bernardo Buontalenti furnished some drawings for galley ship-lights. The arsenal developed considerably during the course of the 17th century to the point of claiming carvers versed in the new figurative style of the day, thanks in particular to the growing prestige of the *Ordine dei Cavalieri di Santo Stefano* (Order of the Knights of St. Stephen) for their repeated naval victories over Muslim raiders. It is hardly a surprise, therefore, that wood sculpture occupied an important place in the academy for young artists, created in Rome by Cosimo III in 1680.

Under the rule of Cosimo I, the city of Pisa, placed as it is between the plain and the sea, held an undeniably important place in the political setup of the State, under whose dominion it had again fallen in 1509 after an attempted rebellion in 1494. The immediate result of Medici domination was a resumption of the city's commercial and cultural activities. Pisa was the seat of a ducal palace which often hosted Cosimo and his family, and would be later transformed into the royal palace of Francesco I and Ferdinando I. In the 16th century, Pisa became the second most important city, first of the duchy and then of the Grand Duchy. Cosimo I acquired new areas for the enlargement of the arsenal, and in 1562 personally founded the Order of the Knights of St. Stephen. His purpose was to create an Order prepared for combat at sea, whose members - nobility native of Tuscany and elsewhere - were embarked on galleys constructed in the arsenal. (E.C.)

Bibliography: F. Paliaga in *Pisa e il Mediterraneo*, 2003, pp. 305-309, 479.

Anonymous
(follower of Filippo Napoletano)

NAVAL BATTLE
1620 ca.
Oil on river stone from the Arno, 39 x 23 cm
Florence, Museo dell'Opificio delle Pietre Dure, inv. 722

The taste for oil paintings on stone slabs which were chosen as a substitute for the traditional supports of wood or canvas, was already known in the 1500's, but reached its maximum popularity in the course of the first half of the 1600's. Initially, this taste was influenced by the propensity of the late Italian Renaissance to experiment with new techniques and diverse art forms, but also by the idea that an inert and stable support such as stone guaranteed a better and longer conservation.

A taste for the "bizarre" in stones found in nature, prevailed in the 1600's; in particular, stones with veins and markings that could suggest to the imagination of the painter, scenery pre-prepared for the placement of the subject through just the right pictorial intervention. It was a kind of competition between the inventiveness of nature and that of the artist, and much esteemed by connoisseurs, including the Medici and in particular Cosimo II at whose court numerous artists from varied provenances both Italian and European, experimented with this genre. Whatever the subject - sacred, historical mythological - it was ambientated in landscapes created almost entirely by the markings of the stone itself. As in the case of this *Naval Battle* which celebrates a victory in 1617 of the Grand Duke against the Turks, the rippled surface of the sea is created by the parallel, undulating streaks of the stone slab, composed of a type of limestone found on the bed of the Arno River. (A.G.)

Unpublished

Glory & Genius at Court

Annamaria Giusti

The "heroic" efforts of Fernando I, who ruled from 1587 to 1609, resulted in financial rehabilitation and expansion of the Grand Duchy during his reign. For his two successors, Cosimo II and Ferdinando II, internal affairs ran smoothly even though the financial solvency and political relevance of their small State started to decline. This did not however prevent the Medici court from being one of the most splendid in all of Europe due to its refined life-style and undying passion for the arts manifested by all family members. Artists and artisans continuously worked on the expansion and embellishment of Palazzo Pitti and other Medici residences; their collections of masterpieces and art treasures continued to grow; and the Opificio continued to produce semiprecious stone objects much admired throughout the entire continent. Great attention and interest was also focused on the sciences and the natural world in the best Florentine and Medici tradition.

During the century spanning the reign of Ferdinando I to that of his grandson Ferdinando II, the Medici court was a many-faceted place peopled with princes and princesses to be sure, but also servants, musicians and household pets as attested to by numerous court portraits that chronicled the passing years of the Medici and events that marked their lives. Formal portraits marked state occasions, but others record personal events such as a young Ferdinando II as a survivor of smallpox, often a fatal disease.

In addition to the strong link between the figurative arts and life at court, another salient artistic reality of the Florentine panorama at the time was the ongoing productivity in the specialized manufacture of mosaics and the cutting of precious stones exclusively for the Grand Dukes. These works of art were admired throughout Europe for the creativity of their design and for the mastery of technique. The complex secrets of their production were passed from one generation of artisans to the next. As new techniques were developed, the typology of the works also expanded from portraits in inlaid mosaics to landscapes, from door panels to large, elaborately decorated cabinets, from paintings on stone to the third dimension of statuettes.

In the Medici scientific traditions born in the late 1500's, merged a taste for the bizarre, both natural and artificial, as testified to in their large collections of still life painting, with more academic approaches reserved for sciences such as astronomy. It is in this field that Galileo's genius is revealed who counted the future Cosimo II of Tuscany among his scholars at the University of Padua. Once invested as the Grand Duke, Cosimo II summoned Galileo to his court, nominating him Master Mathematician and giving him a villa at Arcetri to pursue his astronomy studies. Later Galileo would seek asylum there after the Church's condemnation for his revolutionary theories on the solar system. Some of Galileo's scholars, such as Vincenzo Viviani and Evangelista Torricelli, continued their studies at the *Accademia del Cimento*, founded in 1657 by the brother of the Grand Duke, Cardinal Leopoldo de' Medici. For the ten years that the Academy was active, Florence held the leading role on an international level in the field of scientific research.

GLORY & GENIUS AT COURT

Long before the lavish excesses of Louis XIV at Versailles, the Medici had dedicated space and finances to the staging of spectacular events, a tradition which reached its apex between the 1500's and 1600's. Whether these took form as parties reserved for the court and its guests or events involving, as often happened, the entire city, they all responded to the passion for the "spectacular," common to all the social classes. They were also intended as a political statement that through ostentation reaffirmed Medici prestige. Weddings, celebrations lasting for months, are the best example of an event involving the whole city and not just the court. Even if it was a small group of aristocrats who were invited to see the submerged courtyard of Palazzo Pitti where a naval battle was re-enacted in honor of the wedding of Ferdinando I or the spectacular decor of Cosimo II's nuptial banquets, the entire city could admire the *apparati*, painted or sculpted scenery made with cheap materials, to adorn and transform the normal urban milieu on such occasions. Even equestrian tournaments in which plumed knights performed elegant battle maneuvers could be public or reserved for the court. Theatrical events, which were originally temporarily staged in the public piazzas, were gradually concentrated at the court, leading to the creation of a permanent theater in the Uffizi.

The strong religious faith of the Medic was also manifested with the pomp and ostentation that governed every aspect of the court. In response to the reformist schisms of the 1500's, the Church had decided to present itself as triumphant both in the solemnity and pomp of its ceremonies as well as in the richness of church decors and architecture. The workshops of the Medici produced many liturgical objects of immense value both in material and in design to donate them to sanctuaries and places of worship throughout the city and the region. Many of the Medici second sons became cardinals; to one of these belonged an ingenious traveling altar. A frequent habit of the most devoted (yet not humble) members of the Medici, was that of being portrayed as one of the most venerated saints, or even as the Sacred Family. In particular, the Grand Duchesses, Cristina of Lorraine, Maria Maddalena of Austria, wife of Cosimo II, and her daughter-in-law, Vittoria della Rovere were almost fanatical in their devotion and equally generous in their ecclesiastical gifts.

Anonymous
(Florentine)

COSIMO AT THE AGE OF SIX WITH GOVERNESS
1590
Oil on canvas, 24 x 56 cm
Florence, Galleria degli Uffizi, inv. 1890 no. 2348

Tiberio Titi
(Florence 1578 - 1637)

PORTRAIT OF MARIA MADDALENA OF AUSTRIA
1610 ca.
Oil on canvas, 202 x 106 cm
Florence, Galleria degli Uffizi, inv. 1890, no. 2306

Even if it was customary to have the members of the Medici dynasty portrayed as children, still such a precocious portrait is unusual. The painting presents the son of Grand Duke Ferdinando I and Cristina of Lorraine, future Cosimo II, at only six months of age. Clearly conceived as a celebration of the flourishing health of the heir to the throne, the portrait shows Cosimo already in a "stiff" posture, in the arms of his Governess, Costanza della Gherardesca. The position of Governess, a sort of "tutor" of the young Medici princes, was usually assigned to noble and trusted Ladies of the Court; in this case, Costanza della Gherardesca could also take advantage of a close kinship with the founder of the dynasty, Cosimo I.
She is portrayed in her mourning robes and shows a mature and affable appearance, captured with naturalistic effect by the anonymous painter whose style turns more rigid in the official image given of the young Cosimo. The inscription on the upper part of the painting says: "Cosimo II, G.(rand) Princ.(e) of Tuscany at the age of six months, November 12, 1590". For the first time here is used the title of "Grand Prince", which would become traditional to indicate the heir to the throne of the Grand Duchy of Tuscany.

Bibliography: C. Caneva in *I volti del potere*, Florence 2002, p. 50 (with previous bibliography).

This full length portrait painting of Grand Duchess Maria Maddalena of Austria, who became the wife of Cosimo II in 1608, is an official portrait in the classic pose of a state representative; the elegant dress is enhanced with rich lace at the wrists, an elaborate ruff, and two fine rows of pearls at the neck. The author of the painting, which can be dated about 1610, is the son of Santi di Tito, Tiberio, one of the official portraitists at the Medici court. Maria Maddalena, of the Hapsburg family, gave the Grand Duke eight children. When Cosimo died prematurely in 1621, she became regent of the Grand Duchy with her mother-in-law, Cristina of Lorraine, until her son Ferdinando II came of age in 1629. Like her husband, Maria Maddalena was a competent and intelligent art patron and collector. She encouraged the presence of Flemish, Dutch and German artists at the Florentine court. She created the Reliquary Chapel in the Pitti Palace and bought and decorated Villa Baroncelli, later known as Poggio Imperiale, which she turned into a magnificent residence for the Medici Grand Duchesses. (S.C.)

Bibliography: S. Meloni Trkulja in *Gli Uffizi*, Florence 1979, p. 752, no. Ic 989.

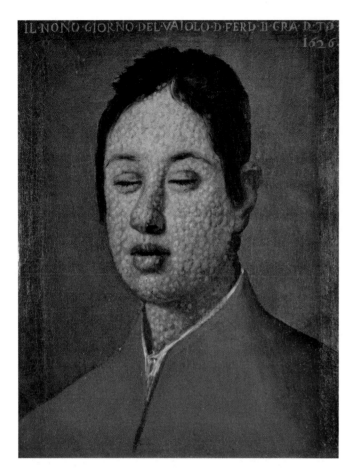

Justus Suttermans
(Antwerp 1597 - Florence 1681)

PORTRAIT OF GRAND DUKE FERDINANDO II ON THE NINTH DAY OF SMALLPOX
1626
Oil on canvas, 43 x 33 cm
Florence, Palazzo Pitti, Depositi delle Gallerie Fiorentine,
inv. Poggio a Caiano, no. 338

Together with another painting, also in the deposits of the Pitti Palace (inv. Poggio a Caiano, no. 337), this is a most rare and unusual scientific record of the illness that afflicted the young Ferdinando II de' Medici in 1626 at the age of 16, when he was not yet Grand Duke. The works represent two successive phases of smallpox, on the seventh and ninth days. In the first painting the face of the prince is quite reddened indicating the start of the outbreak of the rash which, by the ninth day, has erupted fully as seen in the work exhibited. Ferdinando's face (and also his body as can be glimpsed from the open neck of his shirt) is now entirely covered with the smallpox pustles which even prevent him from opening his eyes. At the time, smallpox was a very serious and often mortal illness and it is interesting that it was decided to immortalize the young heir to the throne, still under the guardianship of the two Regents, while in this condition. However, Ferdinando managed to survive the dreadful illness. (S.C.)

Bibliography: G. Pieraccini, *La stirpe dei Medici di Cafaggiolo*, Florence 1942-45; S. Meloni Trkulja in *Sustermans*, 1983, p. 97; K. Langedijk *The portraits of the Medici*, Vol. II, Florence 1983, p. 781.

Gerard Walder, Vittorio Crosten and **Leonard Van der Vinne**

PORTRAIT OF THE GRAND DUKE FERDINANDO II DE' MEDICI
1669
Rock crystal, wood and gilt bronze, 40 x 37 cm
Florence, Museo dell'Opificio delle Pietre Dure, inv. no. 641

During the reign of Ferdinando II, the Medici court was enriched by the presence of craftsmen coming from various parts of Europe, each specialized in rare and refined techniques such as gem engraving, ivory carving or wood intarsia and so forth. This small portrait of the Grand Duke offers a refined culmination of the skills possessed by three different artists: the Argentine Gerard Walder, who engraved a profile of Ferdinando II onto the silver laminated rock crystal; the Dutchman Vittorio Crosten, author of the extremely delicate boxwood carving which forms the garland of roses, into which the Grand Duke's motto "Gratia obvia vitium quaesita" is interlaced; and the Flemish artist Leonard Van der Vinne, specialist in wood intarsia, here responsible for the soberly refined frame of ebony, a highly valued Oriental wood preferred by the Medici court for use with semiprecious stones. (A.G.)

Bibliography: E. Colle, *Arredi delle dimore medicee*, 1993, p. 26; A. Giusti, *Un dorato crepuscolo* in *Tesori delle collezioni medicee*, Florence 1997, p.174.

Justus Suttermans
(Antwerp 1597 - Florence 1681)

PORTRAIT OF VITTORIA DELLA ROVERE
1628 - 1630 ca.
Oil on canvas, 114 x 92 cm
Florence, Museo di Palazzo Martelli, inv. no. 50

Vittoria della Rovere (1622–1694) was the daughter of Claudia de' Medici and Federico Ubaldo della Rovere, Duke of Urbino. The sole heir to the Duchy of Urbino, her father died when she was just one year old, and from an early age she was educated at the court of Florence, marrying her cousin, Grand Duke Ferdinando II in 1637. Vittoria also inherited the artistic treasures of the della Rovere family, consisting of an immense number of masterpieces that were brought to Florence in 1631. These include famous works by Raphael, Titian, Barocci and many other 16th century artists, and still today are some of the most splendid paintings in the museums of Florence. In this official portrait, Vittoria is about 6 or 8 years old and is wearing a magnificent red dress with a beautiful lace collar and fine strings of pearls that had belonged to her mother, Claudia. Later, perhaps between 1639 and 1642, the portrait was transformed into an image of St. Margaret, the protectress of expectant mothers, by adding a crown with halo. (S.C.)

Bibliography: L. Goldenberg Stoppato, C. Contu in *I gioielli dei Medici,* Florence 2003, p. 152 (with previous bibliography).

Giovanni Andrea Ansaldo
(Voltri 1584 - Genoa 1638)

**ALLEGORY OF THE CROWNING OF GRAND DUKE
FERDINANDO II DE' MEDICI**
1629
Oil on canvas, 106 x 97 cm
Florence, Galleria Palatina, inv. Oggetti d'Arte no. 719

The painting is an allegory of the incoronation of the young Grand Duke
Ferdinand II. Born in 1610, while the prince was still a child, his father died
(1621) and he became Grand Duke on coming of age in 1629. His mother,
Maria Maddalena of Austria and his grandmother, Cristina of Lorraine, acted
as regents for the throne during this lengthy period. The painting shows
Ferdinando II in ceremonial garb and with the scepter in his right hand,
seated on the throne and surrounded by the three Virtues - Charity, Justice
and Temperance - who will guide his government, while Minerva, the
goddess of Learning, presents the Arts who offer their gifts to him. The
work has only recently been attributed to Ansaldo and a document has been
traced showing that it was brought to Florence in 1629 by the Marquis
Gianfranco Brignole, perhaps as a gift, but also to introduce the Genoese
artist to the Medici court. (S.C.)

Bibliography: M. Chiarini in *La Galleria Palatina*, Florence 2003, Vol. II, p.
58 (with previous bibliography).

Justus Suttermans
(Antwerp 1597 - Florence 1681)

**PORTRAIT OF VITTORIA DELLA ROVERE
AND COSIMO III AS A CHILD**
1645 - 1646
Oil on canvas, 202 x 122 cm
Lucca, Museo Nazionale di Palazzo Mansi, inv. no. 39

The painting belonged to Cardinal Carlo de' Medici who housed it in the
Casino at San Marco. Grand Duchess Vittoria della Rovere is portrayed in an
elegant black dress with a wide lace collar, with her first son Cosimo III,
future Grand Duke, aged about 3 or 4 years. The style of the dress and the
apparent age of the young prince date the painting to about 1645-46. Many
portraits of Vittoria della Rovere exist and she was also fond of being
represented in the guise of a saint. Most of these portraits were the work of
Justus Suttermans, a Flemish painter who moved to Florence in 1618 and
became the prolific and principal portraitist of the Medici court for some 60
years. This is a fine official portrait in which the Grand Duchess is elegantly
presented as a young woman of 23 years, not beautiful, but fully aware of
her role as a Medici both by birth on her mother's side and by marriage to
her cousin, Ferdinando II. (S.C.)

Bibliography: K. Langedijk *The portraits of the Medici*, Vol. II, Florence
1983, p. 1488, nos. 110, 28.

Tiberio Titi
(Florence 1578 - 1637)

PORTRAIT OF PRINCE LEOPOLDO DE' MEDICI IN A CRADLE
1617

Oil on canvas, 59,6 x 74,2 cm
Florence, Galleria Palatina, inv. 1912, no. 49

Leopoldo de' Medici (1617-1675), the eighth son of Cosimo II and Maria Maddalena of Austria is shown as a baby of a few months, lying in a cradle richly decorated with elaborately embroidered materials and damasks that emphasize his princely status. The painting, previously attributed to Jacopo Ligozzi, is now believed to be by Tiberio Titi, the son of Santi di Tito and portraitist at the Medici court. Leopoldo became a cardinal in 1667 and was one of the most important art collectors in the Medici family, but was also fascinated by scientific experimentation. Even given the numerous types and styles of portraits, including many of children, the image of a newborn prince is unique in the Medici collections. It was probably inspired by a similar portrait of Federico Ubaldo della Rovere as a baby, painted in 1605 by Alessandro Vitali for the Urbino court and also housed in the Palatine Gallery, Florence. (S.C.)

Bibliography: S. Meloni Trkulja in *I principi bambini*, Florence 1985, p. 35; M. Chiarini in *La Galleria Palatina*, 2003, Vol. II, p. 449.

Southern German

BATON WITH THE ARMS OF CARDINAL LEOPOLDO DE' MEDICI
17th century

Engraved ivory, 150 cm
Florence, Museo degli Argenti, inv. Bg. 1878, Armi, no. 1201

The ivory rod, supposedly lathe-made and then engraved, is divided into twenty-three sections, each of which represent a separate scene from the Apocalypse and are connected to each other by gilt silver rings. The way in which the precious material has been handled and certain stylistic details seem to indicate that this object was made in one of the southern German manufactories, renowned for their refined ivory products. Evidently intended for a highly positioned prelate belonging to the Medici family (see the Medici arms held up by two putti and surmounted by the grand ducal crown which decorate the button on the knob), the baton may be connected with Cardinal Leopoldo (1617-1675), son of Cosimo II and Maria Maddalena of Austria. The lack of the Cardinal's hat proves that the rod dates from the years immediately preceding Leopoldo's nomination as Cardinal (1667). Famous collector of art objects and patron of the sciences, Leopoldo was certainly one who would have appreciated such an exquisitely made object. (E.C.)

Bibliography: K. Aschengreen Piacenti, *Gli ultimi Medici*, Florence 1967, p. 152; M. Ciatti in *Opere d'arte della famiglia Medici*, Milan 1997, p. 117.

Tiziano Vecellio (and workshop)
(Pieve di Cadore 1490 ca. - Venice 1576)

VENUS AND CUPID
1550 ca.
Oil on canvas, 139,2 x 195,5 cm
Florence, Galleria degli Uffizi, inv. 1890, no. 1431

Modeled on a classical theme – as well as on the Venus and Cupid composition derived from Michelangelo, dated 1532-33 - the figure of Venus is seen lying on a purplish silk drape. Her pearl necklace and earrings are proof that the young woman's nudity has nothing to do with the attractions of carnal love; common women and courtesans were in fact forbidden to wear pearls which were reserved only for aristocratic married women. The pose of Cupid embracing the shoulders of the goddess has been associated with the antique motif of Eros and the lion, symbol of the victory of love over the forces of nature. In this painting by Tiziano (Titian), the lion is present in the form of the support of a small table, on which a vase of roses is positioned. Venus holds more roses (an attribute of the goddess) in her left hand, while at her feet a little dog (symbol of faithful love) is barking at a bird (a partridge, symbol of fertility and lust). The theme of the work might thus be faithfulness warning against the lure of sensuality.

The painting is mentioned in the Medici inventories since 1635; it came to Florence from Rome in January, 1619 as a gift to Cosimo II de' Medici from Paolo Giordano Orsini. It was often confused with the highly esteemed *Venus of Urbino*, which since 1631 was also to be found in the Medici collections, as part of Vittoria della Rovere's inheritance.

This work of art, painted with the help of the workshop, is usually dated after Titian's sojourn in Rome lasting from 1530 to 1548, and is considered a derivation of the prototype of the Venus cycle conserved in the Prado.

The Medici family fully appreciated Titian as a painter only during the 17th century, while the 16th century Medici court owned only portraits by the artist from Venice (*Pietro Aretino, Cardinal Ippolito de' Medici,*

Philip II of Spain, Baccio Valori, Giovanni dalle Bande Nere, the lost portrait of *Charles V*). Even these, however, did not seem to be always much appreciated, considering the fact that Cosimo I refused, as narrated by Vasari, to have his portrait made by the famous Venetian painter. At the end of the *Cinquecento* (1500's), documents attest to further acquisitions of works by Titian coming into the collection of Ferdinando I. This *Venus*, donated to Cosimo II by Paolo Giordano Orsini, appears after the death of Don Antonio (1621). The major Medici acquisition of works by Titian, however, that furnished the collection with the largest number of certainly attributed paintings by this artist, changing the taste prevalent among Florentine collectors with a new preference for Venetian painting, was the arrival in 1631 of the cases containing the paintings sent from Urbino, inherited by Vittoria della Rovere. This patrimony, which the Grand Duchess conserved until her death in 1694 as her own personal property in the residence at Poggio Imperiale, attests to a very different relationship with Titian maintained by the della Rovere court at Urbino. This connection was destined to last for more than forty years, having begun around 1530, and continuing beyond the death of Francesco Maria (1538), through his son Guidobaldo, up to 1573. Besides the above-cited *Venus of Urbino*, Vittoria della Rovere's inheritance also included among other Titians, such paintings as the *Saviour*, the *Adoration of the Pastors*, the *Magdalene*, the so-called *Bella*, portraits of *Francesco Maria della Rovere, Eleonora Gonzaga, Pope Giulio II* copied from Raphael, *Sisto IV, Giulia Varano della Rovere* and *Paolo III*. (M.B.)

Bibliography: Tiziano nelle Gallerie fiorentine, Florence 1978, pp. 60-65, no. 9; *Venere svelata*, Milan 2003, p. 96.

Anton Domenico Gabbiani
(Florence 1652 - 1726)

PORTRAIT OF FOUR SERVANTS OF THE MEDICI COURT
1684 ca.
Oil on canvas, 205 x 140 cm
Florence, Palazzo Pitti, Depositi delle Gallerie Fiorentine,
inv. 1890, no. 3827

The painting was commissioned from Gabbiani by Cosimo III for his villa at Castello, a few kilometers to the north of Florence and now the home of the *Crusca* Academy, together with other paintings portraying courtiers and lords of the Medici court. The arrival of the painting at Castello in 1684, with another portraying *A Man Playing Two Flutes* is documented in the *Guardaroba Generale* as are its subsequent locations until it was placed in the entrance to the *Guardaroba* of the Pitti Palace. Of the four Medici servants painted by Gabbiani, three are unusual characters, identified in a document dated 1684: the young boy holding the little monkey on a lead is the "young hunchback" who had come to Florence from Livorno; the young boy in a white satin shirt with large yellow flowers and pale green leaves is *il Moro* (the Moor); and the hunchback holding a plate of spinach in his hand is Cristofanino. According to popular tradition, "to eat spinach" meant to act as a spy and is therefore a clear allusion to a certain bad habit of Cristofanino. The character standing behind the "Moor" and pointing to him is identified in the same document as Caporal Buccia. From the early Renaissance on, it was normal for the most important families to have people with unusual physical characteristics, such as hunchbacks and dwarfs, at their court as they were considered to be so rare as to be "wonders". The rich silk clothing, the gilt buttons, the leather shoes and the rustling red silk

curtain behind which we catch sight of a stately building are all elements that allude to the magnificence of the Medici court, even if the subject itself belongs to a genre and is therefore, considered minor.
Not only does Anton Domenico Gabbiani skilfully paint the quality of the cloth - note the glistening white satin of the Moor's clothes that emphasizes the dark color of his skin – but he also succeeds in capturing on the canvas four quite intense portraits. The glances that pass between the two hunchbacks and between Caporal Buccia and the Moor are references to situations that would have been common knowledge at the time in the court, but are unknown to us today.
The artist was influenced by Venetian painting as he had served his apprenticeship in Venice with Sebastiano Bombelli, and given the chromatic quality of the painting, Marco Chiarini places it chronologically in the same period as the *Concerto with Trio* and therefore, before 1687.
(M.D.L.)

Bibliography: M. Chiarini, *Anton Domenico Gabbiani e i Medici* in *Kunst der Barock in der Toskana*, 1976, p. 335, no. 18; M. P. Masini in *Opere d'Arte della Famiglia Medici*, Florence 1997, p. 93, no. 28; E. Scaravella, Scheda Ministeriale OA 0900227248, 1990.

Anonymous

PORTRAIT OF DOGS WITH A CAT AND A RABBIT
Mid - 17th century

Oil on canvas, 81 x 106,5 cm
Florence, Palazzo Pitti, Depositi delle Gallerie Fiorentine,
inv. 1890, no. 4865

The dogs portrayed in this painting are a large griffon pointer surrounded by three other dogs: a bloodhound, a small spaniel and a Molossian wearing a collar "armed" with pointed studs. The group of animals also includes a cat and a rabbit, who appear unusually calm considering that they are posing for this "group portrait" together with their natural enemies. Court painters were often requested to portray family dogs, as in this case, or sometimes depicted animals characterized by exceptional features. That these dogs belonged to the Medici household seems confirmed by the fact that the small short-haired spaniel with bulging eyes also appears in various portraits of ladies and young girls of the family, such as the painting by Suttermans representing Claudia de' Medici (inv. 1890, no. 2267).

The artist shows great capability in capturing the distinctive traits of each animal's personality on the canvas, ranging from the sweet nature of the docile cat to the swaggering ferocity of the Molossian. The composition of the painting is instead rather peculiar, with the painter seemingly worried about leaving empty spaces, to the point of filling the last free area in the upper left hand corner with an iris.

As far as the identity of the artist is concerned, the many doubts remaining make us opt for a generic attribution, as previously suggested by Marco Chiarini, to an anonymous painter, perhaps non-Italian, of the 17th century. (M.D.L.)

Bibliography: M. Chiarini in *Curiosità di una reggia*, Florence 1979, p. 62, no. 31; M. Mosco in *Natura viva in casa Medici*, Florence 1986, p. 94, no. 27.

Tiberio Titi (attributed to)
(Florence 1573 - 1627)

PORTRAIT OF A DOG
Oil on canvas, 51,5 x 66,5 cm
Florence, Palazzo Pitti, Depositi delle Gallerie Fiorentine, inv. 1890, no. 5851

This is a true portrait of a dog, posed on a flat surface covered with red cloth, against a background of a wall also lined in red. Marilena Mosco suggested the name of Tiberio Titi for this work, following its recognition by Evelina Borea among Don Lorenzo de' Medici's paintings in the Villa della Petraia.

The dog, defined as a *moscato* (spotted) in the inventories of the Medici *Guardaroba*, is actually a cross-bred hound. His collar, armed with studs

and points, may also be seen in the painting, lying on the red cloth; it bears the Medici coat of arms, a sure indication that the dog belonged to the family.

Dog collars were considered objects important enough to be listed in the inventories of property together with sculptures, paintings and precious objects. One of the collars mentioned in the inventory of the possessions of Grand Prince Ferdinando, as being "of gilded silver foil over a copper plate, with royal arms and crown", is similar to the one represented in the painting. (M.D.L.)

Bibliography: E. Borea in *La Quadreria di Don Lorenzo de' Medici*, Florence 1977, p. 71, no. 46; M. Mosco in *Natura viva in casa Medici*, Florence 1986, p. 86; *Inventario dei Mobili e delle Masserizie della proprietà del Serenissimo Signore Principe Ferdinando*, 1713.

Grand Ducal Workshops

VASE OF FLOWERS
Mid - 17th century ca.
Hard stone inlay relief, 24 x 19 cm
Florence, Museo dell'Opificio delle Pietre Dure, inv. no. 665

The Medici workshop frequently resorted to relief carving for its semiprecious stone inlays, as in this piece representing a double-handed vase of flowers. The subjects chosen for this type of mosaic were the same already commonly used for similar two-dimensional inlays, as was this floral theme, already well-established in the semiprecious stone repertory at the beginning of the 17th century (see page 162), and reproduced in various versions throughout the entire century and afterwards. The various replicas were all remarkable for the technical perfection achieved by the craftsmen in rendering the elegantly designed vase and the perfectly natural appearance of the flowers. This small panel was probably originally a door of a cabinet whose exterior was lavishly covered with semiprecious stones (see page 184). (A.G.)

Bibliography: A. Pampaloni Martelli in A. Giusti, P. Mazzoni, A. Pampaloni Martelli, *Il Museo dell'Opificio delle Pietre Dure a Firenze*, Florence 1978, p. 293; A. Giusti, *Guida al Museo dell'Opificio delle Pietre Dure di Firenze*, Venice 1995, p. 51.

Grand Ducal Workshops

HEAD OF A CHERUB SURROUNDED BY RAYS
End of the 17th century
Oriental chalcedony relief, 35 x 25 cm
Florence, Museo dell'Opificio delle Pietre Dure, inv. no. 335

Three-dimensional carving of semiprecious stones, already widely practiced in the early period of the workshop's activity, regained vigor during the reign of Cosimo III de' Medici, as was to be expected at this moment of Baroque passion for sculpture. Free-standing sculptures were made combining various pieces of differently colored semiprecious stones; other relief works might be carved from a single piece of stone, as in the case of this cherub made of a precious variety of translucent chalcedony, brought by the Medici from India, whose transparency lets the glow of the gold applied to the rear of the face show through. This head, surrounded by an irregularly shaped nimbus of rays, was probably meant to be inserted in the midst of semiprecious stone clouds in some object meant for a religious destination, left unfinished. (A.G.)

Bibliography: A. Pampaloni Martelli in A. Giusti, P. Mazzoni, A. Pampaloni Martelli, *Il Museo dell'Opificio delle Pietre Dure a Firenze*, Florence 1978, p. 308.

Grand Ducal Workshops

MELCHISEDEK AND THE CANDELABRA
First two decades of the 17th century
Hard stone inlay, 28 x 55 cm
Florence, Museo dell'Opificio delle Pietre Dure, inv. no. 457

This panel, which represents the Biblical scene of the Priest and King of Salem, Melchisedek, awaiting the return of Abraham near the Holy Ark, next to which a candelabra and an altar are placed, seems to completely fulfill the desire manifested by Ferdinando I de' Medici to see the mosaics created in his workshop succeed in being a kind of magical "painting in stone". The scene is set in an open landscape near a river, with a knotty tree trunk to delineate the foreground and under a sky dotted with scudding clouds of chalcedony. This masterful work, produced during the fervent moments of the creation of the altar for the Chapel of the Princes, may be admired both for the shades of the stones and for the perfect cut of the various pieces, which succeeds in making their joints practically invisible. (A.G)

Bibliography: A. Giusti in A. Giusti, P. Mazzoni, A. Pampaloni Martelli, *Il Museo dell'Opificio delle Pietre Dure a Firenze*, Florence 1978, p. 289; R. Przyborowski in *Splendori di pietre dure*, Florence 1988, p. 114.

Grand Ducal Workshops

CABINET WITH LANDSCAPES, FLOWERS AND ALLEGORICAL FIGURES
Third quarter of the 17th century
Ebony, hard stones and gilt bronze, 218 x 50 x 124 cm
New York, Fioratti Collection

This work is a magnificent, imposingly designed monumental, free-standing cabinet from the English royal collections where it entered as a gift made by sir Thomas Liddel to George IV, and was later passed on to Queen Victoria who kept it in Buckingham Palace. The origin of this superb piece of furniture goes back, however, to the 17th century and the grand ducal workshop in Florence, which dedicated itself throughout the period of the Medici to the production of such courtly furnishings. The external part of the wooden structure of this type of object was richly covered with semiprecious stones and gilded bronze decorations.

This furniture type, diffused throughout all of Europe, functioned as a strongbox designed to hold a treasure of jewels, gems, cameos, coins, medallions, etc. It was itself meant to introduce the beholder to the vision of the riches contained within by means of the precious and refined craftsmanship evident in the materials which composed its covering, designed to totally conceal the internal structure in wood. This particular example, which was property of the royal family of England, possesses stylistic features which identify it as being from the period of the Grand Duke Ferdinando II, at a time when the Florentine Baroque style had not yet reached that state of exuberance which would characterize it towards the end of the 17th century. In fact, this piece does not demonstrate any such traits, either when viewed from the front or side, but rather shows the measured qualities of classical spatial values and a limited three-dimensional plasticity. A more Baroque style may perhaps be discerned in the upper part, where six little free-standing statues in gilded bronze, attributed to the well-known sculptor Ferdinando Tacca (1616/19-1686),

pose freely in space, and in the three-faced central frieze with a clock on its front face, devised with far more capricious form and decoration. Twelve panels with semiprecious stone inlays complete, or better to say, actually form the fulcrum of the entire decorative scheme. Three of these panels dominate the front; they show spacious architectural and landscape views, inspired by 17th century painting with its penchant for fanciful visions of buildings and classical ruins. The other panels, in a more traditional fashion and more in line with the usual Florentine mosaic repertory, represent vegetable twines and floral compositions. The flower vases to be seen on the sides of the cabinet have an additional motif of solid geometrical shapes, invented by the semiprecious stone workshop active in Prague during the early decades of the 17th century, at the service of the Emperor Rudolph II of Hapsburg. After all, the Prague workshop had been founded by Florentine craftsmen, one of whom returned to work for the Medici when the laboratory suspended its activity after the Emperor's death. The passion for inlaying semiprecious stones had thus expanded beyond the boundaries of Florence, taking along with it masters of the grand ducal workshop who gave life to other royal laboratories of the sort, in France under the Sun King and in Naples and Madrid under the Bourbons in the 18th century. (A.G.)

Bibliography: H. Clifford Smith, *The complete history of Buckingham Palace*, 1931, p. 140; A. F. Radcliffe, *Ferdinando Tacca* in *Kunst der Barok in der Toskana*, 1976, p. 23; A. Giusti, *Pietre dure*, Turin 1992, pp. 175-176.

Grand Ducal Workshops

FACETED DROPLET-SHAPED QUARTZ
Smoked quartz, 4 x 3 x 1 cm
Florence, Museo di Storia Naturale, Sezione Mineralogia,
inv. no. 13195/4

Grand Ducal Workshops

EMERALD WITH HEXAGONAL MOUNT
Cabochon emerald and gilded silver, 2,5 x 2,5 x 2 cm
Florence, Museo di Storia Naturale, Sezione Mineralogia,
inv. no. 13603/4

Grand Ducal Workshops

FACETED SQUARE-SHAPED QUARTZ
Hyaline quartz (rock crystal), 3,2 x 3,2 x 2,5 cm
Florence, Museo di Storia Naturale, Sezione Mineralogia,
inv. no. 13172/4

The exceptional historical value of these stones, although they are not particularly precious in their own right, derives from their origin in the Medici grand ducal workshops. Their considerable size and unusual cuts have even suggested the personal participation of Francesco I in their making. Although this hypothesis may seem slightly forced, it certainly evokes the fervent climate of the moment, characterized by the research and experimentation conducted in the Casino di San Marco where the young prince of the House of the Medici measured his abilities with those of the more expert cutters working there.

It may be affirmed, in any case, that such stones were probably used to "test" cuts before they were actually attempted on more important or more costly stones. One example might be the large and precious topazes (with which the different varieties of quartz were sometimes confused), which were still present in the inventories of the gems belonging to Anna Maria Luisa de' Medici compiled at the moment of her death (1743). Topazes would be mounted on precious frog clasps or on Crucifixes destined for use in daily rites of devotion, or could be mounted on the many types of precious objects produced in the grand ducal goldsmith workshops, ornate with precious and semiprecious stones.

We do not find unmounted examples of these types of quartz stones in the inventories of the grand ducal gems or of the dowries brought to court by the Grand Duchesses. The same may not be said of emeralds, often cited as mounted in the form of jewelry or as single stones ready to be set; for example, the emeralds described in the inventory of Ferdinando II of 1621 (see *I gioielli dei Medici*, 2003, p. 217). (M.Sf.)

Bibliography: A. M. Massinelli in *Magnificenze medicee: gli stipi della Tribuna*, in "Antologia di Belle Arti", nos. 35-38 (*Studi sul Neoclassicismo II*), 1990, pp.130-131.

Grand Ducal Workshops

FACETED OCTAGONAL-SHAPED QUARTZ

Smoked quartz, 6 x 5.5 x 4 cm
Florence, Museo di Storia Naturale, Sezione Mineralogia,
inv. no. 13175/4

Grand Ducal Workshops

FACETED OCTAGONAL-SHAPED QUARTZ

Citrine quartz, 5.5 x 5 x 2.5 cm
Florence, Museo di Storia Naturale, Sezione Mineralogia,
inv. no. 13184/4

Florentine

WORKBENCH FOR MAKING FLORENTINE STONE MOSAICS
19th century

Wood, metal
Florence, Museo dell'Opificio delle Pietre Dure, without inv. no.

This 19th century workbench faithfully reproduces those already in use in the *Cinquecento* (1500's) for the making of polychrome stone inlays; the type has in fact remained unaltered from the time of the Medici workshop to the present day Opificio. The instruments are quite uncomplicated, making everything depend upon the craftsmen's extraordinary manual dexterity; a clamp simply fastens a thin strip of stone to the bench in the desired position for cutting, which must be done with extreme precision following the complex outline traced from the paper model. The artisan makes simultaneous use of a hacksaw, equipped with iron wire, and a wet abrasive powder to incise the stone so that the hacksaw is able to cut into it. The harder the semiprecious stones are, the slower this operation will be. Once cut out, each section must fit perfectly, or in other words "connect" (*commesso*) with the other pieces of colored stones, to form the final assembled image. (A.G.)

Bibliography: F. Rossi in *Splendori di pietre dure*, Florence 1988, pp. 276-278; A. Giusti, *Pietre Dure*, Turin 1992, pp. 276-29.

THE "FIORENTINO" DIAMOND
1615 (?)
Etching, 13,5 x 8,6 cm
Florence, Biblioteca Marucelliana, Ms. A CCXIII, c. 95

COPY OF THE "FIORENTINO" DIAMOND
Modern
Light yellow-colored crystal, diameter 2,9 cm
Milan, Museo Nazionale della Scienza e della Tecnica "Leonardo da Vinci", inv. no. 5712

When the uncut diamond arrived in Florence, it was assigned to the Venetian diamond cutter Pompeo Studentoli, who had been working in the grand ducal workshops since April, 1605. He was paid with a salary of 50 *scudi* a month for the entire length of time taken to cut the gem which was finished only in 1615; the diamond was cut into an irregular almond shape with 127 facets.
In this etching the diamond is not yet mounted in the setting of a snake biting its tail, made of gold, encrusted with small diamonds, as it was described in the grand ducal inventory of 1621, and as it appears in the official portrait of Maria Maddalena of Austria with her son Ferdinando II, painted by the court artist Jusus Suttermans in 1623. (M.Sf.)

Bibliography: M. Sframeli in *I gioielli dei Medici*, Florence 2003, p. 141, no. 69 (with previous bibliography).

The diamond known as the "Fiorentino" – the second diamond in the world "for size and weight", as Jaen Baptiste Tavernier wrote in 1676 – was purchased in Rome in 1601 by Orazio Rucellai for the Grand Duke of Tuscany Ferdinando I, thanks to the intermediation of the Cardinal Del Monte; the Portuguese owners, Don Lodovico di Castro and his wife, Mexia di Noronha, had deposited the stone with the Jesuits in Rome.
The stone, which remained in the Medici collections until the dynasty died out (1743), was taken to Vienna by the Lorraine heirs together with all the most precious of the crown jewels of Tuscany. The "Fiorentino" remained in Vienna until 1919, when the last Austro-Hungarian Emperor took it with him at the fall of the Empire; since then, all traces of it have been lost. (M.Sf.)

Bibliography: M. Sframeli in *I gioielli dei Medici*, 2003, pp. 140-141, no. 68 (with previous bibliography).

Pietro Berrettini called Pietro da Cortona
(Cortona 1596 - Rome 1669)

STUDY FOR A YOUNG WOMAN IN THE FRESCO OF THE AGE OF SILVER, IN THE SALA DELLA STUFA OF PALAZZO PITTI
1637

Red and black pencil drawing on waxed paper, 35 x 24,6 cm
Florence, Museo Horne, inv. no. 5604

The four scenes of the *Age of Gold, Silver, Bronze* and *Iron* painted by Pietro da Cortona for the Medici in 1637 and 1641 in the *Sala della Stufa* in the Pitti Palace, together form the first great masterpiece of Baroque painting. They represent a new concept in the decoration of interiors; full of color, highly natural, sumptuous yet soft, both in the neo-Venetian tones of the painted outline and in the grandiose stances of the figures. These were to be the model for all future fresco decorations in palaces and aristocratic Italian and European residences during the 17th century. Ferdinando II appreciated the originality of Pietro da Cortona at the right moment following a formative period spent by the artist in Venice and did not hesitate to commission him to decorate the five reception rooms in the Pitti Palace that came to be known as the *Sale dei Pianeti* (Planet Rooms). Numerous drawings by Cortona for the frescoes and plasterwork in Pitti Palace exist including this splendid sketch for a reclining female figure that appears in the *Age of Silver*, the style and technique show the influence of the drawings of Barocci and Cigoli on the artist. (S.C.)

Bibliography: C. Collobi Ragghianti, *I disegni della Fondazione Horne in Firenze*, Florence 1963, p.15, no. 31; M. Campbell, *Pietro da Cortona at the Palazzo Pitti*, Princeton 1977, p. 265, no. 28; C. Garofalo, *Da Raffaello a Rubens*, Livorno 2000, p. 62, no. 23 (with previous bibliography).

Grand Ducal Workshops

PAIR OF CANDLESTICKS
1610 - 1630

Silver foil over a wooden core; embossed, chased and graffito, height 71 cm
Iscribed on the base: "GRA. DUCHESS.a DI TOSCANA CHRISTIANA LOTARINGIA"
Arms: on the base, the Medici coat of arms parted with that of the Lorraine, surmounted by the grand ducal crown
Monsummano Terme, Museo della Città e del Territorio, Chiesa di Santa Maria di Fontenuova

In 1620, upon the death of Cosimo II, his mother Cristina of Lorraine and his wife Maria Maddalena of Austria began to dominate the political scene in Florence. These two highly religious women were frequently engaged in pilgrimages and making donations to religious orders, primarily to the Jesuits, to the point of provoking a financial crisis at court. Under their influence, in fact, the art of the goldsmith enjoyed a period of substantial patronage and achieved excellent technical and creative results in the grand ducal workshops. Grand ducal memorials and documents register repeated visits of the Grand Duchess Cristina of Lorraine to the Sanctuary in Monsummano where for the first time in 1573, the Madonna was said to have appeared to the little shepherd girl, Jacopina Mariotti. This pair of silver candlesticks was donated during one of these pilgrimages. Their refinement distinguishes them from the other objects conserved in the Sanctuary Treasury, rendering plausible the hypothesis that they were made by a goldsmith working in the grand ducal workshops. (E.C.)

Bibliography: C. D'Afflitto, M.P. Mannini, *Oreficeria e arredi sacri a Pistoia tra '500 e '600* in *Pistoia: una città nello stato mediceo*, Pistoia 1980, pp. 279-280; G. Cantelli, *Storia dell'oreficeria e dell'arte tessile in Toscana dal Medioevo all'età moderna*, Milan 1996, pp. 233-234.

Florentine

HOLY WATER PAIL
1621

Embossed and chiseled silver, 23 x 17 cm
Pistoia, Museo Diocesano

Reading the inscription on the base of the pail (IL PRINC. DO. LOREN. MEDICI MDCXXI), we see that the object was donated by Don Lorenzo de' Medici (1599-1648), to the Giaccherino convent in Pistoia. The donation was probably the result of the fact that one of the Medici court confessors, brother Jacopo Peri, who in 1615 was elected personal confessor to Grand Duke Cosimo II and his two sons, Lorenzo and Ferdinando, came from this monastery in Pistoia.

This object for use during religious rites, dated 1621, is a beautiful Florentine example of the art of the silversmith. The small pail was used to contain holy water. (M.B.)

Bibliography: M.P. Mannini in *Pistoia: una città nello stato mediceo*, Pistoia 1980, p. 272, no. 46; D. Liscia Bemporad, *Argenti fiorentini dal XV al XIX secolo*, Vol. II, Florence 1992, p. 154.

Florentine

COPE WITH A GREEN BACKGROUND
1680 - 1690 ca.

Satin brocade, silk, gold and silver thread, 114 x 69 cm
Florence, Galleria del Costume, inv. MAS 1911, no. 861

The cope, complete with stole, muffler, chalice veil and purse, was first described in the inventories of the Medici *Guardaroba* in 1692, registered among the objects in Palazzo Vecchio. Between 1781 and 1785, it was kept in the Palatine Chapel in the Pitti Palace for use during the religious ceremonies celebrated there.

The arabesque-like motif which decorates this magnificent silk liturgical vestment is closely linked to that invented in Florentine workshops, and it is probable that the textile was woven in the "haberdasher's workshop" of the Medici *Guardaroba*. This is also true of an identical cope still conserved today in the Basilica of Santissima Annunziata, a church to which the Medici family was closely tied. (M.B.)

Bibliography: R. Orsi Landini in *I paramenti sacri della Cappella Palatina di Palazzo Pitti*, Florence 1988, no. 3.

Florentine

SMALL PORTABLE ALTAR
Beginning of the 18th century
Wood, textiles and embroidery in various materials, 225 x 177 cm
Florence, Galleria Palatina, inv. MAS 1911, no. 1518

This portable altar may be folded up and fitted into a trunk, which is covered with leather decorated with stamped polychrome floral sprigs, and has gilded bronze handles on the sides. When open, the altarpiece reveals a red velvet front decorated with gold and silver velvet tendrils and vases within areas delineated by gold and silver braid. In the center, there is an oval-shaped painting representing the Immaculate and Sts. Louis of France and Sigismund of Poland kneeling at the sides of the throne, the work of a Florentine painter of the beginning of the 18th century. Two corner elements of carved and gilded wood, designed to contain relics and liturgical objects, are placed on the sides of the altar base. Red cloth woven with gold thread covers the lower part or frontal of the altar; it has a gold ribbon and fringe with the Medici coat of arms surmounted by the Cardinal's hat (that of Francesco Maria 1660-1710) in the middle.

The rarity and refinement of the piece well illustrate the grand ducal workshops' production of objects for devotional purposes. This type of folding altar was used during the frequent travels undertaken by the Medici for economic or political reasons. (M.B.)

Bibliography: M. Chiarini in *Curiosità di una reggia*, 1979, no. 4.

Pieter Paul Rubens
(Siegen 1577 - Antwerp 1640)

COPY OF THE VISION OF EZEKIEL BY RAPHAEL
1605 - 1608 ca.
Sketch in red and black pencil, grey water color and white lead on white
paper, 30 x 22,5 cm
Florence, Museo Horne, inv. no. 5549

The drawing belonged to several important collectors such as Jabach, Crozat and Mariette before it was bought by Herbert Horne in 1904. It reproduces the famous painting by Raphael (Palatine Gallery, Florence) representing God the Father surrounded by symbols of the four Evangelists. Quite strong similarities to classical art can be seen in the figure of God, inspired by representations of Jupiter. The image is usually thought to refer to the biblical vision of the prophet Ezekiel, though it has also been suggested that it could be the apocalyptical vision of Saint John on the island of Patmos. The title of the small painting by Raphael, dated 1516-1518 is now accepted to be the *Vision of Ezekiel* and it first belonged to the collection of the Ercolani family of Bologna, then later to the Medici. From 1589 it was in the Tribune of the Uffizi, and at the end of the 17th century it was moved to the Pitti Palace. The drawing exhibited here is of very high quality and a subtle and complex technique has been used by the artist. The first draft is in lead pencil and this is retouched in red; the drawing was then completed with a painted background of grey watercolor and strokes of white lead. The work is traditionally believed to be a copy by Rubens of Raphael's painting, perhaps made sometime between 1605 and 1608 when the Flemish

artist paused in his journey from Mantua to Rome. The painting was acquired for the Horne Collection in Florence with this attribution and it has been confirmed in more recent times. Other scholars, including Sylvia Ferino Pagden, believe instead that the technique used is not characteristic of Rubens and it could therefore be an original preparatory drawing by Raphael for the Florentine painting, subsequently owned and retouched by Rubens who not only enjoyed collecting and copying antique drawings, but also, in fact, reworking them. The drawing is certainly of excellent quality and reveals a subtle hand more closely related to 16th century works than to the more Baroque, 17th century style of the Flemish painter. However, many authoritative scholars have not accepted the attribution to Raphael, preferring to sustain the traditional attribution to Rubens, as is given here. (S.C.)

Bibliography: M. Jaffé, *Rubens and Raphael* in *Studies in Renaissance and Baroque Art*, 1967; S. Ferino Pagden in *Raffaello a Firenze*, 1984, pp. 302-303; C. Garofalo, *Da Raffaello a Rubens*, 2000, p. 86 (with previous bibliography).

Giulio Parigi (attributed to)
(Florence 1571 - 1635)

SCENERY WITH RIVER ALLEGORIES
Drawing, pen and ink with brown and blue water-color wash,
29 x 39,5 cm
Grassina, Alberto Bruschi Collection

The drawing is most likely a sketch for scenery designed for an "interlude" of a comedy in music. A river god is to be seen in a recess formed by a jutting rock on the upper left, as he makes water spring from the rocks; behind him are a black and white shield and a She-wolf, symbols of the city of Siena. Two other allegorical figures representing river gods make water gush out and flow to the sea on which a galley is floating. Various figures appear on board the ship, among which the three centrally-seated figures seem to be the comedy's main characters. On the right, there is a group of six crowned girls, perhaps a chorus of nymphs. The allusion to the city of Siena probably refers to the fact that the Grand Duchy of Siena had been assigned to Ferdinando I de' Medici (1551-1609) while he was still Cardinal; newly elected, he entered the city through Porta Camollia which was reconstructed for the occasion. Also from Siena was Girolamo Bargagli, author of the musical comedy, *La Pellegrina* commissioned by Ferdinando I in 1560, and put on stage by the *Accademici Intronati* of Siena for the wedding of the Grand Duke and Cristina of Lorraine in 1589. The attribution of the drawing to Giulio Parigi (1571-1635) seems plausible; he was architect to Cosimo II, as well as court scenery designer, and nephew of Bernardo Buontalenti who had made the drawings for the "interludes" of *La Pellegrina*. (M.D.L.)

Bibliography: V. Longo in *Per un regale Evento*, Florence 2000, no. 52, p. 97; S. Bellesi, *La scultura tardo-Barocca fiorentina e i modelli per la manifattura di Doccia* in *Le Statue del Marchese Ginori*, Florence 2003, pp. 1-28

Ferdinando Ghelli
(Design and Construction)

INTERPRETATIVE MODEL FOR A THEATER STAGE, IN THE STYLE OF BUONTALENTI FOR THE TEATRO MEDICEO
1980
Wood, 138 x 241 x 148 cm
Florence, Provincia di Firenze

The conquest of power and the affirmation of the principality under Cosimo I were guided by wise political strategy, which included using exceptionally magnificent spectacles and theatrical representations as an efficient means of propaganda. The prince had various "technicians" on call, specialized in how to best use theatrical spaces, whether organized in temporary locations or in actual permanent theaters created inside the Medici villas. Among the architects who took on such tasks, revealing themselves to be capable of becoming the most ingenious of set designers, were Bastiano da Sangallo, Giorgio Vasari, Bernardo Buontalenti, Giulio and Alfonso Parigi. Bernardo Buontalenti himself (1536-1608) was the inventor of a complex system of machinery which allowed continuous changes of scenery for the comedies played out in the Medici Theater. (E.C.)

Bibliography: L. Zorzi in *Il potere e lo spazio*, 1980, pp. 336 - 342; A. M. Testaverde in *L'ombra del genio*, Florence 2002, pp. 133-143.

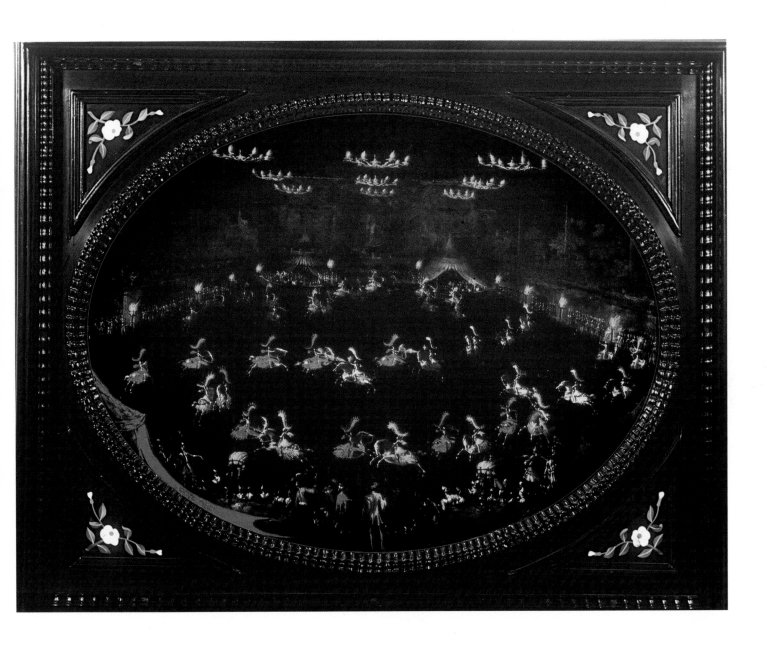

Stefano Della Bella
(Florence 1610 - 1664)

NOCTURNAL CAROUSEL IN THE AMPHITHEATER OF THE BOBOLI GARDENS
1637
Oil on touchstone, 43,5 x 58,8 cm
Grassina, Alberto Bruschi Collection

The scene is set at night in the amphitheater of the Boboli Gardens behind the Pitti Palace, which can just be seen in the background, dimly lit by torches. The nocturnal carousel was held on July 15, 1637 to celebrate the marriage of Ferdinando II de' Medici and Vittoria della Rovere, and was loosely based on the theme of *Gerusalemme Liberata* by Torquato Tasso. Two rows of knights (including many noblemen and guests of the Medici court) confronted each other in a game that was theatrically choreographed by Ferdinando Sarcinelli, director of the celebrations. All important events in the Medici family were traditionally celebrated by magnificent performances in the courtyard or garden of the Pitti Palace. This splendid reproduction of the scene by Stefano della Bella, a Florentine painter who produced few works, presents a dreamlike fantasy image, inspired also by Jacques Callot, that uses the black background of the stonework to suggest the darkness of the night, illuminated by the glow of the lamps and torches. (S.C.)

Bibliography: S. Bellesi in *Bizzarrie di pietre dipinte*, Milan 2000, p. 74 (with previous bibliography).

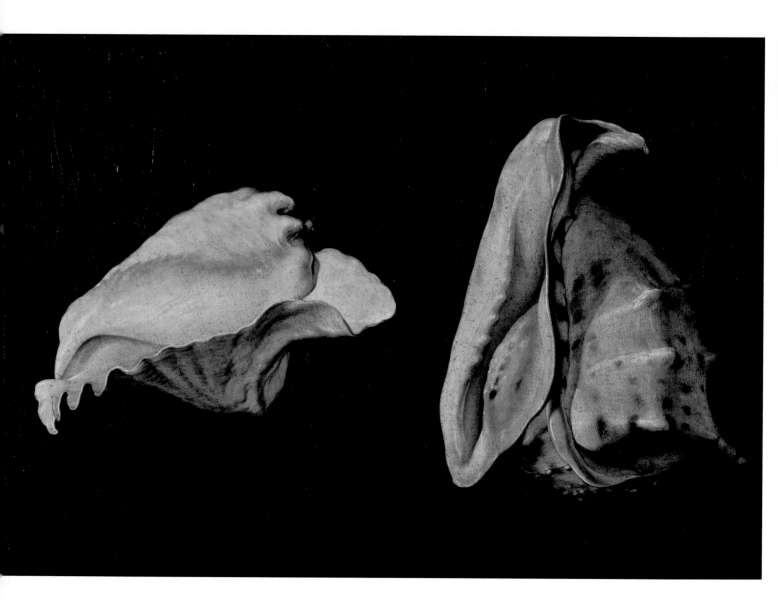

Teodoro Filippo de Liagno called **Filippo Napoletano**
(Rome or Naples 1587/91 - Rome 1629)

TWO SHELLS
1618
Oil on canvas, 39 x 56 cm
Florence, Galleria Palatina, inv. 1890, no. 6580

These two examples of tropical shells (*Tridacna elongata* and *Cassis cornuta*) are faithfully represented here on a black background that highlights the unusual forms, the rare material and delicate colors illuminated by natural light. The image can be considered as a genuine scientific document and may have been a descriptive image for the famous Medici collection of shells kept in a studio in the Uffizi until the 18th century and then dispersed. Archival records show that this fine small painting was given to Cosimo II in 1618 by the painter Filippo Napoletano who resided in Florence from 1617 to 1621. These *Two Shells* are therefore an early and rare example of still life painting which, in the lively cultural atmosphere of the Medici court in Florence, was closely related to the great interest in the natural sciences shared by both Grand Duke Cosimo II and Filippo Napoletano. (S.C.)

Bibliography: S. Casciu in *La natura morta italiana*, Florence 2003, p. 274 (with previous bibliography).

Anonymous
(Bartolomeo Bimbi ?)
(Settignano 1648 - Florence 1729)

LARGE CITRON IN A LANDSCAPE
Late 17th century

Oil on canvas 60 x 65,5 cm
Florence, Galleria degli Uffizi, inv. 1890, no. 9378

Traditionally citrus fruits have always been well represented in Tuscan paintings of natural phenomenon, both in complex compositions illustrating the various varieties and individually as this large citron lemon, displayed on a stone surface, still on a leafy branch, almost like a grand formal portrait. Lemons, citrons, oranges, limes, perfumed lemons, pomegranates and bergamots were always found in Tuscan, and especially Medici, gardens growing in large pots or trellised, and their presence is reflected in these fascinating and highly naturalistic paintings that enjoyed much popularity at the Medici court. Early and important evidence of this fashion for citrus fruits is the painting of two *Citrons* made by Filippo Napoletano in 1618 for Cosimo II. The painter best known for the genre was, however, Bartolomeo Bimbi whose patron was Grand Duke Cosimo III. The style and theatrical arrangement of this painting, probably late 17th century, would suggest Bimbi as the author. (S.C.)

Bibliography: R. Spinelli, *La pittura di Bartolomeo Bimbi* in *Le Belle Forme della Natura*, Bologna 2001, p. 44; *I mai visti*, Florence 2002, p. 64.

Bartolomeo Bimbi
(Settignano 1648 - Florence 1729)

TWO-HEADED LAMB
1721

Oil on canvas, 58 x 72 cm
Florence, Palazzo Pitti, Depositi delle Gallerie Fiorentine, inv. 1890, no. 4854

The painting represents a "monster of nature", a lamb born with two heads or more probably Siamese lambs. In fact the inscription on a stone, below left, records that the animal, born near San Casciano, near to Florence in February 1721, had two of almost all its organs. Painted by Bartolomeo Bimbi for Grand Duke Cosimo III, the picture is evidence of the lively scientific interest of the Medici court for the animal world and for botany, including deformities and "monsters" such as this. Bimbi made other paintings of this kind for the Grand Duke, (the *Two-headed Calf*, for example) and his paintings reveal a fine descriptive ability especially for flowers and fruit as well as animals. Bimbi's skill in the genre of still life and the description of natural events makes him one of the most original and interesting artists of the 17th century in Florence. (S.C.)

Bibliography: S. Meloni Trkulja in *Bartolomeo Bimbi*, Florence 1998, p. 210 (with previous bibliography).

Florentine

COPY OF GALILEO'S TELESCOPE OF THE 17TH CENTURY
Modern

Wood and leather, length 92 cm
Florence, Istituto e Museo di Storia della Scienza, inv. no. 2428

The telescope is formed of a wooden tube, covered with red leather and gold ornaments; the lens is biconvex, with an opening of 16 mm and a focal distance of 96 cm. The first telescope developed by Galileo and offered to the Venetian Senate, had a 9 x enlargement, which could be increased to 20 x by changing the lens. Galileo's detractors, faced with the reality of his invention of the telescope, started to claim that he had plagiarized the invention of a Dutchman, and that in any case the studies carried out on lenses could in reality already be found in the 1593 treatise by Della Porta. The true novelty was in the idea of pointing the instrument towards the sky, thus laying the basis for the use of telescopes in astronomy. Galileo used his telescope to observe for the first time the four satellites of Jupiter, which he baptized "stars or planets of the Medici". Galileo reported his discoveries in the *Sidereus Nuncius*, first printed in Venice in 1610. (E.C.)

Bibliography: M. Miniati, *Il Museo di Storia della Scienza*, Florence 1991, p. 72; F. Camerota in *Nel segno di Masaccio*, Florence 2001, p. 232.

Justus Suttermans
(Antwerp 1597 - Florence 1681)

PORTRAIT OF GALILEO GALILEI
1635

Oil on canvas, 66 x 56 cm
Florence, Galleria degli Uffizi, inv. 1890, no. 745

This is, perhaps, the most famous portrait of the famous scientist, Galileo Galilei (1564-1642). The approach and angle used in the portrayal is extremely direct and dynamic. With a stylistic approach that can be defined as entirely Baroque, Galileo is seen turning briskly to the right as if suddenly attracted by a voice or event, his lively eyes shining and mouth partly open as if talking. Contemporary sources describe the history of the painting fully, especially in the writings of Filippo Baldinucci, who records that the painting was made in 1635 at the request of Galileo himself, by the Flemish painter Justus Suttermans, official portraitist at the Medici court. It was sent to Paris as a gift to his learned friend, Elia Diodati, to whom Galileo felt very close and was also grateful as he had promoted the publication in France that same year of the translation of his *Dialogues*. Suttermans' Baroque dynamism, so evident in the painting, was a direct result of his experience in Rome, where he had been able to study and appreciate the work of Andrea Sacchi, but also of Pieter Paul Rubens and Anton Van Dyck. After Galileo's death, the portrait was given to Grand Duke Ferdinando II in 1656 and was immediately placed in the Tribune of the Uffizi gallery, the most prestigious location for items in the Medici art collections.

Galileo was one of the most important scientists of the 17th century, founder of modern experimental science who also made some of the most important historical discoveries in astronomy and physics and wrote works that are fundamental in the history of science. He was always admired and protected by the Medici, even during the period when he was condemned by the church. One of Galileo's many discoveries was the four satellites of Jupiter, which he dedicated to the Florentine grand dukes, naming them the *Sidera medicea* (the Medici planets). (S.C.)

Bibliography: C. Pizzorusso, in *Sustermans. Sessant'anni alla corte dei Medici*, 1983, pp. 58-59 (with previous bibliography); *Scienziati a corte*, Florence 2001, pp. 68-69.

German

SOLAR-LUNAR CLOCK
Second half of the 16th century
Silver plate and gilt brass, 6,4 x 10 cm
Florence, Istituto e Museo di Storia della Scienza, inv. no. 2481

The Medici collections, although scarce in mechanical timepieces, are quite rich in the field of gnomonics, the category to which sundials belong. These, although they may appear in a great variety of forms (like a little box, a column, horizontal or vertical, polyhedral or flat), actually all have similar characteristics. The sundial is the graphic representation of some of the principal circles of the celestial sphere, traced on the flat plane which forms the dial according to special projections derived from geometrical perspective. The surface of the dial has hour lines onto which the shadow of the gnomon or stylus is projected, after having correctly oriented the instrument with the aid of a compass. It is evident that sundials require clear skies to function correctly. The same is true of lunar dials, which must follow the movement of a star in relation to the pole star seen at night, or the phases of the moon, and therefore function as a lunar calendar. The indications given by a sundial may differ from the simple measurement of the passage of time, and be linked to specific astronomical characteristics, as for example the indication of the position of the zodiacal signs on the ecliptic rather than in relation to the horizon. These are denominated ascending or descending, or sometimes sidereal sundials. Sundials have been used since antiquity to mainly indicate the so-called "natural" hours, derived from the simple division of day and night into twelve equal parts without taking into account seasonal differences. This hourly system may have already been used by the Sumerians, although solid proof of its use is only to be found about one millennium BCE in Egypt, and only in the IV-III century BCE in Greece. The system of natural hours was adopted by almost all ancient populations and in use until the Middle Ages; they were also called Temporary, Judaic, Antique, Saxon, Canonical (because used also by the Church), Planetary hours.
The timepiece exhibited here is in the form of a missal, bearing the monogram of the Company of Jesus, IHS. The lunar dial is placed on the cover, while on its reverse we find the meridians; the sundial was inside, with its revolving gnomon and compass, now missing; on the back plate are the planetary hours. (E.C.)

Bibliography: M. Miniati, *Il Museo di Storia della Scienza*, 1991, pp. 5-6, 10.

Arab

ASTROLABE
13th century
Gilt brass, diameter 18 cm
Florence, Istituto e Museo di Storia della Scienza, inv. no. 1112

The astrolabe is an instrument whose function is both astronomical and topographical. Traditionally attributed to Hipparcus of Nicea (II century BCE) and widely used by the Arabs, it arrived in Europe through Spain during the Middle Ages. Its name, of Greek origin (*astron lambanein*), means "star seeker". An astrolabe is formed of a round case (*mater*) inside which there are one or more plates called *tympanum*, on which are inscribed lines which are the projected representation of the sky in relation to the precise latitude for which the plate has been calibrated. The circle of the Zodiac, the constellations, and the principal stars in each constellation are traced on a web placed over the *tympanum*, while the back of the astrolabe was used for making readings and measuring angles for the determination of heights. The characteristics of the astrolabe vary according to its place of origin. The one exhibited here contains three *tympani* for the latitudes of 24°-25°, 32°-36°, 34°-38°, while the web has silver buttons. (E.C.)

Bibliography: M. Miniati, *Il Museo di Storia della Scienza*, Florence 1991, pp. 4-5, 8.

Tito Lessi
(Florence 1858 - 1917)

GALILEO GALILEI AND VINCENZO VIVIANI
Late 19th century
Oil on canvas, 51 x 48 cm
Florence, Istituto e Museo di Storia della Scienza, without inv. no.

Portrayed according to the Galileo iconography typical of the late 19th century, the elderly, already blind scientist is shown in a somewhat austere interior together with his young and faithful disciple, Vincenzo Viviani, who edited his works for publication and wrote his biography. In the foreground we may see the globe by J. W. Blaeu dated 1622, and the armillary sphere made in 1564 by Girolamo della Volpaia. The patronage of the sciences already offered by the Medici during the 16th century was revitalized during the following century thanks to Galileo. Cosimo II favored Galileo's return to Tuscany and Galileo in return did not hesitate to dedicate his exceptional discoveries to the Medici, contributing to the confirmation of the dynasty's prestige throughout Europe. The objects belonging to Galileo, discoverer of new worlds and father of experimental research, immediately became a worthy part of the Medici collections. (E.C.)

Bibliography: A. Porta, *Galilei: la sensata esperienza*, Florence 1988; M. Miniati in M. Bona Castellotti, F. Gamba, E. Mazzocca, *La ragione e il metodo*, Milan 1999, p. 106.

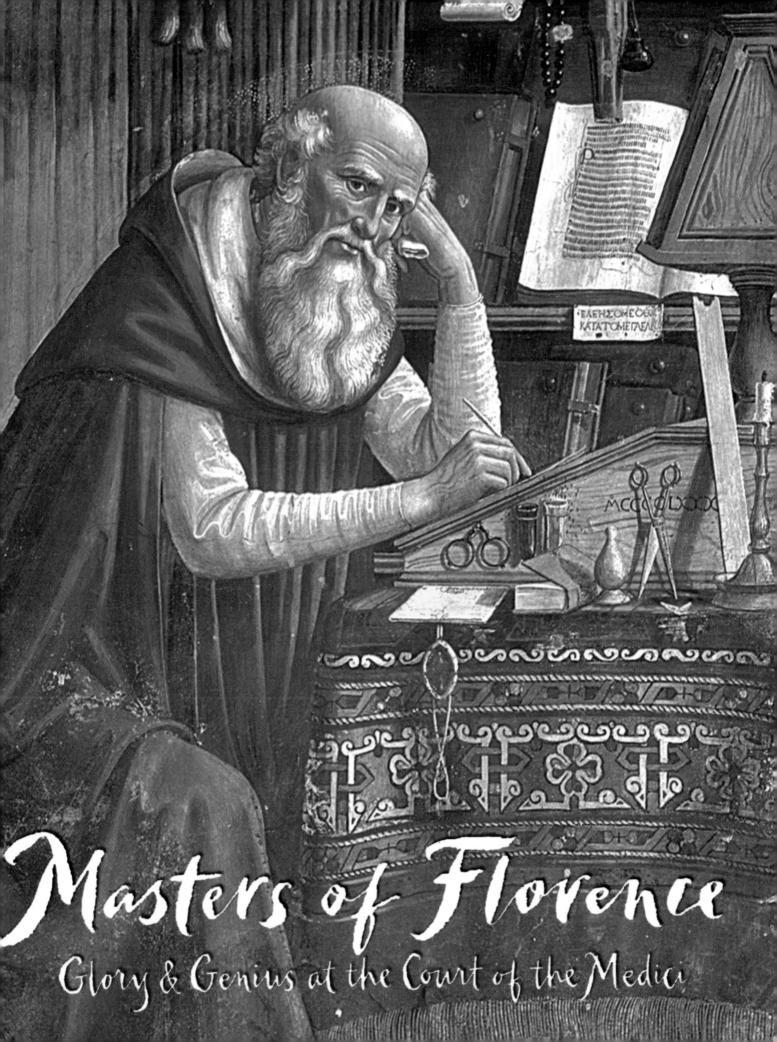

Masters of Florence

Glory & Genius at the Court of the Medici

Twilight of a Dynasty

Annamaria Giusti

"*Certa fulgent sidera*" (Constant shining stars) is the motto which was chosen by the son of Ferdinand II, Cosimo III: in fact fortune seemed to come his way when, as heir to the Grand Duchy of Tuscany, he married Marguerite-Louise of Orleans, cousin of the most illustrious sovereign in Europe, Louis XIV, King of France. Of this union three children were born, but in 1674, four years after Cosimo had succeeded his father, Marguerite returned to France indefinitely as she never accepted the provincial climate of Florence nor the bigotry of the grand ducal court. Cosimo III, who was very close to his mother Vittoria della Rovere and strongly influenced by her, became very religious to the point of fanaticism. He was an undefatigable collector of reliquaries and a patron of numerous furnishings for churches and sanctuaries. He even commissioned from the Opificio a magnificent mausoleum of precious marble and bronze to be sent to a Jesuite church in Goa, India. Apart from his religiosity, Cosimo III had a taste for the magnificent and the ostentatious. Conscious of the political decline of his small State, the Grand Duke tried to counterbalance this by demonstrating grandeur, which although illusory in substance, had a dazzling effect all the same. The Pitti Palace and the Medici art collections were constantly enriched and sumptuous, marvellous objects were manufactured and sent as gifts from the Grand Duchy to all the major European courts. While the finances of the court were constantly dwindling and taxes rising, Cosimo III hurried to obtain the title of Royal Highness. This raised his prestige within the hierarchy of the European courts. His eldest son and heir to the throne had a very different character from his father; he was not interested in government, and almost as if he foresaw his own death prior to that of his father, dedicated himself to music, the arts, to his retreat at the Villa at Pratolino, and to his travels in Italy and Europe. Nor was he interested in his wife, Violante of Bavaria, whom his father had chosen, and thus he died in 1713 without a heir. He thereby left the succession to his younger brother, Gian Gastone who had already divorced his German wife with whom he had lived for a short time in Bohemia, also without having had any children; a forewarning to the Medici that the dynasty would soon become extinct. As a consequence, various courts around Europe became interested in the future of the Grand Duchy of Tuscany.

When Cosimo III died in 1723, Gian Gastone was 52 years old and a profoundly elderly and disillusioned man, who nevertheless, at least during the first years of his reign, took some positive initiatives, such as the abolition of the death penalty and the normalization of the climate both at court and in the city to a less religious, more lively tone. His last years however were marked by an ever increasing dependence on alcohol, illness and lost sense of dignity. He died in 1737. Already in her seventies, his sister Anna Maria Luisa survived him. She had, already as a young child, given evidence of a firm and balanced character, and love for culture. Her marriage in 1691 to the Elector Palatine, Johan Wilhelm, although arranged, was a happy one and at the court in Düsseldorf, they revealed themselves as cultured patrons. Since Cosimo III had sent his favorite child and son-in-law gifts which had been created especially for them in the grand ducal workshops, the Electress acquired an extraordinary collection of jewelry and enriched her residences as well as the churches with works of Italian and German artists.

TWILIGHT OF A DYNASTY

Widowed in 1716 and without children, Anna Maria returned to Florence, taking with her only her personal belongings. Here, she continued her active interest in the arts, receiving among others in 1718, Antonio Vivaldi; one of his works was performed at the Pergola Theater, one of the first music theaters in Europe open to the public. With the years, her devotion increased and many of the works she commissioned from sculptors and painters had religious themes, but she also had an interest in botanical subjects and collected precious objects, thereby continuing the family tradition.

Cosimo III had faith in the qualities of his daughter, involving her in politics during his last years and, in vain, had tried to obtain the right to nominate a successor to the Medici within the Grand Duchy of Tuscany, but he was unsuccessful as the European courts objected. At the death of her brother, Gian Gastone, the last Grand Duke, Anna Maria inherited all the family possessions, including the Pitti Palace, the Medici villas and the prestigious art collections. In 1735, an international treaty designated Francesco Stefano of Lorraine as official Grand Duke of Tuscany, and he took up his new position in 1737. The Electress retired in a wing of the Pitti Palace and dedicated her last years to the completion of the Medici mausoleum, the Chapel of the Princes, which had still been left incompleted. She died in 1743. In 1737, she had written a "Family Pact", a testament that left all the Medici possessions to the new Grand Duke with the binding clause that the collections should be for the embellishment of the State, for public use and to attract foreign interest, nor should any part of it be transported or removed from the capital and Grand Duchy.

With this enlightened act, ahead of her own times, the last of the Medici concluded with great dignity the story of this great family and ensured that Florence would forever keep its unique role as a city of Art.

Giovan Domenico Cerrini
(Perugia 1609 - Rome 1681)

ALLEGORY OF HUMAN FRAGILITY
1656 - 1661
Oil on canvas, 130 x 97 cm
Florence, Museo Bardini, inv. no. 293

Giovanni Camillo Sagrestani (Florence 1660 - 1731)
(drawing)
Giovan Battista Termini
(textile)

DOOR HANGING WITH THE MEDICI COAT OF ARMS AND
AN ALLEGORY OF THE ARNO RIVER
1710 - 1717
Tapestry, wool and silk, 316 x 230 cm
Florence, Archivio di Stato, without inv. no.

A woman, seated on a wooden chair with a child and a dog at her feet, holds in her right hand a fan on which is written, " OGNI COSA QUA / PASSA E NON DURA / OGNI / CONTENTO HUMA(N) / CADE E TRAMONTA" (Everything passes / passes and does not last / All human happiness / fades and declines). It is an allegory therefore of the transience of human life, in which everything, including happiness is destined to come to an end. The theme of the painting is emphasized by the melancholic expressions of the figures and even by the quality of the light. Giovan Domenico Cerrini, an artist born in Umbria, lived in Florence between 1656 and 1661, during which time he was in contact with the Medici court and in particular with Prince Matthias and Cardinal Leopoldo. The painting probably dates from that period. Salvador Rosa also dealt with this theme in a painting now in the Fitzwilliam Museum, Cambridge, but there seems to have been no contact between the two artists. (S.C.)

From the 16th century on, tapestries were used not only for decorative purposes but also to protect and insulate the halls and chambers of palaces from cold draughts by covering doorways and windows. This door covering is decorated with a large Medici coat of arms, supported by two angels and surmounted by a regal crown. Cosimo III was granted the title of Royal Highness by the Emperor in 1691. Below are an elderly bearded man, his hair represented by acquatic plants, symbolizing the Arno River, and the *Marzocco* lion, emblem of the city of Florence. One of a series of similar tapestries, it was made between 1710 and 1717 under the direction of Giovan Battista Termini in the Medici workshops from a design by the Florentine painter Giovanni Camillo Sagrestani. The clearly rococo style shows the influence on Florentine artists of the Venetian painter Sebastiano Ricci, active in the city during the first few years of the 18th century, particularly in the service of Prince Ferdinando de' Medici. (S.C.)

Bibliography: M. Chiarini, *Aggiunte al Cerrini* in "Antologia di Belle Arti", no. 6, 1978, p. 282; *Il Museo Nascosto*, 1991, p. 54, no. 29.

Bibliography: Gli ultimi Medici, 1974, p. 412.

Giovanni Zanobio Weber
(Florence 1737 - 1806)

MEDAL OF GRAND DUKE COSIMO III
After 1785

Bronze, diameter 4,8 cm

Florence, Museo di Palazzo Martelli, without inv. no.

The medal was part of a series dedicated to the Medici, carried out beginning in 1785 by Giovanni Zanobio Weber, grandson of the more famous medalist Lorenzo Maria Weber. The Grand Duke Cosimo III dressed in antiquity-style clothing is portrayed on the front, together with an inscription which includes Weber's initials (I. V.); on the back there is an altar with a flame and the inscription "RELIGIONIS AMOR", which alludes to the Grand Duke's fervent religiosity. The medal has been coined rather than cast, perhaps because Weber was actually more expert in coining money than in making medals. The series which contained this piece was made when the Medici dynasty was already extinct, and was not commercially successful, while a predecessor to it, the famed Medici Series composed of 111 medals almost all designed and cast by Antonio Selvi beginning in 1739, was far more fortunate. Selvi was the most prolific Tuscan medalist of the Baroque age. He prepared a series which included portraits of all the members of the Medici family, starting with Salvestro Chiarissimo, considered the founder of the family in the *Trecento* (1300's), up to the last representative of the dynasty, the Electress Palatine. (S.C.)

Unpublished

Baldassarre Franceschini called "Il Volterrano"
(Volterra 1611 - Florence 1689)

PORTRAIT OF GRAND DUKE COSIMO III
1677

Oil on canvas, 196 x 122 cm

Florence, Provincia di Firenze, inv. 1890, no. 3195

This is a full length portrait of Grand Duke Cosimo III (1642-1723) holding the crown and scepter and clothed in gold damask with an ermine cloak. In the background is the port of Livorno, the most important military base of the Grand Duchy, and center of his mercantile trade, showing the monument to Ferdinand I with the *quattro mori* (the four Moors). This large painting was part of a series portraying all the Grand Dukes in official garb and with the insignia of office, once located in the Hospital of Santa Maria Nuova of which the Medici were patrons. The portrait is by one of the most important Florentine Baroque artists, "Il Volterrano" who, with the sumptuous luxury of the clothing, the damask, the lace, the ermine and the theatrical backdrop of the red curtain, enhanced the majesty of the figure of the Grand Duke. (S.C.)

Bibliography: S. Meloni Trkulja, *Il potere del ritratto* in *Stanze segrete stanze scomparse*, Florence 2003, pp. 72-87 (with previous bibliography).

Giuseppe Antonio Torricelli (attributed to)
(Florence 1662 - 1719)

COSIMO III DE' MEDICI
Early 18th century; mounting, 1952

Hard stone, bronze and wood, height 46 cm
Florence, Museo dell'Opificio delle Pietre Dure,
inv. nos. 594, 610. 611, 3305

This unfinished statuette representing the Grand Duke Cosimo III was perhaps intended for the exterior of a *stipo*, or cabinet, which although never completed, was probably planned as a pendant to another one made at the beginning of the 18th century for the Elector Palatine, son-in-law of the Grand Duke of Tuscany, now conserved in the Museo degli Argenti in Florence.

Cosimo's head, hands and feet have been seemingly effortlessly sculpted in hard chalcedony, probably by the specialist in free-standing semiprecious stone carving, Torricelli. Besides the parts in chalcedony, the bronze flag and military trophies are also original. The object was kept in storage at the Opificio in this fragmentary state until 1952, when the original pieces were mounted, and the Grand Duke's armature was carved in wood following the example of another bronze statuette, property of the forementioned Elector. (A.G.)

Bibliography: A. Pampaloni Martelli in A. Giusti, P. Mazzoni, A. Pampaloni Martelli, *Il Museo dell' Opificio delle Pietre Dure a Firenze*, Florence 1978, p. 307.

Giuseppe Antonio Torricelli
(Florence 1662 - 1719)

COSIMO III AND TUSCANY BEFORE THE TEMPLE OF PEACE
Beginning of the 18th century

Chalcedony cameo, 17 x 11 cm
Florence, Museo dell'Opificio delle Pietre Dure, inv. no. 580

This exceptionally large cameo is the work of one of the major specialists in semiprecious stone relief carving, active in the Medici workshop at the time of Cosimo III. Made from a single piece of chalcedony, shading from pearly tonalities to warmer amber tones, this cameo represents Tuscany shown as a crowned female figure, with the Grand Duke standing in front of her, against a background of a temple consecrated to Peace. An identical allegorical subject appears in a bronze medallion celebrating Cosimo III, by the hand of the sculptor and bronze-caster Massimiliano Soldani Benzi, another artist active in the grand ducal workshop. (A.G.)

Bibliography: A. Pampaloni Martelli in A. Giusti, P. Mazzoni, A. Pampaloni Martelli, *Il Museo dell' Opificio delle Pietre Dure a Firenze*, Florence 1978, p. 306; M. Sframeli in *Splendori di pietre dure*, Florence 1988, p. 176.

Anonymous

VIEWS OF THE FAÇADE OF PALAZZO PITTI AND OF THE AMPHITHEATER IN THE BOBOLI GARDENS
Early 18th century
Pen and brown ink, with brown watercolor wash,
77 x 99 cm (with frame)
Florence, Private Collection

These drawings represent two of the most celebrated views of Palazzo Pitti: the façade, as wide as it would become in the middle of the 17th century, and the central courtyard of the palace in front of a perspective view of the Boboli Gardens. The façade appears as it already did in the 15th century, composed of ponderous blocks of stone, whose jutting effect diminishes going upwards from the ground floor towards the two stories above. According to Vasari, the façade was designed in this fashion by the great Florentine architect, Filippo Brunelleschi towards the middle of the 15th century. It still maintains its original concept today, despite the various projects to re-arrange the piazza and the façade, in particular by architects such as Bernardo Buontalenti and Pietro da Cortona in the 17th century. The building was commissioned by the banker Luca Pitti, who desired a Renaissance style palace entirely made of stone, to be quarried from the hill of Boboli, and which would be the largest and most splendid palace ever built in Florence. Although still unfinished at the time of Luca's death (1472), his name has remained perpetually linked to the Palace.

The Duke of Florence, Cosimo I de' Medici, bought the palace in 1565, and the court architect and pupil of Michelangelo Buonarroti, Bartolomeo Ammannati, was commissioned to enlarge it with the addition of the monumental central courtyard and the palace wings which flank it. These project towards the garden which was taking form on the Boboli hillside behind the palace, according to the plan by Niccolò Tribolo. Ammannati himself provided for the monumental ground floor arches of the façade with "kneeling" windows derived from Michelangelo, characterized by lions' heads surmounted by the ducal crown, as if to validate the "promotion" of the palace to official residence of the Medici family. The palace façade was expanded only at the beginning of the following century, during the rule of the Grand Duke Cosimo II de' Medici, reaching the extension it shows in this drawing in the second half of the century. The piazza represented in the drawing is animated by a procession of carriages which has just come out of the left gate (we may observe the beginning of the corridor which unites Palazzo Pitti to Palazzo Vecchio, constructed by Vasari for Cosimo in 1565). The first of these is undoubtedly the grand ducal carriage: it is in fact a carriage and six, preceded by halberdiers (also to be seen guarding the main portal), who belonged to the guard of the then Grand Duke Cosimo III de' Medici. The view of the courtyard also shows numerous groups of people walking around and conversing; they are wearing clothes which may be dated from the first two decades of the 18th century.

The two drawings seem to be the work of a Florentine artist in anticipation of the style of panoramas typical of the famous specialist in this kind of work, Giuseppe Zocchi (1716/17-1767), who would later represent the same scene of the piazza and Palazzo Pitti. (M.C.)

Unpublished

Baldassarre Franceschini called **"Il Volterrano"**
(Volterra 1611 - Florence 1689)

VENUS AND CUPID
1641 ca.
Fresco on reeds, 80 x 67 cm
Florence, Museo Bardini, inv. no. 866

The fresco, a sensual image of Venus embracing a small Cupid, is not a fragment detached from a larger image but, from the outset, was conceived as a small autonomous work, a decorative room painting, even though the technique used is that of a mural painting. The preparatory plaster on which the fresco painting is laid, is applied to a support of reeds. The technique is characteristic of Volterrano, who was a skilled mural painter. The oval work is one of a pair and the matching piece represents

Ila with the Golden Bowl. The combination of mythological and allegorical subjects with the fresh, bright colors produced by the fresco technique was most popular with Florentine collectors of the day. The work and its pair belonged to Cardinal Giovan Carlo de' Medici and were in the villa at Castello. The style of painting shows the influence of Correggio's soft, clear tones and of Pietro da Cortona's Baroque works. Volterrano was the only painter in 17th century Florence who was fully capable of interpreting the Baroque innovations of Cortona in large scale decorative works. (S.C.)

Bibliography: M. Gregori in *70 Pitture e Sculture del '600 e '700 fiorentino,* Florence 1965, p. 54; S. Mascalchi, *Anticipazioni sul mecenatismo del Cardinal Giovan Carlo de' Medici e suo contributo alle collezioni degli Uffizi* in *Gli Uffizi,* Florence 1982, p. 66; C. De Benedictis in F. Scalia, C. De Benedictis, *Il Museo Bardini,* Florence 1984, Vol. I, p. 248, no. 57.

Florentine

CONSOLE
1800 - 1805 ca.
Carved and gilded wood; table top of yellow Siena marble,
90,5 x 178,5 x 83 cm
Florence, Museo di Palazzo Martelli, inv. Mobili, nos. 164-165

Florentine

TWO ARMCHAIRS
Mid - 17th century
Walnut, carved and partially gilded; seat and back covered with stamped and
partially gilded leather; 140 x 63 x 55 cm
Florence, Museo degli Argenti, inv. MPP 1991, nos. 13268-13273

The style and ornamentation of this lovely console from Palazzo Martelli,
identical pendant of another with which it forms a pair in the same room,
recall certain Baroque prototypes produced in the grand ducal workshops,
inspired by the taste for magnificent and elegant furnishings typical of the
Florentine court and nobility at the beginning of the 17th century. It is
more than likely that this pair of console tables is actually a 19th century
derivation, in substitution of the ones visible in an 18th century painting
conserved in the Martelli Palace which depicts the family in the green
drawing-room (by Giovan Battista Benigni, inv. Martelli, Dipinti no. 40):
the two consoles in the painting are similar, but not identical to the actual
pieces of furniture. (M.B.)

Unpublished

These two chairs are part of a series of six, whose style is based on a late
16th century typology which reached broad diffusion in Florence during the
century to follow, and which was frequently present in the grand ducal
residences. Such armchairs are mentioned in 16th/17th inventories as being
of various types, such as the Venetian, the *Bolognese*, the *Pistolese*, or in
the "comfortable" style. It is extremely difficult to establish a certain date
for them, as the style remained constant, without variations, and only the
covering became more and more refined over time. The oldest reference to
covering them with stamped leather, until now discovered in the records of
the *Guardaroba*, dates from 1617. (E.C.)

Bibliography: E. Colle, *I mobili di Palazzo Pitti. Il periodo dei Medici*,
Florence 1997, p. 256.

Balthasar Permoser (attributed to)
(Kammer 1651 - Dresden 1732)

PAIR OF TORCH HOLDERS IN THE FORM OF MOORS
Last decades of the 17th century
Painted wood, height 154 cm each
Florence, Galleria Palatina, inv. MPP 1911, nos. 4225, 4226

Beginning in the second half of the 17th century, torch holders, until then placed on tall stools for the purpose of lighting the vast and sumptuous halls of the grand ducal apartments, were substituted with painted wooden figures. They could be of a type similar to the "two figures in wood of youngsters dressed like pages in pants and golden jacket, which are used as torch-holders," listed as being in the apartment of Prince Ferdinando in 1713 (ASF, *Guardaroba Medicea* 1222, c. 97), or in the form of Moorish figures

dressed in rich and colorful clothes, or else "semi-nude" figures such as these, dressed only in a little skirt of ostrich feathers and a strip of red material around the waist. These two Moors are shown stepping forward, supporting a cornucopia on top of which the candelabra would be placed; the heads are bent back to look upwards towards where the light would shine. The high-quality carving which models and shapes the chest and head of the two figures, and according to the information supplied by Aschengreen Piacenti that Permoser had made two Moors for Prince Ferdinando in 1683, suggest an attribution to this German sculptor. In those very years (between 1676 and 1690), he was present at the Medici court working as an ivory turner. This pair of Moorish figures has always been recorded, since 1737 as Enrico Colle informs us, as being present in the first floor apartments of Palazzo Pitti. (M.D.L.)

Bibliography: K. Aschengreen Piacenti in *Gli Ultimi Medici*, 1974, p. 380; E. Colle, *I Mobili di Palazzo Pitti*, Florence 1997, p. 246, no. 83.

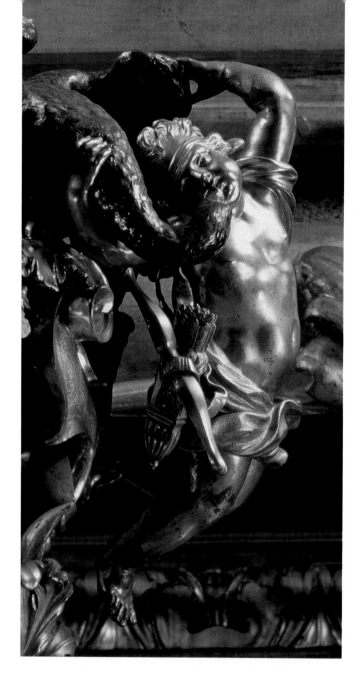

Massimiliano Soldani Benzi
(Montevarchi 1656 - 1740)

**VASE WITH HANDLES IN THE FORM OF SWANS WITH
PUTTI**
1689 - 1693
Black marble of Belgium, gilded silver and bronze, height 80 cm
Florence, Galleria Palatina, inv. O.d.A. 1911, no. 1534

The splendid vase of black touchstone (black marble of Belgium) is one of a group of four, made for the Grand Prince Ferdinando by Massimiliano Soldani between 1689 and 1693. They have always been in the Pitti Palace, and were listed in 1713 among the possessions of the Grand Prince: "Four Touchstone urns...each with handles formed by a putto cast in bronze and gilded, which embraces a swan made of a plate of silver" (ASF, 1222, c.14). It seems from a document cited by Dimitrios Zikos, that Ferdinando commissioned the vases to decorate the Palace chapel where his wedding to Violante of Bavaria was to be held. The theme of the *amorino* kissed by a swan is in fact strictly connected to nuptial events.

Every phase of the making of these four vases is known, thanks to the documentation cited by Sandro Bellesi and by Dimitrios Zikos; from the first step of the turning of a model in wood, to the insertion of clasps and screws to fix the metal parts to the marble.

The pure black marble of the vase exalts the splendor of the gold putti, whose facial features and drapery recall Algardi's sculptural style, and of the silvery wings of the swans, whose refined craftsmanship perfectly evokes their natural lightness. The elegant naturalism of the foliage on the top of the urn and at the four corners of the base is also typical of Soldani's style.

The sculptor in his Florentine works shows great mastery in elaborating the experiences acquired in Rome, where he had attended the grand ducal academy founded by Cosimo III. Soldani's derivations are in particular from the work of sculptors such as Alessandro Algardi, and from the suggestive elegance of French applied arts, with which he had come into contact during the period spent in Paris in 1682.

Other works by Soldani, who was Master of Coinage and Custodian of the Medici Mint for thirty years starting in1688, are listed among the possessions of the Grand Prince. They are all now conserved in the Museo degli Argenti: four bas-relief sculptures in terracotta representing the *Seasons*, two urns in serpentine with handles in the form of two entwined snakes, and a bronze group with the *Christ Child and young St. John*. (M.D.L.)

Bibliography: S. Bellesi, *Precisazioni su alcune opere eseguite da Massimiliano Soldani Benzi per il Gran Principe Ferdinando de' Medici* in "Paragone", no. 497, 1991, pp. 82, 84; D. Zikos in *Palazzo Pitti*, Florence 2003, p. 617, no. 157.

Giovanni Mannozzi called **Giovanni da San Giovanni**
(San Giovanni Valdarno 1592 - Florence 1636)

AURORA E TITHONUS
1634 - 1635 ca.
Detached fresco, 360 x 160 cm
Florence, Museo Bardini, inv. no. 768

The fresco represents the goddess Aurora, sister of Helios, god of the sun, as she sprinkles rose-colored flowers over her elderly husband, Tithonus who, being immortal but not eternally young, remains deep in sleep every morning while the goddess rises from her bed to bring the dawn. The painting was originally at center ceiling of a room in the Pucci Palace in Florence as can also be seen from the much foreshortened figure of Tithonus. In 1633, Alessandro Pucci bought the palace and had Giovanni da San Giovanni frescoe a cycle of various mythological and allegorical subjects in the palace. Some of these have survived (*Night with Aurora and a Cupid; Venus; Fame; The Judgement of Paris; Orpheus and Eurydice*) while others have been lost. The remaining paintings confirm that the cycle was of considerable importance and quality. The particular stylistic characteristics of Giovanni da San Giovanni's painting are his extremely elegant drawing, creative fantasy, skill in organizing the scenes in a theatrical manner, fine handling of the lighter tones, and the originality of the play of light from below upwards that lend his frescoes a charm that is almost 18th century. The frescoes in the Pucci Palace are almost contemporary to the decoration of the large hall in the summer apartments in the Pitti Palace, carried out between 1635 and 1636, the last and most felicitous period in the career of Giovanni da San Giovanni. His absolute masterpiece was the Medici hall in the Pitti Palace where another of his qualities emerges unequivocally – the sense of irony and wit that make his works highly original and free from that heaviness that is sometimes evident in 17th century decoration. Completion of the Medici cycle in Pitti Palace was halted by the unexpected death of the artist in 1636 which however facilitated the rise to fame of Pietro da Cortona in Florence. In 1637, in the *Sala della Stufa* in Pitti Palace, he created the first masterpiece of Baroque painting, the *Four Ages of Man*, continuing thereafter with the decoration of the splendid *Sale dei Pianeti* (Planet Rooms). (S.C.)

Bibliography: F. Scalia, C. De Benedictis, *Il Museo Bardini a Firenze*, Florence 1984, Vol. I, p. 245, no. 47; I. Della Monica in *Giovanni da San Giovanni*, Bologna 1994, pp. 19-20, 84.

Grand Ducal Workshops

HOLY WATER FONT
Beginning of the 18th century
Hard stones and gilt bronze, 78 x 46 cm
Florence, Museo dell'Opificio delle Pietre Dure, inv. no. 615

This holy water font was meant for the wall of a bedroom, therefore for the private devotion and daily prayers of a member of the Medici family, who would thus be able to cross himself with holy water taken from its agate basin. Although precious refinement would always be reserved for objects intended for an important person, even when designed for religious use, here it tends to take on the sumptuous, theatrical forms typical of the Baroque style in the 17th century, similar whether the work was intended for a monumental setting, such as the famous throne of St. Peter designed by Bernini for the Vatican Basilica, or was of limited size such as this font.

As do other particularly exuberant objects created in the grand ducal workshop during the times of Cosimo III de' Medici, the font achieves spectacular effects through the triumphant nimbus of rays, closed on the bottom with a double festoon, and the vivid chromatic scheme which combines the brilliant luminosity of gilded bronze with the warm tones of the semiprecious, multi-colored stones. The fluffy clouds enclosed by the circle of rays are carved from white chalcedony, softly veined in a golden tonality, which almost seems to be a reflection of the sun about to illuminate the dove, symbol of the Holy Spirit. Variously colored stones form the two relief busts, representing the Archangel Gabriel and the Annunciated Virgin which decorate the medallions on the sides of the font. The Annunciation, a scene which had always enjoyed great diffusion in the Catholic tradition, was and still is famous today in Florence as it was

depicted in the frescoed version in the church of the SS. Annunziata; this image, held to be miraculous, has always been venerated since it was painted in the 14th century. The Grand Duke Cosimo III paid special devotion to it, and had various semiprecious stone derivations made of it, both in mosaic and relief form.

Both the Grand Duke's personal taste and that of the age in which he lived showed particular fondness for semiprecious stone sculpture, which was expected to achieve levels of absolute virtuosity. For this reason, the craftsmen in the workshop were divided into specialists in two-dimensional mosaics ("flat inlays") and masters of carving. Among the latter, Giovan Battista Torricelli (see p. 209) excelled, and may well have been the author of the extremely fine relief carvings which adorn the holy water font, carved so sweetly that it almost seems impossible that such results could be achieved handling materials as hard and scarcely ductile as are these silicates. The fine workmanship evident in the heads of the two sacred figures is particularly impressive; they are both carved from a single small block of chalcedony, whose natural color variations, ranging from white to bright yellow, have been exalted to suggest the paleness of the faces and the blond shade of hair. (A.G.)

Bibliography: A. Gonzàlez Palacios in *Gli Ultimi Medici*, Florence 1974, p. 346; A. Giusti in *Splendori di pietre dure*, Florence 1988, p. 170.

Giovan Battista Foggini
(Florence 1652 - 1725)
(and grand ducal workshops)

RELIQUARY OF SAINT SIGISMUND
1719
Ebony, silver, gilded bronze, hard stones, height 57,7 cm
Florence, Museo delle Cappelle Medicee, inv. Tesoro di San Lorenzo, no. 84

This fine reliquary is dedicated to Saint Sigismund, the first Christian king of Burgundy, and the central scene portrays his miraculous appearance to a group of injured youths. The structure of the reliquary is made of ebony, the figures are silver, the decorations in gilded bronze while the small fruits are made of semiprecious stone. This combination of precious materials with different chromatic effects is typical of late Baroque art at the Florentine court and in particular of the style of Giovan Battista Foggini who was the foremost architect and sculptor at Cosimo III's court. Made to his design and under his direction, numerous furnishings, decorations and objects of various kinds, were made in the highly organized grand ducal workshops located below the Uffizi gallery from the end of the 17th century to the beginning of the 18th. Foggini's design was sophisticated and characterized by the Roman Baroque style, careful and original choice of materials, and the highest quality of production. He not only provided the plans and designs for almost all of these items but also undertook the most important phases, especially sculptural, of the work. A beautiful preparatory drawing for this reliquary, which was consigned in September 1719, is in the Louvre and reveals some slight modifications, but the seven elegant figures were modeled, fused and honed by the master. Other specialized craftsmen whose names are also documented, were responsible for the decorative elements, such as the small fruits of semiprecious stone and the gilded bronze decorations. (S.C.)

Bibliography: L. Lankheit, *Florentinische Barockplastik*, Munich 1962, pp. 62-63; K. Aschengreen Piacenti, A. Gonzàlez Palacios in *Gli Ultimi Medici*, Florence 1974, p. 354, no. 198.

Massimilano Soldani Benzi
(Montevarchi 1656 - Florence 1740)
Pietro Motti
(active Florence, 1690 - 1697)

RELIQUARY OF ST. ALEXIUS
1691 ca.
Hard stones, chiseled and cast gold, embossed and chiseled silver, gilded copper and ebony, height 54 cm
Florence, Museo delle Cappelle Medicee, inv. Tesoro di San Lorenzo no. 110

The elaborate structure of the reliquary was inspired by the story of St. Alexius, who had fled his home the day of his wedding, then took a vote of chastity; he later returned to his father's abode to take refuge, but died under a staircase. The composition, work of Soldani as already affirmed by Lankheit in 1962, seems to be scenery viewed foreshortened and with illusionist effects, in part the result of the vivid chromatic combinations of the semiprecious stones. Recent archival research conducted among the volumes of the Medici *Guardaroba* has permitted the reconstruction of all the phases of the crafting of this impressive sacred object; documents attest to the consignment to the artist of the columns of amethyst (September 14, 1690), and of the gold necessary to make the small statue of the Saint, as well as a receipt for payment to Pietro Motti for the frame and other elements of gilded copper (May 10, 1691). (M.Sf)

Bibliography: L. Bertani, E. Nardinocchi, *I tesori di San Lorenzo*, Livorno 1995, p. 60, no. 18 (with previous bibliography).

Anonymous

THE FUNERAL OF GRAND DUKE COSIMO III
1724

Oil on canvas, 67,5 x 81 cm
Florence, Museo Horne, inv. no. 6497

In the painting, the funeral of Grand Duke Cosimo III who died in 1723, is recreated. Funerals or other public ceremonies of the Grand Dukes, members of the Medici family, or other important Florentine or non-Florentine individuals that the government wished to honor, were celebrated in San Lorenzo, the Medici church since the *Quattrocento* (1400's). On these solemn occasions, the interior and exterior of the church was completely transformed by temporary theatrical scenery composed of artificial architectural elements, sculpture, painting and other fittings, created by a group of artists with incredible speed, in low quality but appealing materials (such as wood, painted paper-maché, canvas, tin plate, plaster, fabric). There remains visual documentation that these were often re-utilizations of those from previous ceremonies with a few changes. The scenery effects for the funeral of Cosimo III in San Lorenzo were designed and directed by the architect Alessandro Galilei. (S.C.)

Bibliography: F. Rossi, *Il Museo Horne a Firenze*, Florence 1966, p. 149; L. Bertani in L. Bertani, E. Nardinocchi, *I Tesori di San Lorenzo*, 1999, p. 69; A. M. Testaverde, *San Lorenzo "cantiere teatrale"* in *La morte e la gloria*, Florence 1999, pp. 75-79.

Niccolò Cassana
(Genoa 1659 - Venice 1713)

PORTRAIT OF GRAND PRINCE FERDINANDO DE' MEDICI
1690 -1699
Oil on canvas, 101 x 88 cm
Florence, Galleria Palatina, inv. 1890, no. 5448

Ferdinando, Grand Prince of Tuscany (1663-1713) was the son of Cosimo III and Marguerite-Louise of Orléans. A famous and sophisticated collector, perhaps the greatest in the history of the Medici family, he never became Grand Duke as he died ten years before his father. As well as acquiring numerous paintings and sculptures, now an essential part of the Florentine museums, Ferdinando discovered and protected many contemporary artists, becoming a patron of the arts on an international scale. Cassana was one of the artists at his service, a fine portraitist who made this painting showing the Grand Prince as a man of arms, as well as many other portraits of the last Medici court. At the same time, Cassana acted as agent for Ferdinando, especially during his sojourn in Venice at the end of the 17th century, in the acquisition of many paintings, often adapting the dimensions to fit the new frames designed for the decoration of rooms in the Pitti Palace. (S.C.)

Bibliography: M. Chiarini in *Gli Ultimi Medici*, Florence 1974, pp. 200-201.

Italian

SMALLSWORD OF THE GRAND PRINCE FERDINANDO
1680 - 1690
Steel and silver with niello and gilding, length 99,5 cm
Florence, Museo Nazionale del Bargello, inv. no. M 260

The smallsword exhibited here was the property of the Grand Prince Ferdinando de' Medici (1663-1713); it had a double-edged blade and a steel protective hilt embellished with gold and silver decorations. Commonly used in the 18th century, the smallsword is an often richly ornamented weapon, limited in size, which was usually carried in ceremonies and official receptions (compare it with the one in the portrait of Ferdinando from the Galleria Palatina). Luxury weapons with elements made of gold, silver or other precious metals, were sometimes kept in the Uffizi Tribune designed by Buontalenti, but we also have mention of them, kept as valuable collector's items, in the Grand Dukes' private apartments. (E.C.)

Bibliography: M. Scalini in *Opere d'arte della famiglia Medici*, Milan 1997, p. 115.

Niccolò Cassana

(Genoa 1659 - Venice 1713)

PORTRAIT OF ANGIOLA BIONDI, DWARF IN SERVICE TO PRINCESS VIOLANTE OF BAVARIA

1707

Oil on canvas, 153 x 118,5 cm

Florence, Palazzo Pitti, Depositi delle Gallerie Fiorentine,
inv. 1890, no. 5140

The dwarf, Angiola Biondi, was in the service of Princess Violante of Bavaria, wife of Prince Ferdinando. Angiola was also a gifted singer. Her portrayal as a shepherdess with an Arcadian landscape, at the time internationally fashionable, in the background, helps to evaluate her position at the Medici court. The animals are probably intended to emphasize her height. The portrait was painted for Prince Ferdinando de' Medici who mentions it, with a matching portrait of a cook, in a letter dated 1707. The prince particularly appreciated Niccolò Cassana who was of Genoese origin, though he had developed his artistic skills in Venice, and for some years while living in Florence, he was the preferred portraitist at the court. The animals were probably painted by Niccolò's brother, Giovanni Agostino who specialized in the genre. (S.C.)

Bibliography: M. Chiarini in *Gli Ultimi Medici*, Florence 1974, p. 202, no. 114; S. Meloni Trkulja in *Al servizio del Granduca*, Florence 1980, p. 52, no. VII, 16.

Domenico Remps
(Antwerp, late 17th century - early 18th century)

TROMPE-L' OEIL WITH AN OPEN CABINET
Oil on canvas applied to wooden support, 99 x 137 cm
Florence, Museo dell'Opificio delle Pietre Dure, inv. no. 780

The painting represents a kind of show case with glass windows, known as a *scarabattolo*, used to house and display quite small collectable items of various kinds, both natural and man-made. During the 17th and 18th centuries, the studies of scholars and collectors often had such cabinets, frequently of quite sophisticated craftsmanship. The collection of various precious items was intended to reflect the notion of concentrating the complete variety of creation and of art into an organized microcosm, full of surprises and delights for the minds and eyes of the curious and connoisseurs. Using the trompe-l'oeil technique, created in Flanders in the 16th century, Domenico Remps reproduces one of these collector's cabinets made of a richly veined and knotted wood. Inside, with great skill and illusionistic ability he portrays small pictures, coins, letters and drawings, coral, insects, small bronzes, mirrors, a skull, ivory spheres (*bibelot*), shells, clocks, glass and other items. Many of these refer to the fragility and transience of things, and of life, and the painting could therefore be considered as a *vanitas*. Yet the extreme clarity of the sharp analytical description of the items creates a detached atmosphere, as if of another dimension and almost surreal. The painting belonged to Prince Ferdinando de' Medici, an inquisitive and enthusiastic collector, also of still life images, and he probably kept this work in a special studio in the villa at Poggio a Caiano. The presence of a letter in the painting bearing the name of the Marquis Francesco Riccardi, a Florentine aristocrat and patron of contemporary artists, reveals that Remps made it in Florence in the late 17th and early 18th century, perhaps as a gift from Riccardi to Ferdinando. Such a work would certainly have served as a model for other Florentine artists who produced trompe-l'oeil painting, also in the production of semiprecious stone mosaic work. There is no biographical information for Remps, though he was probably born in Antwerp and may have been a relation of Cornelis Gysbrechts, one of the most important Flemish specialists in trompe-l'oeil during the 17th century. (S.C.)

Bibliography: M. Chiarini in *Curiosità di una reggia*, Florence 1979, p. 61; A. Giusti in A. Giusti, P. Mazzoni, A. Pampaloni Martelli, *Il Museo dell'Opificio delle Pietre Dure di Firenze*, Florence 1978, pp. 335-336; I. Della Monica, *Gran Principe Ferdinando* in *Il giardino del Granduca*, Turin 1997, p. 263.

Anton Domenico Gabbiani
(Florence 1652 - 1726)

PORTRAIT OF THREE MUSICIANS OF THE MEDICI COURT
1687 ca.

Oil on canvas, 141 x 208 cm
Florence, Galleria dell'Accademia, Museo degli Strumenti Musicali,
inv. 1890, no. 2802

This canvas is one of a group of four paintings representing similar subject matter, made by Gabbiani for the Grand Prince Ferdinando de' Medici (1663-1713) for the villa at Pratolino, as mentioned by the early biographers of the artist, Francesco Saverio Baldinucci and Ignatius Hugford. Ferdinando had a theater built in the villa, where music composed specially for him was performed.

The musicians portrayed are members of the Medici court, although their identity is not certain. The harpsichord player, shown with his hands poised above the keyboard as he is about to start to play, has in the past been identified as Antonio Pagliardi, although at the time he supposedly would have been forty-eight years of age, while the painted player appears much younger. The violinist might be the twenty-nine year old Martino Bitti, and the singer Francesco de Castro, called "Cecchino", who entered the court of the Grand Prince in 1687 after having served the Duke of Mantua.

Gabbiani's work demonstrates an admirable ability in capturing the expression on the faces of the three musicians as they await the music to start, their eyes turned towards the onlooker almost as if they are expecting him to give the first stroke of the wand. Just as brilliant is the rendering of the sumptuous fabrics which clothe the figures, especially the flowered white silk satin worn by the Moor seen holding a parrot with his hand. This detail of clothing is very similar to that of the Moor in another painting by Gabbiani, the *Four Servants of the Medici Court* (see page 178).

It is interesting to note that the painted harpsichord and violin correspond to instruments to be found in the vast collection of musical instruments which once belonged to the Grand Prince, part of which is now exhibited in the Museum of Musical Instruments in the Galleria dell'Accademia.

Bartolomeo Cristofori, who was on the payroll of the Medici court, created various keyboard instruments for the Grand Prince Ferdinando, lover of music and himself a musician, among which were the first examples of *forte-piano*, while Niccolò Amati and Antonio Stradivari constructed violas, violins and cellos for him, as is punctually recorded in the inventories of the Medici *Guardaroba*. (M.D.L.)

Bibliography: S. Casciu in *Lo spettacolo maraviglioso*, Florence 2000, p. 148, no. 2.1.8 (with previous bibliography); F. Falletti, *Un museo in mostra* in *La Musica alla corte dei Granduchi*, Florence 2001, p. 13.

Balthasar Permoser
(Kammer 1651 - Dresden 1732)

PORTRAIT OF THE PRINCESS VIOLANTE OF BAVARIA
1689 ca.

Ivory relief carving, 10,5 x 7,8 cm
Florence, Museo degli Argenti, inv. Bargello 1879, no. 80.

The minute ivory oval contains the profile image of a young princess of the House of Bavaria, Violante, who wed the Grand Prince of Tuscany, Ferdinando in 1689. The portrait was a gift to the future bridegroom by the artist himself, Balthasar Permoser, and remained in the residence in the Pitti Palace even after his death, until 1761 according to the palace inventory of that year.

The young princess was sixteen years of age when she arrived in Florence. She was quite beloved by her father-in-law Cosimo III, who in fact invited her to remain in Italy when she was widowed in 1713. The villa of Lappeggi was assigned to her, where she retreated, but at the moment her sister-in-law Anna Maria de' Medici returned to Florence from Düsseldorf with the aspiration of becoming Grand Duchess, she had the government of Siena given to her and moved there with her court.

The art of turning ivory was introduced in Florence by the Grand Duke Cosimo III, who had learned to appreciate this art during his travels in northern Europe, and had even made it become a pleasant discipline of his sons' instruction, Gian Gastone and Ferdinando. A little ivory vase conserved in the Museo degli Argenti has an inscription on the base which tells us that it was made by Ferdinando himself in 1678.

Balthasar Permoser, during his 14 year stay in Florence as official court turner, made various works in ivory for the Grand Prince besides this medallion with the Princess Violante. Among these are four small sculptures designed as knife handles, two with Adam and Eve and two with little putti. The large ivory Crucifix now on the altar in the Palatine Chapel of the Pitti Palace has also been attributed to him. (M.D.L.)

Bibliography: K. Aschengreen Piacenti, *Documented Works in Ivory by Balthasar Permoser* in *Mitteilungen des Kunsthistorisches Institutes in Florenz*, 1963, p.10, pp. 274-283; S. Asche, *Balthasar Permoser* in "Pantheon", 1982, no. 40, pp. 309-316.

Philipp Sengher
(Augsburg ? - St. Petersburg 1723)

PORTRAIT OF THE GRAND PRINCE FERDINANDO
1700 ca.

Ivory relief carving, 8,5 x 6,5 cm
Grassina, Alberto Bruschi Collection

The ivory profile image of the Grand Prince Ferdinando has been framed with a rich and elegant ornament of gilded silver plate, proof of the level of elegance and refinement reached in the arts at the Medici court in the late 17th century. The surface of the ivory, which simulates with its more ductile material the antique art of the cameo, has an almost frothy appearance in the rendering of the curls of the wig and the lavish lace of the tie. The facial features made heavy by time and evident wrinkles (this certainly is not an idealized portrait of the Grand Prince) make about 1700 an acceptable date for the work, as proposed by Alessandro Bellesi.

Philipp Sengher, official ivory turner at court together with Balthasar Permoser, introduced the Grand Prince himself to the art of ivory turning, training him in the time-consuming work of patiently challenging this precious material. A vase made of ivory dated 1678 and signed by Ferdinando at the age of fifteen is conserved in the Museo degli Argenti.

Philipp Senger elaborated furnishings and theatrical machinery for Ferdinando's new theater at Pratolino, establishing a fellowship with the Grand Prince destined to lead him to become official court "right-hand man" and "gentleman of the chamber". (M.D.L.)

Bibliography: S. Bellesi in *Testimonianze Medicee a confronto*, Florence 1997, pp. 60-61, no. 31.

231

Anonymous
(Florentine)

GRAND DUKE GIAN GASTONE IN BED, RECEIVES COSIMO RICCARDI
1736
Oil on canvas, 77,5 x 102 cm
Florence, Museo degli Argenti, inv. 1890, no. 9601

The painting provides a rare record of court life at the time of the last Grand Duke, Gian Gastone de' Medici (1671-1737). A complex character who perhaps has not been entirely understood even today, Gian Gastone has, in the history of the Medici family, been almost entirely blamed for the extinction of the dynasty, becoming the subject of accusations and criticism that may be exaggerated and more generally anti-Medici. Due also to his poor state of health during the last years of his rule, the Florentine court did not have any strong guidance. After 1729, he no longer appeared in public and did not further develop the artistic interests of his predecessors, favoring instead, for example, more frequent contact with Florentine society. This painting represents the presentation to Gian Gastone of the young Cosimino Riccardi, born in September 1735, and recorded in a diary of the time. The Grand Duke is lying on a magnificent four-poster bed in one of the rooms of the summer appartment on the ground floor of the Pitti Palace, now known as the *Sala delle Ambre* (Amber Room). (S.C.)

Bibliography: G. De Juliis in *Curiosità di una reggia*, Florence 1979, p. 58.

Giovan Battista Foggini
(Florence 1652 - 1725)

PORTRAIT OF ANNA MARIA LUISA DE' MEDICI AS A CHILD
1675 - 1677
Marble relief, 20 x 16 cm
Grassina, Alberto Bruschi Collection

Anton Domenico Gabbiani
(Florence 1652 - 1726)

PORTRAIT OF ANNA MARIA LUISA DE' MEDICI AS A YOUNG WOMAN
1685 ca.
Painting on canvas, 87 x 96 cm
Florence, Galleria Palatina, inv. Poggio Imperiale 1860, no. 564

The oval portrays, on a background of black marble, the almost three dimensional bust of Anna Maria de' Medici, as also confirmed by the inscription with her name in capital letters, at eight to ten years of age. The work thus can be dated around 1675-1677. The frame is made from the yellow marble of Siena. The work reveals its refinement in the chromatic rapport of the different stones and in its spirit of recalling the classic portraiture of antiquity. The white bust on a dark background, draped with simplicity, recalls not only the cameos and gems of antiquity, but also the classicism of the Florentine sculpture of Luca Della Robbia or Ghiberti of the *Quattrocento* (1400's). The work has been attributed to Giovan Battista Foggini, sculptor and architect of the Medici court, and was probably commissioned by Vittoria della Rovere, grandmother of the young Princess, whom she educated at the villa of Poggio Imperiale after the scandalous return to Paris in 1675 of her mother, Marguerite-Louise of Orleans. (S.C.)

Bibliography: M. Visonà, *Un Ritratto di Anna Maria Luisa de' Medici bambina e i lari del Poggio Imperiale* in "Paragone", XLIX, 1998, no. 585, S. III 22, pp. 19-30.

Born in 1667, Anna Maria Luisa de' Medici is portrayed here at the age of 17 or 18 years, when her marriage to a European prince who could bring new alliances to the Medici court had already been planned for some time. Negotiations were not to be concluded until 1691 when the marriage to Johann Wilhelm von der Pfalz-Neuburg was celebrated by proxy. The marriage was a happy one, but no heir was born to the couple. Attributed to the Florentine painter, Anton Domenico Gabbiani, the portrait was made for the Princess' brother Ferdinando. The painting is lively and interesting; the young woman, intelligent and thoughtful, is dressed simply and elegantly with a rich blue velvet mantle, lined with ermine and, as fashion then dictated, she wears only two jewels, a fastening at the collar, and a armband, though both are decorated with gems of great value. (S.C.)

Bibliography: L. Goldenberg Stoppato, C. Contu in *I gioielli dei Medici*, Florence 2003, p. 166 (with previous bibliography).

Jan Frans van Douven
(Roermond 1658 - Düsseldorf 1727)

**PORTRAIT OF THE ELECTORS PALATINE
JOHANN WILHELM VON DER PFALZ-NEUBURG AND
ANNA MARIA LUISA DE' MEDICI**
Before 1708
Oil on canvas, 243 x 182 cm
Florence, Galleria degli Uffizi, inv. 1890, no. 2718

This splendid official portrait presents the Electors Palatine of the Rhine, Johann Wilhelm von der Pfalz-Nueburg (1658-1716), and Anna Maria Luisa de' Medici (1667-1743), daughter of Grand Duke Cosimo III. Their marriage took place in 1691 and united the now declining Medici dynasty to the Palatine dynasty, which supported the Hapsburg Empire. With this marriage the Medici hoped to obtain some advantage in the checkerboard of European politics, at a time when the dynasty found itself in some difficulty, but on the whole such hopes were disappointed. In fact the couple did not have any children and on the death of the Elector in 1716, Anna Maria Luisa decided to return to Florence and her father's court. The marriage was a happy one however, and coincided with a period of growth and development for the city of Düsseldorf, the Palatine capital, due also to the couple's shared enthusiasm for the figurative arts, theater and music. Moreover, between 1691 and 1716, there were many artistic contacts between the two cities of Florence and Düsseldorf. The Elector, Grand Duke Cosimo III and his son Ferdinando were all keen and sophisticated collectors of paintings and sculptures with quite similar tastes

on an international level. The constant and courteous presence of the Electress favored the close relationship between the two courts which exchanged quite princely gifts such as paintings by Raphael and Rubens, and important small sculptures in bronze.

In this portrait by Jan Frans van Douven, a Dutch painter and official portraitist at the Electors' court, the Elector Palatine is represented in his role of Vicar General of the Empire as is evident from the presence of the Imperial crown in the center of the painting, placed on a red cushion held by the Prince, while in her right hand Anna Maria Luisa holds an olive branch, symbol of peace. Johann Wilhelm inherited the office of Imperial Vicar General from his father in 1690, but the absence of the emblem of the Order of Saint Hubert, refounded in 1708, leads us to place the portrait prior to that date. (S.C.)

Bibliography: L. Goldenberg Stoppato, C. Contu in *I gioielli dei Medici*, Florence 2003, pp. 168-169 (with previous bibliography).

Jan Frans van Douven
(Roermond 1658 - Düsseldorf 1727)

PORTRAIT OF THE ELECTORS PALATINE AT A FESTIVITY
1695
Oil on canvas, 68 x 52 cm
Pisa, Museo di Palazzo Reale, inv. no. 4960

The small painting shows the two Electors Palatine, Johann Wilhelm and Anna Maria Luisa de' Medici while they dance, dressed in fabulous clothing, richly hemmed with red and gold. On her head the Electress wears a fanciful and precious diadem of pearls and precious stones. Other versions of the work exist (in Florence and in Germany) indicating that it represents a moment during a celebration that may have been particularly important for the couple at the court in Düsseldorf. The version of the painting housed in Palazzo Pitti and dated 1695 is signed by Jan Frans van Douven, a Dutch painter in the service of the Electors' court. The painting is evidence of the great enthusiasm there was for music, dance, and theater during the years of Anna Maria Luisa's residence at the Düsseldorf court, when she also encouraged the presence of many Italian musicians in Germany. (S.C.)

Bibliography: H. Kühn Steinhausen, *Die Feste am Düsseldorfer Hofe* in "Düsseldorfer Heimatblatter", XXII 1939, pp. 125-199; M. Chiarini, *Gallerie e musei statali di Firenze*, Rome 1989, p. 115.

Jan Frans van Douven
(Roermond 1656 - Düsseldorf 1727)

PORTRAIT OF THE ELECTRESS PALATINE AS A WIDOW IN FRONT OF A PORTRAIT OF HER DECEASED HUSBAND
1716
Oil on canvas, 67 x 47,5 cm
Pisa, Museo di Palazzo Reale, inv. no. 4975

Anna Maria Luisa de' Medici, Electress Palatine, is portrayed in sumptuous widow's clothing standing before a death portrait of her husband, Johann Wilhelm von der Pfalz-Neuburg, Elector Palatine of the Rhine, laid on a catafalque with the symbols of his authority. To the right, on a table covered with an elaborate damask cloth, are a clock, symbol of time that passes, and an open book. The author of the painting, and of the portrait of the Elector in death, still housed in the Stadtmuseum of Düsseldorf, is Jan Frans van Douven, a painter of Dutch origin and official portraitist at the Electors' court. After the death of the Elector in 1716, Anna Maria Luisa decided to return to Florence where she lived for 26 more years, witness to the inexorable decline and inevitable extinction of the Medici dynasty which had remained without an heir. (S.C.)

Bibliography: H. Kühn Steinhausen, *Die Feste am Düsseldorfer Hofe* in "Düsseldorfer Heimatblatter", XXII 1939, p. 147, no. 77; *Anna Maria Luisa Medici*, Düsseldorf 1988, p. 259; S. Meloni Trkulja in *The portraits of the Medici,* Vol. I, Florence 1981, p. 273.

Silversmith GAC (Augsburg) and
Conrad Hadernach (Düsseldorf)

PAIR OF TABLE CANDLESTICKS
1710 ca.
Silver, heigth 16 cm, width of the base 10 cm
Florence, Gualtieri Collection

At the base of the pair of candlesticks are the linked arms of the Medici and the Pfalz-Neuburg, surmounted by the electoral crown of the Rhine, evidence that the two objects were owned by Anna Maria Luisa de' Medici. One of the candlesticks also bears the initials GAC, the signature of a workshop in Augsburg, while the other is a copy of the first and was made in Düsseldorf by the silversmith Conrad Hadernach around 1710. They were brought to Florence by the Electress in 1717 and on her death in 1743 were bequeathed to Averardo Serristori, an equerry at her Florentine court as can be seen from the inscriptions added beneath the feet. As was the fashion at all the European courts in the 17th and 18th centuries, Anna Maria Luisa de' Medici commissioned an extraordinary number of silver items, both personal ornaments and furnishings; today almost all are lost as they were smelted to reuse the precious material. Particularly famous was the furniture made almost entirely of silver which decorated the princess' appartments first in Germany and then in Florence. (S.C.)

Bibliography: M. Visonà in S. Casciu, *Anna Maria Luisa de' Medici Elettrice Palatina*, Florence 1993, p. 68.

Gaspare Lopez (Naples ? - Venice 1740)

TWO VIEWS OF A STEM WITH THREE MULTI-PETALED TULIPS
1730
Oil on canvas, 56 x 70,2 cm
Florence, Palazzo Pitti, Depositi delle Gallerie Fiorentine,
inv. Castello, no. 278

The single stalk that has produced three striped and multi-petaled flowers is presented from two different angles in order to highlight their beauty and exceptional size. The center scroll records that the tulips flowered in the Boboli gardens in April 1730 and were immediately painted for Anna Maria Luisa de' Medici by the Neapolitan painter Gaspare Lopez who lived in Florence at the time. By commissioning works such as this, the Electress Palatine was continuing the practice of her father Cosimo III of documenting natural phenomena (flowers, fruit, animals) that were of particular beauty, size, rarity, or occasionally even freakish, in paintings by court artists. In this case, the Princess commissioned the pictorial documentation from a Neapolitan artist who was capable of adapting his style of painting to the Florentine environment, which required particular attention to the natural details, emphasized by a strong light. (S.C.)

Bibliography: S. Casciu in *La natura morta italiana*, Florence 2003, p. 286 (with previous bibliography).

Giuseppe Piamontini
(Florence 1664 - 1742)

PLAYFUL FAUN AND SATYR
Marble sculptural group, height 85 cm
Montecarlo, Private Collection

A young faun with just the hint of a tail is holding down a little goat-footed satyr, while teasingly showing him a couple of bunches of grapes. The satyr replies by sticking out his tongue and making that vulgar and insulting gesture of putting his thumb between forefinger and index finger that the thief, Vanni Fucci shows to Dante Alighieri when they meet in the *XXV° Canto* of the *Inferno*.

A name and date are inscribed on the ribbon next to the bagpipe: "G.PIAMONTINI F.L.MDCCX."

Pellegrino Antonio Orlandi in his brief autobiography of Giuseppe Piamontini (1714), after having spoken of the sculptor's principal works in Florence, mentions "Other Groups and statues of marble and Bronze sent to Rome, Bologna, Prussia, London, to the Rhein, to Scotland, and England". Perhaps this group of a *Playful Faun and Satyr*, which recently reappeared on the antique market in London, was among those sculptures sent to England. At the moment when Sotheby's put the marble on auction, it was completely over-painted with a white ground, making it appear more Neoclassical than Baroque, and concealing the brown veins of the marble which vertically and insidiously streak the figure of the faun.

There are numerous similarities between the *Playful Faun and Satyr* and the group of two playful cupids exhibited in the Museo degli Argenti in the Pitti Palace; the subject is of the same sort, name and date are inscribed on a ribbon on both, the bases are similarly formed sculpting part of the marble block itself as a rock, the height is also the same. The locks of hair entangle in a similar way on both groups, and similar is the consistency of the cloth draping the little nude body of the faun, and which, with a swirl in the air, accompanies the diagonal formed by the

arms. Also comparable is the way in which the sculptor has handled the rough surface of the rock, as well as that of the satyr's wing feathers and hairy goat hoofs, contrasting with the smoothness of the nude flesh. It should be noted, however, that the group exhibited here appears to be treated in general in a slightly less refined way, especially the grapes and grapevine foliage, which do not reach the material elegance of the quiver in the Pitti *Amorini*.

Although the starting point may be identified in the "eroti" of classical antiquity, filtered through the interpretation of such early 17th century artists as Duquesnoy and Algardi, Piamontini's invention of groups of *amorini* or satyrs and fauns playing together created, in a certain sense, a new "genre", one more reflecting popular taste, in which mythological figures were represented in activities ranging from the lascivious to rather heavy practical joking as was popular among "common people".

All this made his groups extremely popular, whether made in marble or bronze. Numerous requests for them consequently arrived, especially from Florentine collectors, who at the beginning of the 18th century were mostly members of the nobility, such as the Pandolfini, Feroni or Borri families. Especially the latter, and in particular Giuseppe Borri, had a great number of sculptures by Piamontini in their collection, as is proven by the list of works belonging to them that they proposed for acquisition to the Grand Duke. (M.D.L.)

Bibliography: S. Bellesi, *La scultura tardo-Barocca fiorentina e i modelli per la manifattura di Doccia* in *Le Statue del Marchese Ginori*, Florence 2003, p. 18.

Italian

LADY'S EMBROIDERED DRESS
1730 ca.
Silk and gold, 205 x 150 x 15 cm
Florence, Galleria del Costume, inv. G.A. 1913, no. 1117

The dress is a rare example of an aristocratic lady's gown dating from the early 18th century, made of linen, silk and gold. It has a V-shaped neckline, elbow-length sleeves, a pleated bust, and a wide skirt. A basket of fruit has been embroidered in the center: it holds spikes of wheat of golden thread and an assortment of flowers and fruit, such as iris, king's spear, roses, buttercups, cherries and wild strawberries, satin-stitched with silk threads of various colors. Minute "rocaille" flower and foliage motifs are embroidered on the bodice with gold thread.
The unusual and complex structure of the dress has suggested that it was worn as a costume on some special occasion or festivity. The fabric and its decoration are similar to those of certain liturgical vestments, many more of which have survived than actual clothing. (M.B.)

Bibliography: M. A. Carlano in *Curiosità di una reggia*, Florence 1979, no.1.

Dutch
(Amsterdam)

JEWEL IN THE FORM OF A BABY AND CRADLE
1695 ca.
Gold filigree, enameled gold, blister pearls, diamonds, pearls, silk embroidered with pearls, 4,9 x 5,5 cm
Florence, Museo degli Argenti, inv. Gemme, no. 2566

The gondola also displayed in this exhibition and this small cradle of gold, pearls and precious stones are part of the *galanterie gioiellate* (jeweled favors) that belonged to Anna Maria Luisa de' Medici, only a few of which have survived until today. Unlike other favors, the cradle would seem to have a direct reference to the Electress Palatine herself. The words "AUGUROR EVENIET" are written in gold filigree and clearly refer to the wish for the birth of an heir that however, was never to be. The baby in the cradle is formed by a large blister pearl with the addition of a smaller pearl with an engraved face. The fashion for these items - precious but bizarre to the point of being grottesque - was typical of northern European courts from the late 17th century to the early 18th century. (S.C.)

Bibliography: Y. Hackenbroch in *I gioielli dell'Elettrice Palatina al Museo degli argenti*, Florence 1988, p. 148; M. Sframeli in *I gioielli dei Medici*, Florence 2003, pp. 172-173.

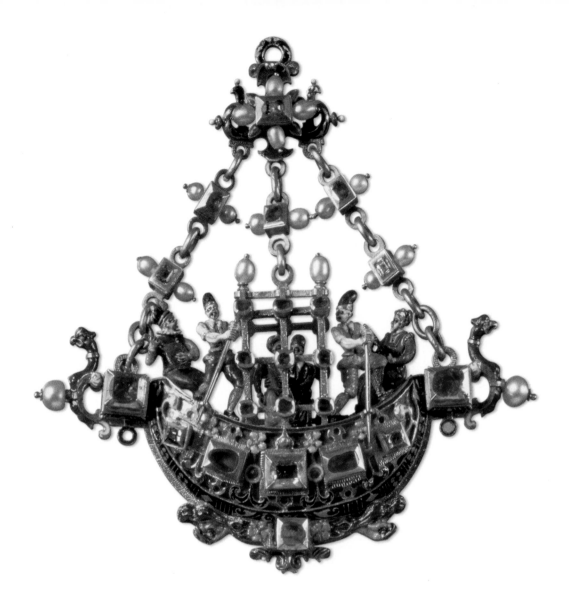

German
(Munich)

PENDANT IN THE FORM OF A GONDOLA
1570 ca.

Enameled gold, pearls, rubies, diamonds, 7,5 x 7,3 cm
Florence, Museo degli Argenti, inv. Gemme, no. 2500

This pendant is part of a group of gems conserved in the Museo degli Argenti in Florence, known as *galanterie gioiellate* (jeweled favors), once belonging to the Electress Palatine, Anna Maria Luisa de' Medici. These pieces are small precious objects fashioned in various ingenious ways from gold, pearls, ivory, enamel, and stones. Although not exceptionally valuable from an economic point of view, since the 16th century, collectors have always been very fond of them for the cleverness of their design, the rarity of the materials, and their special uses. The real jewels belonging to the Electress Palatine, both those property of the Tuscan crown (that is, of the Medici family), as well as her own personal jewelry, were certainly held in much higher esteem. Her own personal possessions in jewelry were undoubtedly very numerous and immensely high in value, making the Princess one of the richest collectors of gems in Europe. After 1743, however, the new Lorraine dynasty either sold off or had taken apart all of the Medici jewels, and only a small group of about seventy gallantry pieces survived. Having been sent to Vienna in 1750, they returned to Florence in 1921 after World War I, and are now in the Museo degli Argenti.

The group includes pendants, buttons, small animal figures (some of which are invented), little human figurines and various other types of objects. It is often difficult to date the pieces, as they were produced from the 16th to the 18th centuries. It is just as difficult to identify the craftsmen who made them, most of whom came from the German, Flemish and Dutch workshops of goldsmiths, silversmiths and jewelers operating for the northern European courts. Very seldom do we know their names.

This pendant, fashioned in the form of a gondola on which a couple of lovers are seated, accompanied by the gondoliers and two musicians, is particularly fascinating for the precious stones, rubies and diamonds, used to decorate it. Pendants in the shape of gondolas or boats are quite frequently mentioned in archival documents, and are also represented in portrait paintings. Most of these objects date from the late 16th century, as does this particular piece. On the basis of its typology and technique of crafting, it was almost certainly made in a southern German workshop around 1570. Another important example of a gondola-shaped pendant is the one conserved in the Florentine Museo degli Argenti, dated about 1568, which may be attributed with certainty to the Bavarian court goldsmith, Giovanni Battista Scolari, who was originally from the area around the city of Trent. (S.C.)

Bibliography: Y. Hackenbroch, *Le "Galanterie" al Museo degli Argenti* in *I gioielli dell'Elettrice Palatina al Museo degli Argenti*, Florence 1988, pp. 62-63, no. 2 (with previous bibliography).

Carlo Ventura Sacconi
(active Florence, 1692 - 1747)

DEATH OF THE VIRGIN, MOURNED BY THE MEDICI FAMILY
1730 ca.
Oil on canvas, 190 x 267 cm
Florence, Villa La Quiete, inv. O.d. A. 1810

Commissioned by the last of the Medici, the Electress Palatine Anna Maria Luisa, in 1730, the painting shows the death of the Virgin surrounded by twenty figures who represent all the most important figures of the grand ducal family. Their names are all recorded on the back of the painting. The Madonna is portrayed by the mother of the Electress, Marguerite-Louise of Orléans who scandalized the courts of Europe by abandoning Cosimo III, the husband she so detested, and returning to Paris. The painting is the only, and an extreme, homage to her mother by Anna Maria Luisa who, in all her life, never showed any sign of having suffered from having been abandoned at the age of eight. Though of no great artistic quality, the painting is of importance, even if funereal in style, as the final representation of the once glorious Medici family, almost a presage of the extinction of the line in 1743 with the death of the Electress. (S.C.)

Bibliography: S. Casciu, *Dalla villa al giardino* in *Villa La Quiete*, Florence 1997, pp. 153-154; S. Casciu, *La morte della Vergine*, 2004.

Florentine

LORRAINE-MEDICI COAT OF ARMS
18th century
Painted and gilt wood carving, 200 x 150 cm
Florence, Museo dell'Opificio delle Pietre Dure, without inv. no.

In 1737, after Gian Gastone de' Medici passed away without leaving heirs, the Grand Duchy of Tuscany passed to Francesco Stefano of Lorraine, husband of the Austrian Empress Maria Teresa of Hapsburg. The new dynasty of the Hapsburg Lorraine governed from this moment until 1859, when Tuscany became part of the newly united Italian nation. This large coat of arms carved in wood was exhibited throughout the 18th and 19th centuries inside the semiprecious stone manufactory, which had not ceased its activity under the new dynasty; the crowned emblem of the Lorraine is shown together with that of the Medici, as if to affirm not only the continuity of the Grand Duchy, but also that of the artistic undertakings fostered by the Medici themselves. (A.G.)

Unpublished

BIBLIOGRAPHY

Acidini Luchinat C., *La scelta dell'anima: le vite dell'iniquo e del giusto nel fregio di Poggio a Caiano* in "Artista", 1991, pp- 16-25.

A critical and historical corpus of Florentine painting, by R. Offner and K. Steinweg. Continued under the direction of M. Boskovits and M. Gregori. New ed. with aditional notes and bibliography by M. Boskovits: Vol. III, *The works of Bernardo Daddi*, Florence, 1989; Vol. IV, *Bernardo Daddi, his shop and following*, Florence 1991; Vol. V, *Bernardo Daddi and his circle*, Florence 2001.

Alberti L.B., *On painting* (1435-36); trans. with introduction and notes by J. R. Spencer, New Haven 1970.

Al servizio del Granduca. Ricognizione di cento immagini della gente di corte, catalogue of the exhibition, edited by S. Meloni Trkulja, Florence 1980.

Anna Maria Luisa Medici Kurfüstin von der Pfalz, catalogue of the exhibition, Düsseldorf 1988.

Armand A., *Les Medailleurs italiens des quinziéme et seiziéme siécles*, vol I, Paris 1883.

Asche S., *Balthasar Permoser. Ein Hauptmeister des Barock*, in "Pantheon", no. 40, 1982, pp. 309-316.

Aschengreen Piacenti K., *Documented works in ivory by Balthasar Permoser and some documents related to Filippo Sengher*, in "Mitteilungen des Kunsthistorischen Institutes in Florenz", no. 10, 1963, pp. 273-285.

Aschengreen Piacenti K., *Il Museo degli argenti a Firenze*, Milan 1967.

Avery C., *Giambologna. La scultura*, Florence 1987.

Baldini U., Giusti A., Pampaloni Martelli A. (edited by), *La Cappella dei Principi e le pietre dure a Firenze*, Milan 1979.

Barbaglia S., *L'opera completa del Cellini*, Milan 1981.

Barocchi P., Ristori R., *Il carteggio di Michelangelo*, posthumous edition of G. Poggi, III, Florence 1973.

Bartolomeo Bimbi. Un pittore di piante e animali alla corte dei Medici, edited by S. Meloni Trkulja and L. Tongiorgi Tomasi, Florence 1998.

Bec C., *Firenze mercantile e i Medici* in *Idee, istituzioni ed arti nella Firenze dei Medici*, edited by C. Vasoli, Florence 1982.

Becherucci L., Brunetti G., *Il Museo dell'Opera del Duomo a Firenze*, 2 vols., Milan 1969-70.

Becker U., in *Von allen Seiten Schön*, 1995.

Bellesi S., *Precisazioni su alcune opere eseguite da Massimiliano Soldani Benzi per il Gran Principe Ferdinando de' Medici*, in "Paragone" no. 497, 1991, pp. 80-85.

Bellesi S., *La scultura tardobarocca e i modelli per la manifattura di Doccia* in J. Winter, *Le statue del Marchese Ginori*, Florence 2003, pp. 1-28.

Belli Barsali I., *I forzieri e gli scrigni dei mercanti* in *I palazzi dei mercanti nella libera Lucca del '500. Immagine di una città-stato al tempo dei Medici*, catalogue of the exhibition, Lucca 1980, pp. 516, 518

Bernocchi M., *Zecche di imitazioni e ibridi di monete fiorentine* in *Le monete della Repubblica fiorentina*, Florence 1978, p. 76.

Bertani L., Nardinocchi E. (edited by), *I tesori di San Lorenzo. 100 capolavori di oreficeria sacra*, Livorno 1995.

Bertani L., *San Lorenzo dai Medici ai Lorena* in *La morte e la gloria. Apparati funebri medicei per Filippo II di Spagna e Margherita d'Austria*, catalogue of the exhibition, edited by M. Bietti, Florence 1998, pp. 68-70.

Bertelli S., *Leone X e Clemente VII* in *Giovanni delle Bande Nere*, edited by M. Scalini , Florence 2001, pp. 42-101.

Berti L. (edited by), *Palazzo Davanzati a Firenze: il Museo dell'antica casa fiorentina*, Florence 1958.

Berti L., *Il Principe dello Studiolo: Francesco I dei Medici e la fine del Rinascimento fiorentino*, Florence 1967.

Berti L., *Il Museo di Palazzo Davanzati a Firenze*, Milan 1971.

Berti L., Cecchi A., Natali A., *Michelangelo*.

I disegni di Casa Buonarroti, Florence 1985.

Bigi E., Lorenzo de' Medici e la letteratura in La Toscana al tempo di Lorenzo il Magnifico. Politica Economia Cultura Arte (Acts of the Conference 1992), Pisa 1996, Vol. II, pp. 341-355.

Bizzarrie di pietre dipinte dalle collezioni dei Medici, catalogue of the exhibition, edited by M. Chiarini and C. Acidini Luchinat, Florence 2000.

Bona Castellotti M., F. Gamba, E. Mazzocca (edited by), La ragione e il metodo. Immagini della scienza nell'arte italiana dal XVI al XIX secolo, Milan 1999.

Borea E., La Quadreria di Don Lorenzo de' Medici, Florence 1977.

Botticelli F., Rifacimenti e falsificazioni in L'Architettura civile in Toscana, Milan 1997, p. 398.

Burresi M., L'abito della Granduchessa. Vesti di corte e di madonne nel Palazzo Reale di Pisa, Pisa 2000.

Cadogan J., Domenico Ghirlandaio, Florence 2000.

Camerini L. Il Fiorino: un giglio a ventiquattro carati in 1492: un anno fra due ere, Florence 1992, pp. 198-199.

Camesasca E. (edited by), Vita of B. Cellini, Milan 1985.

Campbell M., Pietro da Cortona at the Pitti Palace. A Study of the Planetary Rooms and Related Projects, Princeton 1977.

Caneva C., Botticelli. Catalogo completo dei dipinti, Florence 1990.

Cantelli G., L'arredo, la dimensione privata dell'abitare. Mobilia e suppellettili nelle dimore di patrizi, contadini e borghesi in L'architettura civile nel Medioevo, Milan 1995, pp. 443-493.

Cantelli G., Storia dell'oreficeria e dell'arte tessile in Toscana dal Medioevo all'età moderna, Florence 1996.

Cantelli G., La vita sociale e la nuova dimensione dell'abitare in L'architettura civile in Toscana. Il Rinascimento, edited by A. Restucci, Milan 1997, pp. 231-403.

Casciu S., Anna Maria Luisa de' Medici Elettrice Palatina (1667-1743), Florence 1993.

Casciu S., Dalla villa al giardino. Trasformazioni settecentesche della Quiete per l'Elettrice Palatina in Villa La Quiete. Il patrimonio artistico del Conservatorio delle Montalve, edited by C. De Benedictis, Florence 1997, pp. 129-155.

Casciu S., La Morte della Vergine ed altri dipinti di Carlo Ventura Sacconi per l'Elettrice Palatina, 2004 (in print).

Catalogo del Museo civico di Pisa, edited by A. Bellini Pietri, Pisa 1906.

Catalogue des objets composant le Musée Municipal des Beaux-Arts., Nantes 1876.

Cecchi A., "Invenzioni per quadri" di Don Vincenzo Borghini in "Paragone", nos. 383-385, 1982, pp. 89-96.

Cecchi A., L'ingresso di Carlo VIII in Firenze: nuovi documenti e ipotesi sulla committenza in "Paragone", no. 439, 1986, pp. 41-48.

Cesati F., I Medici: storia di una dinastia europea, Florence 1999.

Chiarini M., Anton Domenico Gabbiani e i Medici in Kunst der Barok in der Toskana, Munich 1976, pp. 333-335.

Chiarini M., Aggiunte al Cerrini, in "Antologia di Belle Arti", II, no. 6, 1978, pp. 278-280.

Chiarini M., Gallerie e musei statali di Firenze. I dipinti olandesi del Seicento e del Settecento, Rome 1989.

Chiarini M. (edited by), Firenze e la sua immagine. Cinque secoli di vedutismo, Florence 1994.

Clifford Smith H., The complete history of Buckingham Palace, London 1931.

Colle E., Arredi dalle dimore medicee, Florence 1993.

Colle E. (edited by), I mobili di Palazzo Pitti. Il periodo dei Medici 1537-1737, Florence 1997.

Collobi Ragghianti L., I disegni della Fondazione Horne in Firenze, Florence 1963.

Conforti C., Vasari architetto, Milan 1993.

Cresti C., La cappella dei Principi. Un pantheon foderato di pietre dure in Splendori di pietre dure. L'Arte di corte nella Firenze dei Granduchi, catalogue of the exhibition, edited by A. Giusti, Florence 1988, p. 68.

Cristalli e gemme, catalogue of the exhibition, edited by L. Dolcini and B. Zanettin, Venice 1999.

Cultura neoclassica e romantica nella Toscana granducale, catalogue of the exhibition, edited by S. Pinto, Florence 1972.

Curiosità di una reggia. Vicende della guardaroba di Palazzo Pitti, catalogue of the exhibition, edited by K. Aschengreen Piacenti and S. Pinto, Florence 1979.

D'Afflitto C., Mannini M. P., Oreficeria e arredi sacri a Pistoia tra '500 e '600 in Pistoia: una città nello stato mediceo, catalogue of the exhibition, Pistoia 1980, pp. 235-290.

Danti Riccardiani. Parole e figure, catalogue of the exhibition, edited by G. Lazzi and G. Savino, Florence 1996.

Della Monica I., Gran Principe Ferdinando in Il giardino del Granduca. Natura morta nelle collezioni medicee, edited by M. Chiarini, Turin 1997, pp. 238-239.

De Luca M. in Florença: Tesouros do Renascimento. Firenze: Tesori del Rinascimento, Il Museo di Palazzo Davanzati a Firenze, edited by C. Poggi, Milan 2000, pp. 49-56.

Falletti F., *Un museo in mostra* in *La Musica alla corte dei Granduchi. Guida alla mostra*, catalogue of the exhibition, edited by G. Rossi-Rognoni, Florence 2001, p. 13.

Fanelli G., *Firenze Architettura e città*, Florence 1973.

Fiderer Moskowitz A., *The sculpture of Andrea and Nino Pisano*, Cambridge 1986.

Fiderer Moskowitz A., *Italian Gothic sculpture: ca.1250 - 1400*, Cambridge 2001.

Firpo M., *Gli affreschi di Pontormo a San Lorenzo: Eresia, politica e cultura nella Firenze di Cosimo I*, Turin 1997.

Fox S. P., *Domenico di Polo* in *Dizionario biografico degli Italiani*, no. 40, Rome 1991, pp. 659-661.

Francolini S., Vervat M., *Il gioco del civettino dello Scheggia. Il ritrovamento di un ulteriore dipinto e la tipologia dell'oggetto*, in "Kermes", no. 42, 2001, pp. 51-63.

Fraticelli P., *Delle antiche carceri di Firenze denominate le Stinche*, Florence 1834.

Frey K., *Studien zur Michelangelo Buonarroti und zur Kunst seiner Zeit*, III in "Jahrbuch der Koniglich Preussischen Kunstsammlungen", Beiheft, XXX, 1909, pp. 103-180.

Garofalo C., *Da Raffaello a Rubens. Disegni della Fondazione Horne*, Livorno 2000.

Giotto. Bilancio critico di sessant'anni di studi e ricerche, catalogue of the exhibition, edited by A. Tartuferi, Florence 2000.

Giotto e Dante, catalogue of the exhibition, edited by C. Gizzi, Milan 2001.

Giovanni da San Giovanni, catalogue of the exhibition, Bologna 1994.

Giuliano A., *I cammei della collezione medicea nel Museo Archeologico di Firenze*, Rome 1989.

Giusti A., Mazzoni P., Pampaloni Martelli A. (edited by), *Il Museo dell'Opificio delle Pietre Dure a Firenze*, Florence 1978.

Giusti A., *Pietre Dure. L'arte europea del mosaico negli arredi e nelle decorazioni dal 1500 al 1800*, Turin 1992.

Giusti A. *Guida al Museo dell'Opificio delle Pietre Dure di Firenze*, Venice 1995.

Giusti A., *Un dorato crepuscolo. Il regno di Cosimo III* in *Tesori dalle collezioni medicee*, edited by C. Acidini Luchinat, Florence 1997, pp. 173-195.

Gli ingegneri del Rinascimento da Brunelleschi a Leonardo da Vinci, catalogue of the exhibition, Florence 1996

Gli Uffizi. Catalogo generale, Florence 1979.

Gli Ultimi Medici. Il tardo barocco a Firenze 1670-1743, catalogue of the exhibition, edited by K. Aschengreen Piacenti and A. Gonzàlez Palacios, Florence 1974.

Goldenberg Stoppato L. in *Mittelungen des Kunsthistorisches Institutes in Florenz*, 2004 (in print).

Gonzàlez Palacios A., *Il gusto dei Principi*, 2 vols., Milan 1993.

Gori O., Sbrilli M., *Due famiglie implicate nella congiura del 1478: i Pazzi e i Salviati* in *Consorterie politiche e mutamenti istituzionali in età laurenziana*, edited by M.A. Morelli Timpanaro, R. Manno Tolu and P. Viti, Florence 1992.

Gregori M., Ruotolo R., Bandera Gregori L., *I quaderni dell'antiquariato. Il mobile italiano dal Rinascimento agli anni '30*, Milan 1981.

Hackenbroch Y., *Le "galanterie" al Museo degli Argenti* in *I Gioielli dell'Elettrice Palatina al Museo degli Argenti*, catalogue of the exhibition, edited by Y. Hackenbroch and M. Sframeli, Florence 1988, pp. 62-63.

Haskell F., Penny N., *Taste and the Antique. The Lure of Classical Sculpture 1500-1600*, New Haven-London, 1981.

Hochrenaissance im Vatikan: Kunst und Kultur am Rom der Päpste I 1503-1534, catalogue of the exhibition, Bonn 1998.

Inventario dei Mobili e delle Masserizie della proprietà del Serenissimo Signore Principe Ferdinando di Gloriosa ricordanza...1713 (Archivio di Stato di Firenze, Guardaroba Medicea 1222, c.1).

I Della Robbia e l'"arte nuova" della scultura invetriata, catalogue of the exhibition, edited by G. Gentilini, Florence 1998.

I gioielli dei Medici dal vero e in ritratto, catalogue of the exhibition, edited by M. Sframeli, Livorno 2003.

I gioielli dell'Elettrice Palatina al Museo degli Argenti, catalogue of the exhibition, edited by Y. Hackenbroch and M. Sframeli, Florence 1988.

I mai visti. Sorprese di frutta e fiori. Capolavori dai depositi degli Uffizi, catalogue of the exhibition, edited by A. Natali, Florence 2002.

I principi bambini. Abbigliamento e infanzia nel Seicento, catalogue of the exhibition, Florence 1985.

I restauri nel Palazzo Medici Riccardi. Rinascimento e Barocco, edited by C. Acidini Luchinat, Milan 1992 .

I tesori di un antiquario. Galleria di Palazzo Mozzi Bardini, Florence 1998.

I volti del potere. La ritrattistica di corte nella Firenze Granducale, catalogue of the exhibition edited by C. Caneva, Florence, 2002.

Il Giardino di San Marco: maestri e compagni del giovane Michelangelo, catalogue of the exhibition, edited by P. Barocchi, Florence 1992.

Il Museo Horne. Una casa fiorentina del

Rinascimento, Florence 2001.

Il Museo nascosto. Capolavori della Galleria Corsi nel Museo Bardini, catalogue of the exhibition, edited by F. Zeri, A. Bacchi, Florence 1991.

Il potere e lo spazio, catalogue of the exhibition, edited by F. Borsi, Florence 1980.

Il primato del disegno, catalogue of the exhibition, edited by L. Berti, Florence 1980.

Il Rinascimento in Italia, catalogue of the exhibition, edited by M. Sframeli, Rome 2001.

Il tesoro di Lorenzo il Magnifico, II. I vasi, catalogue of the exhibition, edited by D. Heikamp and A. Grote, Florence 1972.

Jaffè M., *Rubens and Raphael* in *Studies in Renaissance and Baroque Art, presented to Anthony Blunt on his 60th Birthday*, London 1967.

Kecks R. G., *Ghirlandaio*, Florence 1995.

Kent D., *Women in Renaissance Florence* in *Virtue and Beauty*, catalogue of the exhibition, Washington 2001, pp. 35-39.

Keutner H. in *Giambologna, Ein Wendepunkt*, 1987.

Kreytenberg G. in *The Dictionary of Art*, no. 24, 1996, pp. 874-876.

Krejtemberg G., *Orcagna-Andrea di Cione. Ein Universelle Küntler der Gotik in Florenz*, Mainz 2000.

Kühn-Steinhausen H., *Die Feste am Düsseldorfer Hofe*, in "Düsseldorfer Heimatblätter", XXII, 1939.

Langedijk K., *The Portraits of the Medici 15th- 18th Centuries*, 3 vols, Florence 1981-1987.

Lankheit K., *Florentinische Barockplastik*, München 1962.

Lazzi G., *La moda alla corte di Cosimo I de' Medici* in *Moda alla corte dei Medici, gli abiti restaurati di Cosimo, Eleonora e don Garzia*, catalogue of the exhibition, Florence 1993, pp. 27-34.

Lazzi G., in *Biblioteca Riccardiana e Moreniana in Palazzo Medici Riccardi*, Florence 1998.

Lensi A., *Il Museo Bardini: stucchi e terrecotte*, in "Dedalo", IV, 1923-24, pp. 752-753.

Lightbown R., *Sandro Botticelli*, 2 vols., London 1978.

Liscia Bemporad D. (edited by), *Argenti fiorentini dal XV al XIX secolo. Tipologie e marchi*, 3 vols., Florence 1992.

Liscia Bemporad D., *Gli orafi di Santa Maria del Fiore* in *Alla riscoperta di Piazza del Duomo in Firenze. I tesori di Piazza del Duomo*, edited by T. Verdon, Florence 1997, p. 104.

Longo V., *Per un regale Evento. Spettacoli nunziali e opera in musica alla corte dei Medici*, Florence 2000.

Lorenzo dopo Lorenzo, La fortuna storica di Lorenzo il Magnifico, catalogue of the exhibition, edited by P. Pirolo, Florence 1992.

Lorenzo Ghiberti materia e ragionamenti, catalogue of the exhibition, Florence 1978.

L'Adolescente dell'Ermitage e la Sagrestia Nuova di Michelangelo, catalogue of the exhibition, edited by S. Androsov and U. Baldini, Siena 2000.

L'architettura civile in Toscana. Il Rinascimento, edited by A. Restucci, Milan 1997.

L'architettura di Lorenzo il Magnifico, catalogue of the exhibition, edited by G. Morolli, C. Acidini Luchinat and L. Marchetti, Milan 1992.

L'eredità di Lorenzo il Magnifico, catalogue of the exhibition, Florence 1992.

L'età di Masaccio. Il primo Quattrocento a Firenze, catalogue of the exhibition, edited by L. Berti and A. Paolucci, Florence 1989.

L'officina della maniera. Varietà e fierezza nell'arte fiorentina del Cinquecento fra le due repubbliche 1494-1530, catalogue of the exhibition, edited by A. Cecchi, A. Natali and C. Sisi, Florence 1996.

L'Ombra del Genio. Michelangelo e l'arte a Firenze 1537-1631, catalogue of the exhibition, edited by M. Chiarini, A.P. Darr, C. Giannini, Florence 2002.

L'opera completa del Bronzino, edited by E. Baccheschi, Milan 1973.

La Galleria Palatina e gli Appartamenti Reali di Palazzo Pitti. Catalogo dei dipinti, edited by M. Chiarini and S. Padovani, 2 vols., Firenze 2003.

La morte e la gloria. Apparati funebri medicei per Filippo II di Spagna e Margherita d'Austria, catalogue of the exhibition, edited by M. Bietti, Florence 1998.

La natura morta italiana. Da Caravaggio al Settecento, catalogue of the exhibition, edited by M. Gregori, Florence 2003.

Les Français et la table, catalogue of the exhibition, Paris 1986.

Lo spettacolo maraviglioso. Il teatro della Pergola: l'opera a Firenze, Florence 2000.

Magnificenza alla corte dei Medici. Arte a Firenze alla fine del Cinquecento, catalogue of the exhibition, edited by D. Heikamp and M. Gregori, Florence 1997.

Maestri e botteghe. Pittura a Firenze alla fine del Quattrocento, catalogue of the exhibition, edited by M. Gregori, A. Paolucci, C. Acidini Luchinat, Florence 1992.

Marani P. C., *Leonardo. Catalogo completo*, Florence 1989.

Marani P. C., *Leonardo. Una carriera di pittore*, Milan 1999.

Masaccio e le origini del Rinascimento, catalogue of the exhibition, Milan 2002.

Mascalchi S., *Anticipazioni sul mecenatismo del Cardinal Giovan Carlo de' Medici e suo contributo alle collezioni degli*

Uffizi, in *Gli Uffizi: quattro secoli di una Galleria*, papers of the international conference, *Fonti e documenti*, Florence 1982, pp. 41-82.

Masini M. P., Salvadori D., *Museo di Palazzo Davanzati. I cassoni dal XIV al XVI secolo. Itinerario e proposte didattiche*, Florence 1991.

Massafra M. G., *Il portone in legno a Firenze nella seconda metà del XV secolo: evoluzione e sviluppo dell'ornamentazione classica* in *Giuliano e la bottega dei da Maiano*, congress of studies, Florence 1991, pp. 200-208.

Massinelli A. M., *Bronzi e anticaglie nella Guardaroba di Cosimo I*, Florence 1991.

Massinelli A. M., *Magnificenze medicee: gli stipi della Tribuna*, in "Antologia di Belle Arti", nos. 35-38 (*Studi sul Neoclassicismo II*), 1990, pp.130-131.

Meloni Trkulja S., *Il potere del Ritratto in Stanze segrete stanze scomparse. Frammenti di una residenza-museo*, catalogue of the exhibition, edited by C. Giannini, Florence 2003.

Merson O., *Inventaire général des richesses d'art de la France. Histoire et descriptions du Musée de Nantes*, Paris, n.d (1883).

Miniati M. (edited by), *Il Museo di Storia della Scienza*, Florence 1991.

Moda alla corte dei Medici, gli abiti restaurati di Cosimo, Eleonora e don Garzia, catalogue of the exhibition, Florence 1993.

Monete fiorentine dalla Repubblica ai Medici, catalogue of the exhibition, edited by B. Paolozzi Strozzi, Florence 1984.

Montrésor C., *Il Museo dell'Opera del Duomo a Firenze*, Florence 2000.

Morolli G., *L'architettura del Battistero e l'"ordine buono antico"* in *Il battistero di Firenze*, edited by A. Paolucci, Modena 1994, p. 54.

Natura viva in casa Medici, catalogue of the exhibition, edited by M. Mosco, Florence 1986.

Nel segno di Masaccio, catalogue of the exhibition, edited by F. Camerota, Florence 2001.

Neri Lusanna E., in *Il Museo Bardini a Firenze, Vol. II. Le sculture*, Florence 1986.

Nicolle M. (edited by), *Ville de Nantes. Musée Municipal des Beaux-Arts. Catalogue*, assisted by E. Dacier, Nantes 1913.

Opere d'arte della famiglia Medici, catalogue of the exhibition, edited by C. Acidini Luchinat and M. Scalini, Milan 1997.

Orsi Landini R., *I paramenti sacri della Cappella Palatina di Palazzo Pitti*, Florence 1988.

Orsi Landini R., *L'amore del lusso e la necessità della modestia. Eleonora fra sete e oro* in *Moda alla corte dei Medici, gli abiti restaurati di Cosimo, Eleonora e don Garzia*, catalogue of the exhibition, Florence 1993, pp. 35-45.

Palazzo Pitti. La reggia rivelata, catalogue of the exhibition, Florence 2003.

Palazzo Vecchio: committenza e collezionismo medicei, catalogue of the exhibition, edited by P. Barocchi, Florence 1980.

Paolini C., *Della sedia e dell'arte di sedersi* in *Il Museo Horne. Una casa fiorentina del Rinascimento*, Florence 2001, pp. 82-83.

Petrini G., *Gli stampi dei mattoni grandi per la cupola di Santa Maria del Fiore a Firenze*, in "Parametro" no. 239, 2002, pp. 88 - 89.

Pezzarossa F. (edited by), *I poemetti sacri di Lucrezia Tornabuoni*, Florence 1978.

Pieraccini G., *La stirpe dei Medici di Cafaggiolo*, 3 Vols., Florence 1942-45.

Pisa e il Mediterraneo. Uomini, merci, idee dagli Etruschi ai Medici, catalogue of the exhibition, Milan 2003.

Pistoia. una città nello stato mediceo, catalogue of the exhibition, Pistoia 1980.

Pollard J. G., *Medaglie italiane del Rinascimento nel Museo Nazionale del Bargello*, I Vol, Florence 1984.

Pons N., *Botticelli. Catalogo completo*, Milan 1989.

Pope-Hennessy J., *Cellini*, Milan 1986.

Porta A., *Galileo. La sensata esperienza*, Florence 1988.

Posate, pugnali e coltelli da caccia, catalogue of the exhibition, edited by L. Salvatici, Florence 1999.

Preti M., *Il Museo dell'Opera del Duomo di Firenze*, Milan 1989.

Pulchritudo, Amor, Voluptas. Pico della Mirandola alla corte del Magnifico, catalogue of the exhibition, edited by M. Scalini, Florence 2001.

Radcliffe A. F., *Ferdinando Tacca, the missing link in Florentine Baroque bronzes* in *Kunst der Barock in der Toscana*, Munich 1976.

Raffaello a Firenze. Dipinti e disegni nelle collezioni fiorentine, catalogue of the exhibition, edited by M. Gregori, Florence 1984.

Ragionieri P. (edited by), *Casa Buonarroti*, Florence 1987.

Ravanelli Guidotti C., *Ceramiche occidentali del Museo Civico Medievale di Bologna*, Bologna 1985.

Riflessi di una Galleria. Dipinti dell'Eredità Bardini, catalogue of the exhibition, Florence 2001.

Rinascimento da Brunelleschi a Michelangelo. La rappresentazione dell' architettura, catalogue of the exhibition, edited by H. Millon, V. Magnago Lampugnani, Milan 1994.

Romanticismo storico, catalogue of the exhibition, edited by S. Pinto, Florence 1974.

Rosenberg R., *Beschreibungen und Nachzeichnungen der Skulpturen Michelangelos*, Berlin 2000.

Rossi F., *Il Museo Horne a Firenze*, Florence 1966.

Rossi F., *Il commesso e la glittica all'Opificio delle Pietre Dure* in *Splendori di pietre dure. L'Arte di corte nella Firenze dei Granduchi*, catalogue of the exhibition, edited by A. Giusti, Florence 1988, pp. 276-278.

Sandro Botticelli pittore della Divina Commedia, catalogue of the exhibition, Rome 2000.

Savonarola e le sue reliquie a San Marco, edited by M. Scudieri and G. Rasario, Florence 1998.

Scalia F., De Benedictis C., *Il Museo Bardini a Firenze*, 2 vols., Florence 1984.

Scalini M., *Armature da Cosimo I a Cosimo III de' Medici*, Florence 1990.

Scaravella E., Ministry Report, OA 0900227248, 1990.

Scienziati a corte. L'arte della sperimentazione nell'Accademia del Cimento di Firenze, catalogue of the exhibition, Florence 2001.

Scudieri M., *Miniatura del '400 a San Marco. Dalle suggestioni avignonesi all'ambiente dell'Angelico*, Florence 2003.

Sframeli M., *Il centro di Firenze restituito*, Florence 1989.

Simon K., *I Gonzaga. Storia e segreti*, Rome 1990.

Spinelli R., *La pittura di Bartolomeo Bimbi tra eredità e innovazione* in *Le Belle Forme della Natura. La pittura di Bartolomeo Bimbi (1648-1730) tra scienza e "maraviglia"*, catalogue of the exhibition, edited by D. Savoia and M. L. Strocchi, Bologna 2001, pp.

40-50.

Splendore dei Medici: Firenze e l'Europa, catalogue of the exhibition, edited by C. Acidini Luchinat and M. Scalini, Florence 1999.

Splendori di pietre dure. L'Arte di corte nella Firenze dei Granduchi, catalogue of the exhibition, edited by A. Giusti, Florence 1988.

Stefanini Sorrentino M., *Arazzi medicei a Pisa*, Florence 1993.

Sustermans. Sessant'anni alla corte dei Medici, catalogue of the exhibition, edited by M. Chiarini and C. Pizzorusso, Firenze 1983.

Tartuferi A., *Una mostra e alcune spigolature giottesche* in *Giotto. Bilancio critico di sessant'anni di studi e ricerche*, Florence 2000, p. 27.

Tesi M., *Biblioteca Medicea Laurenziana*, Florence 1986.

Testaverde A. M., *San Lorenzo "cantiere teatrale"* in *La morte e la gloria. Apparati funebri medicei per Filippo II di Spagna e Margherita d'Austria*, catalogue of the exhibition, edited by M. Bietti, Florence 1998.

Tessuti serici italiani 1450-1530, catalogue of the exhibition, Milan 1983.

Testimonianze Medicee a confronto, catalogue of the exhibition, edited by G. Lazzi, Florence 1997.

Tiziano nelle Gallerie fiorentine, catalogue of the exhibition, Florence 1978.

Tolnay C., *Corpus dei disegni di Michelangelo*, Novara 1975-1980.

Tondo L., Vanni F. M., *Le gemme dei Medici e dei Lorena nel Museo Archeologico di Firenze*, Florence 1990.

Torresi A. P., *Neo-Medicei. Pittori, restauratori e copisti dell'Ottocento in Toscana. Dizionario biografico*, Ferrara 1996.

Trento D., *Benvenuto Cellini. Opere non*

esposte e documenti notarili, Florence 1984.

Vannel F., Toderi G., *La medaglia barocca in Toscana*, Firenze 1987.

Vasari G., *Le Vite*, edited by G. Milanesi, Florence, Vol.VII, 1878-1885.

Vasari G., *Lives of the Artists*, 2 vols., edited by G. Bull, London 1965.

Venere svelata. La Venere di Urbino di Tiziano, catalogue of the exhibition, edited by O. Calabrese, Milan 2003.

Ville de Nantes. Musée Municipal des Beaux-Arts. Catalogue des peintures, sculptures, pastels, aquarelles, dessins et objects d'art, Paris 1903.

Ville de Nantes. Musée des Beaux-Arts. Catalogue et Guide, edited by L. Benoist, Nantes 1953.

Visonà M., *Un ritratto di Anna Maria Luisa de' Medici bambina e i lari del Poggio Imperiale (riflessioni sul Foggini)*, in "Paragone", XLIX, no. 585, S. III 22, 1998, pp. 19-30.

Zanieri S., *Un gioco ottico di Ludovico Buti al Museo di Storia della Scienza di Firenze* in "Nuncius", XV, 2000, pp. 665-670.

70 pitture e sculture del '600 e '700 fiorentino, catalogue of the exhibition edited by M. Gregori, Florence 1965.

PHOTOGRAPHY CREDITS:

RESTORATION CREDITS:

WONDERS

The Memphis International Cultural Series